Social Sciences

Social Sciences: The Big Issues 2nd edition offers an introduction to the big debates within the social sciences and to what the social sciences can provide as a means of explaining the changing world. The social sciences focus upon people as individuals and as members of wider communities and networks, and looks at all aspects of human relationships from the personal and intimate to the public and political. The book covers contemporary concerns with identities, citizenship, migration, diversity, new technologies and the changing and often uncertain impact of globalisation. The second edition has been extensively updated with new illustrations and examples and additional discussion of the responses of the social sciences to the mobilities of contemporary life, such as migration, living in multi-ethnic and often rapidly changing communities, new forms of citizenship, the impact of the material world, the perception that we live in a more insecure and dangerous world and the role of the media in presenting ideas about the changes that might be taking place.

Kath Woodward is Professor of Sociology at the Open University. Recent publications include, *Boxing, Masculinity and Identity* (2007), *Embodied Sporting Practices* (2009) and *Why Feminism Matters* (2009). She chaired the Open University, level 1, Introduction to the Social Sciences and currently chairs This Sporting Planet, a level 1 course on sport and the social sciences. She works on gendered, racialised identities, at CRESC and on Sport Across Diasporas at the BBC World Service for the AHRC Diasporas, Migration, Identities programme.

Social Sciences

The big issues
2nd Edition

Kath Woodward

Routledge
Taylor & Francis Group

LONDON AND NEW YORK

First edition published 2003
by Routledge
2 Park Square, Milton Park, Abingdon, Oxon, OX14 4RN

Second edition published 2010
by Routledge
2 Park Square, Milton Park, Abingdon, Oxon, OX14 4RN

Simultaneously published in the USA and Canada
by Routledge
270 Madison Ave, New York, NY 10016

Routledge is an imprint of the Taylor & Francis Group, an informa business

© 2003, 2010 Kath Woodward

Typeset in Times New Roman by
Keystroke, Tettenhall, Wolverhampton
Printed and bound in Great Britain by
TJ International, Padstow, Cornwall

British Library Cataloguing in Publication Data
A catalogue record for this book is available from the British Library

Library of Congress Cataloging-in-Publication Data
Woodward, Kath.
Social sciences : the big issues / Kath Woodward. – 2nd ed.
p. cm.
1. Social sciences. I. Title
H61.W68 2009
300–dc22
2009006353

ISBN10: 0–415–46660–1 (pbk)
ISBN10: 0–415–46661–X (hbk)
ISBN10: 0–203–87289–4 (ebk)

ISBN13: 978–0–415–46660–8 (pbk)
ISBN13: 978–0–415–46661–5 (hbk)
ISBN13: 978–0–203–87289–5 (ebk)

For Steve, Richard, Tamsin, Jack and Sophie
and my sister Sarah

Contents

Illustrations

Acknowledgements

The author and publishers would like to thank PA Photos for permission to reprint the following photographs: Plates 2.1, 2.3, 6.2, 7.2, 7.3, 7.4 and 7.5.

Acknowledgement is also made to HMSO (Crown copyright) for Figures 4.1, 4.2 and 4.3, and Table 5.2, and to Brendan Ingle of St Thomas's Gym, Sheffield, for Plate 6.1.

The photographs in Plates 5.1 and 7.1 are by the author.

Thanks to Sylvia Lay-Flurrie for her support and help with getting it all together.

Chapter 1

Introduction

Getting started

This is a book about big issues. Big issues about world politics, environmental degradation, social and economic inequalities and cultural change inform debates in the social sciences and our everyday lives. Recent developments range from concerns about global terrorism, which has, in some instances, replaced conflicts between nation states as a major cause of anxiety across the entire world, to the growth of transnational corporations, economic crises and the threat of climate change. Change is taking place with a new intensity through the progress of technological developments and the increased mobility of people. Changes are specific as well as sometimes unpredictable and some of the transformations of recent years have led to increasing anxieties (for example, about jobs, pensions, physical safety and health). The second edition of *Social Sciences: The Big Issues* takes on board both the direction of some of the changes that have taken place since the first edition was published and the particular nature of some of these changes, in order to accommodate the development of debates within the social sciences in recent years. Increasingly, social scientists are arguing that there is no single explanation of change, but many different stories that can explain the different forms change takes, the extent of change and consistencies and continuities in social life.

The big issues remain those which have arisen as a result of some of the changes that have taken place at the beginning of the twenty-first century in power relationships, in global and local politics and economics as well as through the development of new technologies and working practices and changes in intimate, personal relations. In a sense this is also a book about little issues, in that global transformations impact upon routine encounters and everyday practices, and the domestic and personal lives of individuals and the local communities in which they live. The social sciences are concerned with making sense of change and of the links between the big debates and those that are the concern of individuals in our daily lives. These are the big issues that concern us in our daily routines. These everyday matters include our sense of who we are in our exchanges with families, partners, friends, neighbours, faith communities and at work. Dealing with health, welfare and ill health, securing accommodation, shopping and all the leisure activities in which we might engage, all matter, as well as the global big issues relating to big business, corporate finance and banking, global credit, international politics, conflicts between states and ethnic groups, environmental degradation and risk. My concern in this book is to demonstrate the links between the two, between global events and everyday experience and, in particular, to introduce some of the ways in which the social sciences help us make sense of everyday life and offer ways of understanding what matters. These are the big issues, the things that matter, the areas of experience which are changing and those about which there is most debate and contention. The social sciences offer critical ways of thinking and of making sense of social, political, cultural and economic life. The approach taken in this book is to highlight some of the concepts used in the social sciences to classify and explain different social phenomena, and to introduce some of the questions that the social sciences pose. Knowing which questions to ask is a most important stage in the process of doing social science.

Getting started involves asking questions

Change, and especially the speed with which some transformations in the social, economic, political and cultural patterns of our daily lives are taking place, has characterised the contemporary world. Within a single generation it is possible to trace very different patterns of family life, experiences of paid work, of sexual relations and experience of ethnic and cultural diversity. Exploring the extent to which such changes are taking place is crucial to understanding the range and extent of changes and moving towards an understanding of what they mean. What sorts of changes are taking place in the contemporary world and how important are these changes in human social relations? Where could we look to find out what is happening?

Changing people: changing lives

One of the areas in which changes are taking place is in everyday lives. This is an area which is well documented through people's lived experience and in official statistics of demographic changes which governments gather to inform their policies. Demographic changes have had an enormous impact upon our daily lives. Demography involves all aspects of human populations, including growth and decline, different patterns of movement across the globe and within nations, births and deaths, the ratio of women to men, young to old, ill health and dependency. One of the ways of accessing information about demography is to look at the official statistical data produced by government-sponsored sources. In the UK there is a range of such sources, including annual surveys produced as the census and its updates, data from the Office of National Statistics and publications like *Social Trends* and *British Social Attitudes*. Some of the evidence cited in this book draws upon such sources.

Population changes include not only an increase or decrease in overall numbers, but the numbers of people within particular age categories; all of the information required by governments in order to manage populations and provide the necessary services, such as health care, accommodation, training and education. For example, in most Western countries there has been an increase in the elderly and, in some cases, a decrease in other age groups, notably the under-sixteens; in the UK out of a population of 60.2 million in 2007, the under-sixteens constituted only 19 per cent, a percentage that had fallen from 25 per cent in 1971 (*Social Trends*, 2007). By 2008, the UK population comprised more elderly people than those under 16. In August 2008, the Office for national Statistics reported 11.58 million pensioners, classified as men over 65 and women over 60 compared with 11.52 million under-sixteens. With life expectancy improving, the number of deaths recorded each year dropped from 599,000 in 2001 to 571,000 in 2007. The number of over-eighties almost doubled from the 1970s, reaching 2.7 million in 2008 (ONS, 2008).

Population trends in countries like the UK have involved both a shift towards an ageing population and migration replacing births as the major source of population growth. The 2001 census demonstrated the ethnic mix of the UK as including 88.2 per cent of what the census classified as 'white British' and a total of 11.8 per cent from different ethnic groups. The growth of more diverse, multi-cultural and multi-ethnic societies raises wider issues about who we are and about social, cultural and political policies. Fertility patterns have changed in a variety of ways. There has been a trend towards an overall decline in the birth rate in the UK, with 20 per cent fewer births in 2005 than in 1971 and a rate of 1.79 births per woman in the UK as in most other European countries (*Social Trends*, 2007). However, in each year from 2003 there has been an increase, which may be attributed to the age profile of young migrants, a category of the population which is predicted to decline, so it is too soon to predict a trend. For example, figures published in 2008 suggest that the biggest wave of Eastern European workers registering for jobs in Britain in recent history has peaked; there were 40,000 applicants mainly from Poland between April and June 2008 compared with 54,000 over the same period in 2007 (Travis, 2008). There has, however, been an increase in births to foreign-born mothers, which comprised 23 per cent of all UK births in 2007, and the Office of National Statistics reports that there has been an increase in the number of women of child-bearing age in the UK (ONS, 2008). The UK birth rate has been rising more significantly since 2003 and, in 2008, stood at 1.9 per woman which is the highest it has been for a long time (Travis, 2008). Later marriage or cohabitation, women's increased participation in higher education and in the labour market, and the increased availability of contraception have all contributed to an increase in the average age of giving birth, as well as a more general trend towards a decline in the birth rate, although it is interesting to note that not only does migration boost overall population, it may also contribute to an increase in the birth rate owing to the age of those migrating. Recent developments suggest an uneven picture and not a single story of a declining birth rate, but changes in one area of social life, such as the birth rate, may be attributed to changes in another, such as migration patterns.

The proportion of teenage (under-18) pregnancies and births remains high in the UK which tops the European league tables, having a teenage birth rate that is six times that of Holland, four times that of Italy and three times that of France (Donnelly, 2007) and indeed those of the developed world, along with the US (NCHS, 2007). Births to teenage mothers are most likely to take place outside marriage (*Social Trends*, 2007), although there is an overall increase in the number of births outside marriage. What constitutes a family is changing, as is the composition of households. People live in a variety of households during their lifetime, but the trend in recent years has been towards greater diversity. Birth rates are now given 'per woman' and not 'per couple' as they were in the past (ONS, 2008). The traditional notion of a married couple living together with their children as the dominant form of household has been transformed, although this remains the predominant form in, for example, Indian Pakistani and Bangladeshi households. Increasing numbers of children are born to cohabiting couples, although most people do still marry in the UK. Twenty-four per cent of non-married people under 60 were cohabiting in 2005, twice as many as in 1986 (*Social Trends*, 2007: 19). Family size has declined as has the proportion of UK households comprising a couple with dependent children, with 24 per cent of children living in lone-parent families, three times as many as in 1971. Young adults (between 20 and 24), however, are more likely to remain in the parental home with 58 per cent of men in this age group and 39 per cent of women living at home. This is a trend which is clearly linked to another social trend, notably that of the increase in house prices, markedly up by 204 per cent between 1995 and 2006, a period during which pay rises fell far behind and the demand for housing increased, owing to the growing number of smaller households, including lone-person households (*Social Trends*, 2007). This, however, is another trend noted in 2008 *Social Trends* which is then countered by a changing economic climate brought on by the 'credit crunch' of that year, which has led to the same outcome, namely fewer people being able to afford to buy their own homes, but because of unemployment and the lack of availability of mortgages, rather than rising house prices. The dramatic fall in UK house prices in 2008 led to a Bank of England estimate that 1.2 million UK households, 10 per cent of mortgage holders, would be in negative equity in 2009 (in Conway, 2009). This means that people are living in a house that is worth less than the amount they borrowed to pay for it. This is a phenomenon which is happening at the same time as instability in the labour market with increasing unemployment and credit restrictions meaning that there are limitations on borrowing, which often costs more.

The overall trend has been for fewer people to marry although there is some fluctuation. It remains the case that 70 per cent of families include a married couple, although marriage, like child-bearing, on average takes place later than in the past with the average age of men at first marriage being 32 and for women 29. While divorce rates in the UK reached a peak in 1971 and 1972 following the Divorce

Reform Act of 1969, which introduced the irretrievable breakdown of marriage as the sole ground for divorce, removing the concepts of 'guilty party' and 'matrimonial offence', divorce remains part of the experience of family life. Divorce is also often followed by remarriage so that 10 per cent of children in the UK live in step families (*Social Trends*, 2007: 20). Again there are fluctuations in these social trends. For example, 2008 saw the lowest divorce rate since before the Divorce Reform Act, although this could most likely be due to the vastly reduced numbers of people marrying than to the contentment of the marriages that had previously taken place.

As is evident from the number of marriages ending in divorce, changes in the law contribute to and facilitate social trends. The year 2005 saw the legalisation of civil partnerships for same-sex couples, and 15,700 people in the UK took advantage of this between December 2005 and September 2006. The majority of these civil partnerships were made in England and Wales (with London seeing a large number of the 93 per cent), with only 6 per cent in Scotland and 1 per cent in Northern Ireland, suggesting that the law is not the only force in play, but legalisation does demonstrate changing patterns. The evidence points to changes in the patterns of social and economic life and in everyday living, all of which indicate the need for policy makers to address the changing needs of the population. Patterns of domestic living and demographic trends all lead to the need for governments to amend their policies, especially in terms of welfare, education and health care. An increasingly elderly population means greater demands for health and social care; fewer young people in the working population and more of pensionable age reduce the pool of taxation upon which governments can draw.

Changing places: changing times

As may be seen from some of the discussion of demography, there are changes taking place in people's everyday lives, but these changes are uneven and, although there are identifiable patterns of change there are also continuities and some marginal shifts rather than massive changes. An increasingly elderly population, more women in the workplace, later and fewer marriages and the postponement of child-bearing among some sections of the population seem to constitute discernible patterns which impact both upon everyday life and governments and policy makers. The overall trend has been for a reduction in the birth rate in what can be called the West, but there have been recent blips in this general reduction in the number of babies being born. This evidence is drawn largely from official statistics. As I shall demonstrate later in this book, statistical data offer one source of evidence, but, of course, social scientists also use qualitative data drawn, for example, from interviews and observation to understand and explain social life. Qualitative data provide rich material which captures people's own experience and how they feel about their lives. Media accounts also provide a source of evidence for patterns of social change. The media offer an important source of information, although social scientists do have to be sceptical because such versions of recounting social change tend very much to focus on the sensational values of news and to emphasise both what is dramatic about the changes that are taking place and the extreme nature of any identified changes. Sensation and drama will sell newspapers, and raise viewing, listening and accessing figures.

One of the most significant areas of change in social life in recent years has been the mobility of peoples, for example across Europe. There have always been migrations of people for a number of reasons; motivated by economic factors, to gain a better life, or to escape an oppressive regime and political persecution. Post 9/11 and the destruction of the twin towers in the US, the 2004 Madrid train bombings and 7/7, the London bombings, discussion of migration has taken a different turn and has become mixed up with talk of the politics of national security and risk. This is a trend that has been enthusiastically embraced by the press, especially the tabloid press in recent years, where migration has been read as 'swamping' the community which is host to migrant people who may be described as 'scrounging'; those who leave their country of origin are seen as threatening the way of life of their new home or draining its resources, and the economic and cultural contributions they make are often overlooked. Again, the evidence of such mobility, which we will look at in more detail in Chapter 6, is much more complicated than the sensationalist popular press would suggest. The UK population is increasingly diverse, for example, with young people being six times more likely than adults to be mixed race. The Equality and Human Rights Commission reported in 2009 that there had been a dramatic shift over the past ten years with as many as one in four primary schoolchildren in some inner city areas, for example in London, being mixed race (Asthana and Smith, 2009). The term 'mixed race' is not one that everyone so described embraces, but the evidence does point to both the speed of change and the diversity of contemporary life.

Case study: life in the tower block

One device for exploring a slice of life in contemporary society is to focus upon a particular location. A study of a single street has been used as such a device in the social sciences to undertake research into the experience of everyday life and how this might be changing. 'The street' is often the focus of everyday claims about society; 'the man in the street' often serves as a metaphor for the ordinary person; 'the woman in the street' is less often invoked, although her views are increasingly important to governments, many of whom have translated the ordinary woman into the woman at work juggling the demands of home and paid employment. 'The street' is often perceived as representative of local communities and, as such, is the focus of popular culture, as in soap operas like *Neighbours* and *Coronation Street*, and it is accessible to children, as in *Sesame Street*. In this section I describe a tower block in London which serves a similar purpose.

ACTIVITY

First of all think about where you live. Who lives around you? Do you know your neighbours? What do you think has changed about this place over the period you have been living there? If you haven't lived there very long think about how this place is different from where you lived as a child.

COMMENT

Of course, it depends on where you live and how long you have lived there, but it is very unlikely that the community in which you live has remained untouched by the demographic changes of recent years and the shifts in housing policies. Many of the changes you note are likely to be examples of some of the shifts noted at the start of this chapter. People live in very diverse forms of families and relationships; many people live alone. Urban areas, where the vast majority of Western populations live, have seen the greatest transformations through migration and changes in domestic living. Rural areas have remained less ethnically mixed than urban areas and many are predominantly white in the UK, for example, but even in traditionally settled communities you may well not know your neighbours, and 'the street' may no longer provide a strong sense of belonging to a place.

The example which follows is of a place that is in many ways a typical urban site in the twenty-first century. The example is not at the top end of the market, being a block of flats which was formerly social housing in the UK. It is not occupied by the more affluent members of British society, although some of those who own the flats which are let out may have made money from doing so, even though they do not live in the property they own, but in a different part of town or even in a different country. What does it tell us about how local everyday life might be changing and how do any of these changes relate to wider changes across the globe? What questions does this example raise and what are the big issues?

The housing estate

Social housing in the UK for much of the twentieth century was provided by local council housing. This was housing owned and maintained by local authorities and let to tenants at an affordable, low rent. Following the election of the Conservative government led by Margaret Thatcher in 1979, legislation was passed heralding a 'social revolution' in housing called 'The Right to Buy', which allowed council tenants to purchase their own council house. In 1979 42 per cent of the British population lived in council housing. In 2008 the figure was 12 per cent (Harris, 2008). My purpose in exploring the example of a block of flats where tenants were given the 'right to buy' is not to debate the rights and wrongs of this policy but to look at the links between everyday life in all its diversity and the wider social world.

The Becontree housing estate in Dagenham, east London was such a case of tenants having the 'right to buy' their own homes at a very competitive price; in fact a very low price, which took the form of flats in a high-rise building. Who lives there in 2009?

Whereas, in 1979, 66 per cent of homes in the borough were owned by the council, by 2008 it was a different picture, with a very limited supply of social housing which had been largely taken over by the private rented sector and a very diverse population, reflecting the expansion of the UK's multi-racial postwar population. Those who live in flats in the tower block represent a diverse range. For example, one flat is occupied by three Kosovan families who rent the flat from their employer. This is in sharp contrast to the occupant of a flat on the floor above which is owned by a landlord, who has now retired to Spain, who bought the flat at a 50 per cent discount in 1982 and sold it for twenty times as much in 2007 to a struggling first-time buyer. A flat below the Kosovan families has been repurchased by the council from its private owner for emergency housing, so the occupiers of this flat represent a transient population. On the other side of the building there is a single woman who bought her flat for £50,000, a bargain until she was subsequently asked for another £50,000 by the council for essential repairs. Another woman who came to the UK from the Caribbean in the 1960s bought her flat in the early 1980s and still lives there. However, another resident notes change over time, and comments on the rapid increase in the number of former tenants buying, so that, from a position of just a minority buying their own flat and remaining resident, there is now a very high and fast turnover of people living in the block.

Not all council tenants availed themselves of the right to buy. One white woman who had lived in one of the flats for 32 years was unable to do so because even at the heavily discounted rate she knew that she and her sick husband would not be able to access a mortgage to purchase the property. As she says:

> The people who bought the properties don't live in them anymore . . . they do them up, they sell them, and they get rented out. A lot of them go and live abroad . . . you might have two or three families in one three-bedroom flat. I've seen that happen on our estate. We get a lot from Africa. A lot of short-term people from Kosovo. The problem is the sense of community is utterly eroded. Once, you could walk down the road and everybody spoke to you; you'd know who they were. People still say 'Good morning', and I'll say Good morning back . . . But I couldn't tell you who they are, because with 95 per cent of them, it's the only time I've seen them.
>
> (in Harris, 2008: 9)

This woman cites the impact of the particular 'right to buy' policy on the local community and one aspect of the mobility of tenants and new owners in her experience.

One Kosovan-Albanian refugee who gained British citizenship in 1992 explains that he was happy with buying the flat he lives in with his wife and two children: 'I thought my kids would have a roof above their heads when we are not around . . . now we have our own place, no one can kick us out' (in Harris, 2008: 10).

However, this dream of security was shattered when, in 2005, the council's property management company requested payment of a large sum (more than the initial cost of the flat in 2002) in payment for maintenance and repair work on the block's exterior, payable within three years and way out of the budget of this family. There is little hope of a solution for this family beyond attempting to appeal against the council's decision at a tribunal, since selling might not be an option given the lack of popularity of lending on such properties by mortgage lenders.

COMMENT: WHAT DOES THIS CASE STUDY TELL US?

This is a partial story about a place to live and how that place has changed over the past 30 years. What are the social issues here? What sorts of concepts do social scientists offer to explain what is happening in terms of patterns of living and of social change?

First, this case study illustrates the links between everyday life and government policies and practices. Changes in government policies impact upon people's lives in very real ways, in this example in relation to where they live. A change in policies can create opportunities for some people and problems for others. Legislation in democracies may change in response to popular demand, but laws can also shape people's lives in ways which they may not welcome. This particular case study presents an example of what has come to be called **neoliberal governance**, a form of government that has become increasingly common across the globe, especially with the breakup of the former USSR and of the communist states of Eastern Europe. Neoliberal governance is characterised by free market economies and a supportive but largely non-interventionist state which encourages its **citizens** to be self-governing and to act independently. The shift from council housing, which is owned by local government and which played a key role in the postwar social democratic settlement implemented by the Labour Party in government in the UK in the late 1940s and 1950s to the 'right to buy', is typical of this transformation. Neoliberal governance presents citizens with opportunities to conduct their lives without constant regulation by the state. Thus, citizens are left to organise their own lives as far as they can with the state providing back-up for those who are unable to do so, for example with a limited pool of social housing. These policies, with their strong reliance on the strength of the market, were associated with the Ronald Reagan presidency in the US and with Margaret Thatcher's administration in the UK in the 1980s, although they have continued into the twenty-first century and have been pursued enthusiastically by more left liberal governments too, including the Blair Labour governments in the UK. This case study demonstrates some of the problems of this trend at a time of economic crisis when, however positive the possibilities of neoliberal opportunities such as the right to buy your own home, limited resources resulting from job losses and lack of availability of credit mean that people may be in financial trouble and even lose their homes without a more proactive government, which is, of course, what happened in 2008. In 2008 and 2009 financial support was more dramatically channelled into the banking system and the big banks than directly to households and people with mortgages which they had been encouraged to take out as part of earlier policy initiatives.

Another social dimension of this example of life in a tower block is the importance of cultural assumptions and ideologies. For example, in the UK there is a powerful discourse that suggests that 'an Englishman's home is his castle' and ownership of one's own home is a right or at least something to which citizens could and even should aspire. This is less the case in other parts of Europe where renting a property to live in is more routine, although the ideology of ownership is more pervasive in the US. This is an aspect of culture and is part of tradition and of the ways in which people make sense of their lives through shared values. This may be construed as ideology or as a set of discourses which make up the common sense of a society and pass for truth; the idea that everyone should want to own rather than rent their own home becomes taken for granted and taken for the common sense that everyone shares.

Second, this case study illustrates demographic trends, one important feature of which in contemporary life is the impact of migration and mobility. Recent years have seen an increase in the movement of peoples across the globe and in particular from what was Eastern Europe. This mobility is not of course a new phenomenon but it has taken particular forms in recent years since the breakup of the USSR and the movement of peoples from Eastern to Western Europe often for economic reasons. Migration has also increased for political reasons and the number of political refugees into parts of Europe (e.g. the UK) has also increased. Several of the occupants of this tower block are from such states and have often come to the UK to avoid persecution or deprivation in their homeland. Matters of security are primary to the concerns of people who are refugees and who have left their country of birth to seek a better life for themselves and their families. Thus ethnicity and mobility are key concepts in explaining social trends and practices in this example.

The occupancy of these flats also demonstrates other demographic trends. There is a more diverse population in terms of **ethnicity**. Ethnicity includes the language, customs, rituals and practices that are associated with a particular group of people, the identity that they share. The term **race**, sometimes expressed as 'race', is used in the social sciences to cover the social identities which are often based on visible differences between people and possibly some physical characteristics they may share. The term race is sometimes preferred because it retains a political dimension, whereas ethnicity is mostly descriptive, and race allows for recognition of racism which is often involved in the relations between people from different ethnic groups. The use of inverted commas, or 'scare quotes', around 'race' allows for a focus on racial difference which shows that the concept is not fixed and biologically rooted, but is a dynamic, socially influenced category. The UK is a multi-ethnic society characterised by citizens from diverse ethnic groups. One of the problems of thinking about race and ethnicity which has been demonstrated by social scientists in recent years is that neither concept addresses whiteness and the particularities of white communities. For example, the white woman who has lived on the Becontree estate for 32 years is part of a local community that has increasingly felt itself to be marginalised, for example in the provision of housing, in recent years. White, working-class communities may feel that their needs have been overlooked and policy priorities favour newer members of the community, many of whom are migrants. This perceived marginalisation is not always supported, for example, because many migrant families and individuals rent in the private sector and do not live in council accommodation, but what is important is that white people also constitute ethnic groups and in many areas are not an assumed majority, but are themselves a numerical minority. **Multiculturalism** and diversity are outcomes of change in the contemporary world in which there has been massive movement of peoples over the past century and especially in recent years with political upheavals following the breakup of the USSR and events in what was Eastern Europe as well as Africa. Migration has led to the advantages of multi-culturalism and the enrichment of **diversity**, but it is also distinguished by hostility and racism. Migrants are not always well received and **racism** is also a feature of most Western societies like the UK. One factor in this is the failure of governments to address the problems of white communities and the resultant resentment which is inevitably an outcome. Whiteness also matters and is an area of research that has important implications for the well-being of the wider society, especially given some of the disadvantages, real and perceived, in traditional white, working-class communities.

Other demographic trends demonstrated in this example are manifest in different forms of domestic living; for example, more people who are lone parents, especially mothers, more single people, living alone as a result of choice or, increasingly, of a relationship breakdown. Several of the occupants of these flats are women; some are single parents, some are women living alone, others are in relationships. Another organising concept that social scientists apply to explaining social organisation, and especially social divisions, is **gender**. The term gender is used in preference to sex owing to the social and cultural connotations which it carries. Although there is no clear-cut distinction between the two, sex and gender are closely related, but gender allows for an accommodation of all the social and cultural meanings that go with being assigned the gender of female or male, rather than seeing these attributes as purely biologically given and fixed. Feminist critics have pointed to the primacy of gender, that is, the expected behaviour and power structures that accompany particular gender divisions, in organising society. Gender is a key factor shaping life chances and is closely linked to other aspects of difference. The main point about theories that foreground gender as a key dimension of difference is that they see power as operating through gender difference, significantly in the power which men are able to exert over women in patriarchal societies. In recent years the emphasis has shifted from a focus on women, whereby gender is seen as being about women, to an examination of how masculinity is constructed. Gender articulates with other social divisions such as generation or age and ethnicity and race. **Generation** is another key factor; for example, older people of pensionable age constitute a growing section of the population who are also likely to experience financial difficulties, especially in times of economic crises. People at different points in the life course have different needs and different levels of dependency as well as different opportunities for looking after themselves. This is also clearly linked to the role of the state in supporting those whose needs are greatest, and is an important aspect of neoliberal policies which promote the self-governing citizen and the ideology of 'looking after yourself'.

Economic factors underpinning many of the social aspects of this case study

Third, these economic materialities often take the form of socioeconomic class. Ownership of the flats is spread across a wide population, although occupancy is restricted to those on limited incomes. Social **class** is an important concept in this case. Social class is defined in different ways within the social sciences, but all approaches include some understanding of differential life chances and opportunities. Class may be understood as being based on employment, income and personal wealth or poverty. Class may be seen as relational; that is, one class is defined in relation to another and in relation to its position in the economy. Those who took advantage of 'right to buy' policies, whether as tenants or through other strategies, and then sold the property at a profit, purchased further properties and benefited financially, may be seen as occupying a privileged position in the capitalist economy that makes this possible. Those who were either unable to purchase their home because of ill health or low income, or who did so and were unable to keep up payments, occupy a very different class position without any ownership of capital or possibility of benefiting from that ownership. They have only their labour to sell in whatever employment they are able to get and cannot invest capital which they do not have. Class covers a person's socio-economic grouping. Class is defined in many different ways by social scientists, and in recent years has been a less popular category of classifying social divisions. Class focuses on economic position, for example in relation to the labour market and a person's position within the economic system. Class includes access to resources and is a crucial factor in understanding social divisions. In recent years, more emphasis has been given to other aspects of difference, such as race and ethnicity, gender, sexuality and place, and some social scientists have used the notion of 'lifestyle' rather than class to incorporate a wider range of factors. However, class is a very important way of positioning people regarding their social and economic standing in relation to others; to those with whom they share a class position in relation to those who are classified differently. Discussion of the concept of class is taken up in more detail in Chapter 4 but it is signalled here as an important concept within the social sciences, which has a long history and makes significant contributions to debates about equality and inequality and the ways in which societies are divided.

Fourth, a social science concept that is closely connected to class but which encompasses a wider area of study, the example illustrates the importance of

materialities. These materialities include the material environment such as the place where people live, including the actual building and how that building, its facilities, décor and situation can impact upon experience. Materialities also include bodies; that is, the physical body of the person. Bodies can have varying degrees of disability and bodily competence. Disability is another aspect of difference that can lead to exclusion and inequality and economic disadvantage. Physical and mental impairments carry social meanings and material outcomes. The experience of disability may be shaped by social factors, including the physical environment, how it is organised, whether or not it is structured to facilitate mobility and freedom for everyone, and social and cultural attitudes, which may greatly constrain those suffering some impairment. Understandings of disability may accord greater or lesser weight to social factors, although there may still be limitations which lie outside social meanings. Disability and ill health can limit people's access to financial security and economic success, in this case to accessing the benefits of buying their own home. This invokes a relationship between the body and the environment, between what could be called 'inner nature' and 'outer nature'. Inner nature is the body, its biology, physical and psychological aspects, and outer nature is the environment in which we live, which includes social organisation and structures. This has been called the '*nature versus nurture*' debate, which is a shorthand and simplified summary of the tension between the 'inner nature' of innate characteristics, skills and propensities and the 'nurture' which includes factors in the social world outside the anatomical body. However, it is very difficult to disentangle what is social and what is natural, and many social scientists prefer to explore how the social and the natural interrelate rather than suggesting that they are separate and distinct.

The emphasis upon materialities in the social sciences as a means of addressing the impact of material things raises questions about the extent to which people are able to exercise agency. While neoliberal governance poses the idea that we are self-governing citizens who can make choices and look after ourselves, this case study demonstrates that we are severely constrained by materialities that are outside our control. This issue has been described as the relationship between individual and collective **agency** on then one hand, and social and natural **structures** on the other. To what extent do human beings shape their own world and how far are they subject to factors outside their control, whether natural materialities, either of inner or outer nature such as their own embodied experience and make-up, or external, environmental factors which impinge upon them or structures within the societies in which they live? Social structures include some of the concepts identified above, such as class, gender and race and ethnicity as well as the social, political, economic and cultural organisation and the institutions of the societies in which we live.

Although I have identified some concepts which inform social science explanations, it is important to note that they interconnect, and social meanings and explanations overlap and combine to provide an understanding of social change and everyday experience which create the big issues in contemporary society that this book addresses.

Conclusion

In this chapter I have set out some of the issues which this book will address and have introduced some of the key ideas employed by the social sciences for exploring changing times. Using the example taken from everyday life, I have attempted to draw out some of the different aspects of the narrative which make it social. By unpacking this case study we have seen some of the ways in which knowledge is produced within the social sciences and highlighted the importance of locating everyday experience within the wider social context. This illustrates the interrelationship between the personal and the social and between the private and the public. A person's own home may seem to be a clear example of a private space, especially if they own that space, or at least that part of the building, but whether or not this private ownership or even access to this space we call home is possible is the result of public policies and wider economic factors that operate very much within the public realm, of the state or of the wider global economy.

The concepts briefly introduced in this chapter are those which will inform the discussion in the rest of the book. The approach taken is one that starts with questions, the kinds of questions posed within the social sciences in order to unpack what is involved in processes of change and upheaval, as well as presenting a sceptical critique of the extent of change. The chapters which follow take a key issue concerned with change in contemporary society and explore some of the ways in which knowledge is produced about this issue and the different claims that are made within the social sciences.

Summary

- *Questions* provide the starting point for the investigation. What is going on? What are the implications of this? What else do we need to know?
- *Concepts* provide an organising framework with categories and concepts covering the key ideas.
- *Debates* present different views and different perspectives which form *theories*.
- *Knowledge* illustrates the ways in which the social sciences inform and relate to policies; social science relates to action and what we do about social issues, and is part of societies where knowledge is of prime importance.

The chapters that follow take a key issue concerned with change in contemporary society and explore some of the ways in which knowledge is produced about this issue and the different claims that are made within the social sciences.

Chapter 2, Identity matters: us and them, focuses on a particular concept, that of identity, which brings together the interrelationship between the personal and the social and focuses upon how the self and how subjects are made. The big issue here, which is of considerable importance in the contemporary world, is the growth of uncertainty about 'who we are' and the attempts that have been made to secure identity. This chapter introduces the concept of identity through exploring some examples covering the areas of place and mobilities, gender and the impact of new technologies on the formation of identities. It addresses the relationship between the public and the private arenas, for example using the idea of electronic communication to look at the different ways in which people present themselves online. Cyberspace may appear to offer a space of enormous possibilities, not only for speed of communication but as a democratic space in which people are not constrained by financial constraints and the material limitations of everyday life including the gender, race and disabilities of the material bodies that they inhabit in their lives offline.

The key questions of the chapter are:

- What is identity?
- Are we more uncertain about our identities in the contemporary world and if so, how do we try to establish and confirm some certainties?
- Why are social scientists interested in identity? What alternative concepts are there to use to think about who we are?
- How can the social sciences contribute to our understanding of personal and collective identities?

Chapter 3, Citizenship and social order, involves an exploration of what is meant by citizenship in the twenty-first century in relation to community and political action. The big issue addresses the changing nature of citizenship and the question of who is excluded and who is included within the category of citizens. The focus is on equality, difference and diversity in the construction of citizenship and the role of the state in relation to inclusion and exclusion as well as the denial of rights and citizenship to those who are dependent on the state.

Key questions for this chapter are:

- How is citizenship constructed?
- Who is included and who isn't, and why not?
- How is citizenship changing?

Chapter 4, Buying and selling, explores the relationship between consumption and production and the emerging importance of consumption-based identities, for example in terms of the shift away from traditional class-based categorisation and the use of lifestyle classifications. The big issue concerns the power relationship between consumption and production, and addresses the question of how far it is possible to focus on patterns of consumption and lifestyle as the key sources of social divisions.

Key questions for this chapter are:

- What is the relationship between production and consumption and how do they influence each other?

- How much control is exercised by consumers in this process; where does power lie and how does it operate?
- Are we what we buy?
- What is the importance of class in the relationship between production and consumption?

Chapter 5, We live in a material world, explores the social science concept of materialities, starting with a review of what is material about what has been covered so far, notably markets and the materiality of wealth and resources and associated inequalities. This chapter will focus upon one of the more negative aspects of the expansion of consumption, namely the status of material resources and ecosystems, by using the example of current debates about waste disposal in the UK in order to show how materialities are a key area of concern and debate within the social sciences and in our lives.

Key questions include:

- What is the influence of the material world on our lives?
- How do people and objects relate to each other?
- How are material objects cultural?
- How is the material world changing?

Chapter 6, Mobilities: place and race, considers the importance of place in shaping social relations, connections and attachments. It explores the impact of diverse ethnicities, using the UK as an example of a multi-ethnic society, and looks at the tension between racism and multi-culturalism and how diversity could be seen as enriching and beneficial at this historical moment. The big issue is the importance of mobilities in the contemporary world and debates about questions of multi-culturalism and diversity, and how place can be rethought in a climate of mobility.

Key questions include:

- What is the importance of mobility in shaping life chances?
- What do we mean by race and ethnicity; how do we use the terms?
- How useful is the concept of multi-culturalism? Is it still possible in the contemporary world?
- How far is diversity constrained by social exclusion and racism?

Chapter 7, Globalisation: opportunities and inequalities, examines some of the key debates about globalisation, focusing especially on the tension between those who see the process as positive and beneficial and those who see it as destructive, for example of local culture as well as of the environment. The big issue is about the impact of globalisation. How far do the phenomena associated with it have beneficial outcomes or how far are they damaging? Is it a uniform process? How far does globalisation produce homogeneity so that we are all the same now? Or, on the other hand, are diversity, resistance and creativity still possible in the face of the ubiquity of global capital? The chapter focuses upon discussion of uneven development and the inequality involved in the globalisation project.

Key questions include:

- What do we mean by globalisation?
- How does it affect different groups and communities; are some more equal than others?
- What are the positive and the negative aspects of globalisation?
- Has globalisation contributed to the 'risk society'?
- Is it a uniform process?
- What is the scope for resistance and for diversity?

Chapter 8, Conclusion, reviews the argument and evidence presented in this book and looks at how far we have come. The 'big issues' have been identified and some discussion of what study in the social sciences can contribute to debate has been introduced. The concluding chapter revisits the key debates in the book about the role of the social sciences, and reflects upon the ways in which the social sciences can enhance and challenge common-sense understandings of the social, political, economic and cultural world. It also suggests ways in which an interest in the social sciences might be developed and pursued with some discussion of the concerns of the different social science disciplines and their application, indicating the links between knowledge produced in the social sciences and political action and policies as well as social change. Knowledge produced within the social sciences is part of the social transformations that are taking place. Social science knowledge is deeply implicated in social change, both in responding to material circumstances, for example in economic life, and as part of the knowledge revolution that is an outcome of new technologies, and social and cultural transformations. So what are these transforming big issues?

Chapter 2

Identity matters

Us and them

Introduction

One of the key debates within the social sciences which was identified in Chapter 1 in the context of changing times is the question of who we are and where we belong. As communities change and re-form, identities become mobile and mobilised. These mobilities focus on the relationship between the personal and the individual on the one hand, and the social on the other. What links are there between individuals and the societies in which they live? How does the one influence the other? Is it possible to distinguish between the one and the other? This issue has been addressed within the social sciences through the concept of identity. Identity offers a means of thinking about and understanding how the personal and the social are connected.

Having an identity is one of the ways in which we fit into the social world and are marked as having distinctive membership of one group rather than another within society. Identity is also a word with which we are familiar in the contemporary world on the global as well as the personal scale. It has been quite a fashionable word, for example, in the media where we read of 'identity crises', new identities and the need to secure our identities, such as national identities, for example as British or English or as European. Is it meaningful to talk about British when the increased mobility of people makes Britain a very diverse society? What does it mean to be English at a time when Welsh, Scottish and Irish identities are reclaimed and there is devolution of power in the UK? Identity is not only in common use, it has deep and often very powerful meanings. What does it mean to be British, French or German at a time of large-scale migration across the boundaries of nation states, for example by refugees and those seeking asylum from repressive regimes and economic deprivation, as well as the movement of skilled labour that is required by global capital? What meanings are attached to the identities of US citizens in the aftermath of 11 September 2001 and the wars in Iraq and Afghanistan? Conflict in the global arena has often been described in terms of competing or conflicting identities; Croats, Serbs and Bosnians, Tutsi and Hutu in Rwanda and, in the twenty-first century, in what is one of the most serious of conflicts in the global arena, Israelis and Palestinians. These conflicts can be between ethnic groups or between explicitly religious groups such as Catholics and Protestants or Muslims and Jews. The assertion of collective identities can lead to conflict and even violent hostilities. The September 11 attacks on Washington and New York were described in the most polarised of terms, as an extreme conflict between 'us' and 'them' which, in some of the political rhetoric, divided the world into the 'free world' and terrorism, which has had enormous global repercussions. These attacks on 9/11, as this occasion has come to be known, were significant in making a shift in the classification of identities at times of conflict and war. Identity became a big issue when the identity of the enemy was terrorism, but had no clear identity marked by membership of a nation state, or even a specific territory or ethnic group. The second Iraq war which followed was a desperate response on the part of the US in particular to locate its enemy in a particular place: a nation state. The contemporary world offers examples of many such conflicts arising from uncertainties about identities.

In other situations identities are linked to the movement of peoples across the globe, whether this arises from the need to seek asylum, economic transformations or the demands of new technologies and the labour market.

New technologies also offer challenges to certainties about identity at a personal level. Cloning of human beings becomes ever more possible if not necessarily desirable or practical. When a French woman gave birth to a child using the egg of an anonymous donor which had been fertilised by her brother's sperm in 2001, alarm was expressed at this development. At the same time, the Italian Professor Severino Antinori announced that 200 couples were participating in an experiment to produce cloned babies. Both events were greeted with considerable anxiety, much of which was centred on the identity of the people so created. The first case showed how reproductive technologies might be used to challenge hitherto securely held certainties about origins and the identity of the mother and the father of a child. It was further complicated by the suggestion that the technology could permit a child to be born whose father was her or his uncle even though no actual incestuous behaviour was involved. Cloning seems even more troubling for our sense of who we are. Who are you if you are not genetically unique? Such developments illustrate some of the uncertainties with which we are beset in the contemporary world. People's responses indicate their desires to attain some kind of certainty in the face of these insecurities. In this chapter we are going to look at the relevance of identity in the contemporary world, what we mean by identity, whether there is more uncertainty than in the past, and the ways in which people seek to establish and secure their identities, both within a group, as having a collective identity, and as individuals, fitting into the world in which they live.

What do we mean by identity?

Identity involves aligning ourselves with one group of people; saying that we are the same as them, as well as marking ourselves out as different from other groups of people. We can have a collective identity at the local or even the global level, whether through culture, religion or politics, as well as having an individual identity, as a mother, father or worker. Identity is not only a word used to make sense of 'who we are' in the global arena; it is what links the personal to the social, the 'I' to the 'me'. Identity includes the idea of 'I', that is, the subject of a sentence. When we say 'I' we have some notion of who it is who is speaking and that it is the same person on each occasion who says 'I'. Identity involves how I see myself and how others see me. The social philosopher George Herbert Mead used this idea to show how the personal and individual was linked to the social in the development of children (1934). Mead argued that we only learn self-awareness through connecting the 'I' to the 'me'. The 'I' is the unsocialised child who is a collection of needs, wants and desires, and the 'me' is the social self. Children become autonomous adults who are able to take up different identities and develop self-consciousness, having moved from imitating the actions of others as small children, to understanding how others see them and being able to look at themselves from the outside, ultimately from the perspective of the society in which they live. In 2008 a self-identified man, Thomas Beattie, aged 34 (BBC, 2008) gave birth to a child, a scenario which illustrates even more powerfully the mixing of the natural and the social and uncertainty about gendered identities. The 'man' had been born a woman, and following hormone treatment had developed external male characteristics such as facial hair and body shape, but had not had either uterus or ovaries removed. Through this process the personal and the social combine and interconnect.

As an individual, each of us has a whole range of identities; as a worker, as a parent, daughter or son, as a consumer, as a member of a community and of an ethnic group, as a fan of a football team, or of a particular form of music or entertainment. These are all part of everyday life. We experience a whole range of different identities in our daily interaction with others. The sociologist Erving Goffman (1959) described these different parts which we play, which I called identities here, as **roles**. Goffman's focus on everyday life is useful in exploring the ways in which people present themselves to others and for exploring the detail of everyday interactions. Taking on an identity may go further than acting out a role. We have personal investment in the identities which we adopt. For most people, holding on to some sense of 'who we are', and sometimes more particularly of 'who I am' is very important. In the contemporary Western world this is manifest in different ways; at the personal level people may turn to 'expert' advice to sort out their sense of who they are. This may be through personal counselling or through the pages of magazines and newspapers, with their problem pages and self-help guides. Television, radio and the Internet also provide us with public spaces in which we can identify with the personal crises of other people. Sometimes we can join in through phone-ins or Internet chat rooms, or through being an actual participant, as on 'reality TV'. We can vote for the eviction of those individuals we dislike from the *Big Brother* household. The coverage of 'reality' TV pro-grammes such as *Big Brother* strongly encourages identification with some individuals alongside the often extreme vilification of others. Identities are the common currency of popular television, offering apparent, if superficial and distorted certainties about 'good' and 'bad'. At the wider level uncertainties about who we are and the need to protect the certainties of one group can lead to conflict, which can take the form of extreme violence, as has been experienced in the heart of corporate North America, in the tourist resort of Bali in Indonesia, in the heart of the Spanish rail system in Madrid, on central London's transport system on 7 July 2007, in Palestine in 2008 and 2009, as well as previously in Bosnia, Chechnya, Israel and Northern Ireland. Whether we delve deeper into ourselves in search of greater certainty about 'who we are' or take to the streets in bitter conflict to protect our identities, identity is an important feature of the contemporary world. This chapter looks at why identity is such an important matter in contemporary societies and why it is important as a concept within the social sciences. This will involve picking out the key features of identity and of what matters in the formation of identity as well as addressing some of the debates within the social sciences that make identity such a big issue.

Summary

- Identity links the personal to the social.
- Identity involves how I see myself and how others see me.
- Each of us has many different identities.
- We have collective and individual identities.
- Identity is a key concept in the social sciences and of major importance in our lives.

Who am I?

Before we move into the broader arena of identity, let us start with an exercise that provides a focus on the more immediate question of 'Who am I?'

ACTIVITY

Stop for a moment and write down five things about yourself; just the first five that come into your head that say something about you.

COMMENT

You may already have done an exercise like this one. It is quite often used in order to highlight the ways we think about ourselves and to suggest what individuals might think is important about their own identities. There may be several different points that you have made. You may have thought consciously about your identity and described your social position as mother, Scottish, student, made reference to the job which you do, or you may have listed your visible and embodied characteristics: tall, thin, black hair, wear glasses. One factor which many people note when they do this exercise is gender. Gender is a little different from other social features because it is also usually a visible characteristic; like hair colour or height, it is something others are likely to observe when they first meet us. You may well have noted some physical characteristics, that is those which are visible and which relate to your body. Age or disability are other features you may have noted. These too may be visible features although this is not always the case. People may not always indicate their age in their appearance; disabilities such as deafness are not visible. One of the other social features is race or ethnicity, which is also likely to be something others notice; race and ethnicity are often visible too. Gender and race are important features that are both visible and social. You can observe these features and they are socially significant. Did you include some reference to these two features in your list? It is still likely to be the case that people who are white are less likely to have included 'I am white' in their list as a distinguishing feature of themselves. Why is this? Is it because being white is taken for granted as what is normal? As Ruth Frankenburg argues, 'white people are "raced" just as men are gendered' (1993: 1); that is, gender is not just women's concern and race is not just about black people. However, in the West it is more likely that 'race' is seen to be the concern of people who are black than of people who are white. Although whiteness has increasingly come under the scrutiny of social scientists, especially due to the growing disaffection of some white communities, such as underperforming white youth in schools, and traditional white working-class communities where there is resentment at the disruption of social life and perceived lack of support and government resources which they feel is invested in this social group. Your ethnicity may relate to the place you come from or to your national identity, or perhaps to your religion. Many aspects of 'who we are' are not likely to be visible in the ways that gender and 'race' are, for example the job you do and even how wealthy or poor you are, except perhaps at the extremes of affluence or poverty, as well as your religious or political beliefs.

This exercise raises issues about the social categories through which we describe and make sense of ourselves. First, considerable importance is accorded to visible differences between people; how far do we differentiate on the basis of visible features? Difference is an important feature of identity. We share an identity with those who are similar to us and are different from those who take up different identity positions, and these differences are represented so that others can understand them. Second, it is apparent that these visible features are social; that is, they have social implications, and the meanings that are attached to them come from the societies in which we live. Some visible features matter more than others and may have social and economic consequences. For example, it may not matter very much if you have black or brown hair, but being a woman or a man, being black or white may have significant consequences for your life chances, even for your earning potential. Some disabilities may be visible and may affect how other people treat you. These visible differences have social implications that are also the result of social, cultural, economic and political practices. The features that are relevant to our identities, indeed those that make up an identity, are the elements that have some social significance.

Factors which contribute to our identities are shown in Figure 2.1. The self is influenced by a number of factors, which have to be negotiated, such as gender, race, ethnicity, visible signs of difference, what is different and what is the same, place, body, employment and life chances. The influence of course is not all one-way.

Some aspects of difference are much more relevant to what is called identity than others. You may have noted aspects of your personality, for example, as extrovert or introvert, or even your mood, whether you are happy or depressed. Personality differs from identity in respect of the degree of agency that we exert in adopting particular characteristics. For example, there may be some links between my personality and the type of identity positions I take up. However, whereas I may engage in some activities such as following football and going to matches every Saturday and shouting loudly, because I am an extrovert sort of person I follow a particular team, because I want to identify with that team and not with another. This allegiance may be the outcome of media coverage of a team and its players and what used to be called 'fair weather' support. Manchester United has massive support worldwide as a result of the team's success and the promotion of its image. There may be several other factors in play. I follow the team that represents the community in which I have lived for some time; it may have cultural, political and even religious links with my own community, as in the case of supporters of Glasgow Celtic or Glasgow Rangers in Scotland. In these examples, identification with one team or the other reflects deep-seated, long-held and occasionally very oppositional, conflictual beliefs. What is important is that to identify and take up an identity position there has to be some engagement.

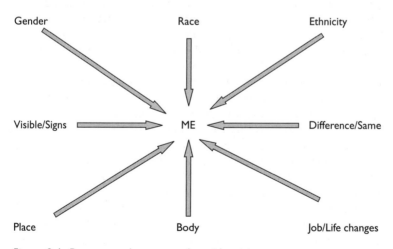

Figure 2.1 Processes that re-produce identities

Identification

Having an identity involves being active in some way, even though for many people there is only limited choice. **Identification** is the term often used in psychoanalysis to describe the process of taking up an identity. Many social scientists now prefer this term to that of identity because identification suggests something of the dynamic of the processes that are involved in taking up an identity position, although they do not necessarily draw upon its associations with psychoanalysis (Gilroy, 2005). This process goes much further than just copying the behaviour and attitudes of others. Identification involves taking an identity into yourself. Identity is not only about what others see, for example as behaviour and outward observable expressions of who we are. It is also about the inside, about feelings and the inner space where emotions and desires are played out. Sigmund Freud (1905) used the concept of identification to describe and explain the ways in which children adopted gender identities through this psychological process. One aspect of Freud's account shares similarities with that of Mead, although Freud was much more concerned with the problems and conflicts which can occur in the formation of identity than Mead. Freud was also particularly concerned with the impact of the **unconscious** mind on our experience, whereas this is not a concern in Mead's discussion. Freud focused on male children and argued that small boys identify with their fathers, taking in what they perceive to be masculine traits and ultimately a male identity. This process of identification is very powerful, and Freud emphasised the importance of early identification with the parent of the child's own sex as forming the basis of gender identity in adult life. One aspect of Freud's analysis that is particularly important is the extent of the investment that is made in gendered identities (Bocock, 1982). The characteristics that are adopted create the person's sense of who they are. Identification may be conscious or unconscious. Freud uses the notion of the **unconscious** to explain the area of the mind into which we deposit repressed feelings and desires. For example, all the times a child's wishes are not met, these unmet desires are repressed into the unconscious mind, from which they may emerge at a later date. They can emerge in dreams or jokes, or in slips of the tongue; those little mistakes that have come to be called Freudian slips. You can probably think of several examples of these. They often involve some sexual innuendo, like the occasions when someone says orgasm instead of organism or sexiest instead of sexist. The Freudian argument is that these slips are more than people having difficulty getting the words out; they represent hidden feelings which are present in the unconscious mind.

It was suggested earlier that we are recognised and recognise others often by appearance. Appearance can give some clue to our identity. Think about it: you might identify with someone who is wearing clothes that signify an identity, such as those which conform to your own religious practice. At sports events we recognise and identify with those who wear our colours or at international events those who carry our national flag and sing appropriate songs. When you are travelling abroad, we recognise as the same those who speak the same language as we do. These involve visible, or audible, outward signs of an identity. How do

Plate 2.1   England football fans display St George's flag in the main square in
Gelsenkirchen, Germany, during the Fifa World Cup 2006
Source: © PA Photos

we indicate our identities to others? By the clothes we wear, by badges, by signs
of belonging such as team colours, logos, designer labels, flags, uniforms, by how
we speak, not only language but through accents and regional dialects. These are
all signs of belonging to a particular group. It is through these signs or symbols
that we represent ourselves to others and come to recognise them. A symbol
involves making one object, word or image stand for another. For example, wearing
a particular scarf or rosette, shirt or insignia indicates membership of a particular
football team. It frequently goes further, by fans wearing a team shirt which carries
the name and number of their favourite player. This has become a global currency,
especially in the case of some celebrity players. Mead (1934) emphasised the
importance of symbolisation in the formation of identity and the representation of
ourselves to others. We have to be able to think symbolically, using language and
visual symbols, in order to imagine ourselves from others' points of view.

Representations

Social scientists have increasingly addressed the question of representational
systems in developing understanding of how identities are constructed and how

people come to take up particular identity positions. Of course it is not only social scientists who have these concerns. Politicians, commercial enterprises and advertising agencies have employed the insights of social science in developing promotional and marketing strategies which will encourage the voter or consumer to identify with a lifestyle or image which is being promoted and, most importantly, to sign up for the political party or buy the product in order to do so.

ACTIVITY

Can you think of examples of products that in their advertising invite the consumer to identify with a particular – attractive – lifestyle, rather than simply extolling the properties of the product? What sorts of links are being made?

COMMENT

Car advertising often uses attractive, affluent, well-dressed young people to represent a lifestyle. The implication is that if you buy the product you will assume the identity of a good-looking, well-off, thirty-something professional. Advertisements promoting food or household products often connote both a desirable lifestyle and caring, successful parenthood, especially motherhood. Much contemporary advertising plays with ambiguities, for example the Calvin Klein images of androgynous young people, where it is difficult to distinguish between those who are female and those who are male. Some companies offer contradictory messages which challenge any simple association between the product and the image presented. The more radical and controversial of these have included the Benetton clothing advertisements, which promoted the 'unlimited colours' of Benetton clothing with images as unexpected as those of a person dying of AIDS and a new-born baby covered in blood. Images deployed in advertising are carefully considered, according to criteria which derive from social science research as well as that of marketing. Meanings are constructed through representations, not all of which are quite so easily readable as the ones I have suggested here. Of the images presented below, further, more expert interpretation may be required to 'read' them successfully.

These are examples of visual images which appear to mark out a person – even before that person has been born. What does the visual image tell us? What meanings does it produce? Do such images reveal a 'truth' which may be seen as reflecting something which is real, something which presents a faithful reflection of reality? This image, of the foetus in utero, is one that many parents in many parts of the world cherish as the first true reflection of the baby that the woman is carrying. Whereas, prior to the arrival of foetal ultrasound scanning, the proof that a woman was carrying a child would be through her own experience of the movement of the child in her body, endorsed by the experienced hands of a midwife, 'proof' in the twenty-first century is visual. The baby would only be seen after delivery. Does the foetus have an identity? Does the mother have an identity?

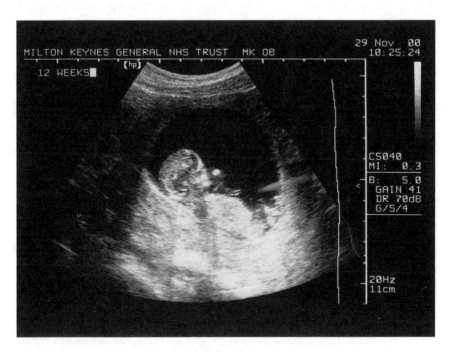

Plate 2.2 Seeing is believing: foetal image

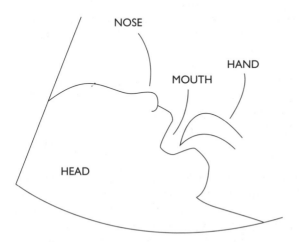

Figure 2.2 Foetal image interpreted

The foetus may be deemed to have an identity having been captured in this visual image.

Think about how many occasions there are in the contemporary world when your identity is secured through a visual image. This could be the photograph on the ID card, the passport photograph, driving licence or security card. Facebook sites include images and personal websites as well as those of organisations and institutions. People often rely on a photograph to confirm that they really are who they say they are, even that they exist at all. In the case of foetal ultrasound imaging the picture is both proof that the foetus exists and that the foetus apparently has a separate identity from the mother. This image of the free-floating foetus gives no indication of its dependent symbiotic status. It is possible to provide an image that is separate, suggesting an independent identity too. This suggestion is exaggerated by the absence of the mother in the image. We know the foetus is entirely dependent and cannot exist without the mother. Rosalind Petchesky ([1985] 2000) argues that the photographic image was produced through ultrasound scanning; it connotes wider social and cultural meanings, that is, it produces meanings by association. She argues that photographs are not simple reflections of something real.

Petchesky uses this example to show the privileging of the visual image. If you have a picture of something or of someone, then it must be real and that must be 'how it is'. However, it is the technology that makes possible the representation of an embryo inside the womb and the representation of foetus and mother as separate, independent beings.

The specific example which Petchesky uses is taken from a US anti-abortion film *The Silent Scream*, which clearly has a particular political position. However, her arguments apply to the privileging of the visual as the primary means of knowledge in Western traditions of knowledge. As she says, the visual has a peculiar property for detachment and apparent objectivity and creating a distance between the person who sees and what is seen (1985). She cites her chosen example as relying

> on our predisposition to 'see' what it wants us to 'see' because of the range of influences that are out of the particular culture and history in which we live. The aura of medical authority, the allure of technology, and the cumulative impact of a decade of foetal images . . . make it credible.
>
> ([1985] 2000: 174)

Visual representation may have a particular place in constructing identities but they are also closely linked to other discursive fields and senses other than the visual. Representations involve the images, words, sounds and practices through which meanings are expressed. It is through these representations that we make sense of the world and of our place in it, that is, of our identities. It is little wonder that advertisers are interested in how systems of representation work! The cultural theorist Roland Barthes (1972) argued that what he called texts include all forms of **representation**, not just words and images but ceremonies, rituals, clothes, films, buildings, hairstyles and television programmes. This gives us plenty to work with, but new technologies provide additional texts and we could add the Internet as another site for the production of meanings about who we are and who we could be.

In the rest of this chapter we look in more detail at the processes involved in the formation of identity and at the factors which can be included. These involve different dimensions of identity, such as gender, ethnicity, where you come from or where you live, the body and life chances, which are the sorts of aspects you might have picked out when describing yourself. All of these might suggest aspects of who we are which could provide some stability. In an uncertain and changing world, perhaps being a woman or a man and having a particular national identity or religion could offer some security and a basis for establishing our identities. Or do they?

Summary

- Identities are made up of different dimensions which include gender, race, ethnicity, work, life chances, body and place.
- These dimensions link the personal and the social and mark difference and sameness.
- Different identities are represented and may be shown through visible differences and signs.
- Identity involves personal investment through identification.

Changing media, changing messages

Different media have different codes of communication. There are different registers. Text messaging on mobile phones may be cryptic and reveal little of who we are, but it represents a shift in methods of communication and changing times in which the advent of computer technology and the speed of newly developed communication systems may be changing the ways in which we represent ourselves to others. Text messaging goes far beyond sending details of meeting times and dates, or times of arrival. Texting has its own codes and meanings, and provides a means of establishing a shared identity with those with whom we communicate.

There has been a massive expansion in Internet sites that provide personal communication mechanisms. Home pages and chat rooms offer a means for ordinary people, as well as the rich and famous, to represent themselves in a public space, which is accessible to everyone who is able to log on to the Internet (for example, Web Ring (2009)). Home pages and Facebook, the free access social networking site founded in 2004, are indications of how people seek to present themselves to others. People have to select those aspects of themselves which they want to present to the outside world. This means the aspects of your own identity to which you would like to draw the attention of others and the methods by which you would hope to achieve this.

Online?

Electronic mail provides a rapid means of communicating (and allows for much more elaborate text than the messages of the mobile phone, although the style is often just as minimalist) and the Internet offers sites on which we can represent ourselves and adopt a range of different identities. People can deploy avatars as computer users' representation of themselves as an alter ego in a three-dimensional computer game model or a two-dimensional picture on Internet or online communities. Sites such as Facebook, with pictures, graphics, music and photographs, are used to give some indication of who we are. The web has, of course, presented much more in terms of convenience and opportunities for communication. Clay Shirky argues that the web is primarily a democratising force (2008) which will ultimately replace other media. He accepts that there may be some preference for magazines with glossy pictures but he argues that the web has so many advantages, including free access, that it must supersede all other media of communication. The web is a motor for change.

> Mobile tools will change the landscape again. Open spectrum may unleash the kind of creativity we've seen in the internet and of course there will be many more YouTube/Facebook-class applications. But the underlying change was the basic tools of the internet. The job of the next decade is mostly going to be taking the raw revolutionary capability that's now apparent and really seeing what we can do with it.
>
> (Teodorczuk, 2009: 1)

This is an expression of the possibilities of the web that are driven by technological advances and offer enormous benefits and possibilities. The Internet is part of everyday life, but is it a political force that promotes equality? Are its advantages all that they are cracked up to be?

ACTIVITY

Think back over the past two weeks and consider how you have been involved in websites and the Internet. It is so much part of everyday life that you may have to think hard about particular examples.

Does the web make your life easier or more convenient? Is the arrival of the World Wide Web a force for the greater democratisation of society?

COMMENT

The Internet provides a space in which the personal and the social are interconnected. We provide personal information online, through shopping, banking, paying bills as well as through social networking sites and electronic communication. The Internet is both ordinary in that it is part of everyday life and extraordinary in the speed and distance that it covers. We can conduct close and intimate relationships with people around the world very quickly and without ever actually meeting them. Communication may never include physical presence, but we are the same embodied selves offline as we are online whatever new identities we may assume, for example, in a chat room.

The Internet can offer valuable means of communication for people with disabilities. Mike Featherstone (2000) cites examples of people with severe physical disabilities who are able to use their computer to engage in mobility and sensory exploration. By mixing computer technology with the body, people are able to achieve greater freedom in shaping their own identities. Online, people can reconstruct and create their identities. Martin Wroe cites the work of John Suter, Professor of Psychology at Rider University in the US, who claims on his website that online discussion encourages people to feel free about expressing themselves. Suter claims that text talk is unencumbered by the interferences of face-to-face communication such as gestures, facial expression and appearance. It is because 'cyberspace presents an alternative social reality, participants take on roles they might never dream of in real life . . . a shy person comes to realise the delight of spontaneously opening up, and how that leads to friendships' (in Wroe, 2002: 50). These views present very optimistic readings of the opportunities afforded by cyberspace!

However, as Wroe notes, online identities are not all positive. 'The peculiar on line cocktail of intimacy and anonymity, immediacy and distance encourages visitors to become abusive much more rapidly than in real life' (2002: 50). The web does, however, provide opportunities for intimacy that are welcomed. Internet dating has become ubiquitous in recent years.

The Internet offers a site for the presentation of sexual identities which can be a valuable resource for those who feel that the pressure of their lives is so great that they lack the time for traditional forms of networking and those who are sexually marginalised by the society in which they live (Tsang, 2000). For example, coming out online is an important stage in defining sexual identity. Although computer communication offers a public space for the expression of intimate feelings, the 'real' embodied person may feel more confident in this disembodied space. However, traditional assumptions are made about speaking as a woman or as a man online. While offering a space for the exploration of new sexual identities or the possibility of greater freedom of expression than are experienced offline, most bulletin board systems where people communicate involve presentations of the self which draw on existing gender roles. They also involve descriptions of real-world circumstances and the establishment of some context that relates to the 'real' world. Some participants use communication on the web to express their offline anxieties, treating the bulletin board as a kind of counselling service.

People may also enjoy the speed and intimacy of email communication even in situations where they frequently meet the people with whom they are communicating. Young people notoriously run up high bills texting their friends on their mobile phones, even while in the same room! The web may be disembodied but it is still 'real' bodies who press the keys and write the scripts. It is 'real' bodies who live offline. The 'real body' may belong to a man of 47, who is passing as a youth and communicating with a girl of 13 while she enjoys the privacy of her bedroom. The anonymity of virtual reality is only called into question when the 'real man' attempts to meet up with the child of 13, what is euphemistically called 'offline'.

On TV?

The Internet does, however, offer a new, public space in which to explore and reconstruct identities. Increasingly, private feelings and personal identities are presented in such public spaces. People are encouraged to explore and reveal their own feelings in public spaces such as those offered by 'Reality TV', for example in programmes such as *Big Brother*, *The Oprah Winfrey Show* and *Jerry Springer*, and radio phone-ins, as well as in chat rooms and on bulletin boards on the web. Television shows like *Big Brother* have become more and more sensational in their desire to recruit audiences through dramatic revelations. Aware of the tedium of 24-hour CCTV cameras covering the ordinariness of everyday exchanges and routine practices such as eating and sleeping, the producers sought to encourage drama by including transsexuals, for example, as a particular attraction. The formation of identities can be illustrated through the link between such public and private spheres.

The Oprah Winfrey Show has become a forum where ethical and social issues are aired. For example, in 2008, a US woman who had reassigned her gender to become a legal male by having her breasts removed and taking hormone treatment to alter her appearance, which involved facial hair and a more masculine appearance, conceived a baby by artificial insemination, and appeared on the show to make her case (Oprah News, 2009). Thomas Beattie, although legally male, retained [his] female reproductive organs and so was able to conceive, carry and deliver (by caesarean section) a baby. The story was newsworthy, with headlines such as 'Man has baby' (*The Times*, 2008), making it worth a feature on *Oprah* as well as a whole television programme. It is not only about the apparent 'shock value' of the story, it is also about airing personal issues and negotiating ethical agendas in public. It is as if the embodied, gendered identity of a person can only be secured by validation on prime-time television; legal gender reassignment is not enough. It is also a way to sensationalise experience and accrue not only attention but financial rewards.

Expressions of the personal in public may suggest a new phenomenon. However, there are other ways in which personal relationships and experiences may be seen as changing. As we saw in Chapter 1, there is evidence of changing social trends in patterns of domestic living, of child-bearing and rearing and of patterns of sexual relationships, which might imply shifts in personal and private relationships. In the West, high rates of divorce, increased numbers of people cohabiting rather than marrying, increased numbers of children born to unmarried parents or lone mothers and of single-person households, the greater recognition (if reluctant in some societies and not fully accepted in most) of same-sex relationships all point to social change. Not only is it now possible to advertise surrogacy or babies for adoption on the Internet, other aspects of technological development may be seen to transform the mother–child relationship.

Hi-tech babies

New technologies make even child-bearing, the most embodied of human relations, when one body is enclosed within another, seem both disembodied and distanced. Artificial reproductive technologies have created the possibility of a woman carrying a foetus which was produced in vitro by the fusion of another woman's egg and the sperm of an anonymous man. The baby, if carried to term, could become the child of yet another, adoptive parent or parents. Who is the child's mother in this situation? Is it the host mother who carries the foetus and gives birth to the baby? Or is it the genetic mother who provided the egg, or the person who puts in the love and long-term hard work and provides care for the child? In such a scenario the possibilities of technoscience confuse existing understandings of parental identities.

In 2002 a dispute arose over the birth of black twins to a white couple who had undergone fertility treatment and in vitro fertilisation. A black couple who were involved in the same IVF programme were unsuccessful in having a baby and it seems most likely that the white woman had given birth to their genetic babies. At the time of writing there has not been a court hearing at which a decision has been made about the identity of these babies. However, an appeal to law is most likely. As the Secretary of the British Association of Adoption and Fostering, Deborah Cullen, said, 'the law is having trouble in keeping up. When the 1984 Warnock inquiry produced its recommendations leading to the 1990 Human Fertilization and Embryology (H.F.E.) Act and the establishing of the H.F.E. Authority, donor conceived children were looked upon very differently and the technologies were nowhere near as advanced as they are today' (in Lee, 2002: 3). Now courts are faced with new problems, as Allan Levy, QC says: 'The woman who carries the embryo is in law the mother. If the other couple lay claim to the children, the twins may be made wards of court' (ibid.: 3). Thus new technologies have created new identities, and new categories of person, with whom the legal system has to deal. Before IVF the 'biological' mother would have been the genetic mother as well, and there would have been just two possibilities – the biological and the social mother.

In this instance the case of the woman who gave birth to the children might be stronger because the longer the babies stayed with her, the greater would be the bonds of social mothering. Courts have to pay primary attention to the needs of children, and a change in circumstances and of carer could be disadvantageous. However other factors are taken into account which include 'the child's age, sex, background any characteristics that the court considers relevant, perhaps including race. An analogy may be drawn with adoption cases, where local authorities have said black children should be with black carers' (Gieve in Lee, 2002: 3). In some senses mobilities are recognised and can encompass the diversity of family relationships, such as same-sex civil partnerships in the UK, but this is countered by attempts to stabilise identities and embed them in traditional relationships and values.

What is at issue here? How have technologies affected our understanding of identity and our attempts to secure it? What is the problem for the courts? This example brings in a whole range of factors which impact upon identity. This case is one which seems to highlight contemporary changes and technological advances and combine biology, technologies and the legal dimensions of identity. However, visible difference as classified by 'race' in the discussion above, which is not a new dimension of identity, is of considerable significance here. Would the identities of the twins and the identity of their 'real' mother be at stake if it were not for the recognition of visible difference and the social impact of 'race'? Courts have to acknowledge the impact of race and of ethnicity and belonging on a child's well-being.

While biology may appear to offer some certainty in establishing identity whether in terms of gender or other embodied features, this example makes a simple notion of 'biology' highly problematic. Does biology mean genetic inheritance, in which case security might be offered by the children being brought up by the mother whose genetic imprint they carry? However, 'biology' also involves the processes of gestation, birth and lactation, which, because of IVF, belong to a different woman. Genetic inheritance is also contributed by the father, which raises a further question about the primacy of the mother or the father, again a largely social and possibly legal question.

This example illustrates the complexity of identity claims and especially of the difficulty of attempting to claim certainty by appealing to biology. It also shows that it is impossible to disentangle the 'biological' and the social, or the natural and the social. The two are interconnected at every point, and in this case we have to appeal to legal processes as part of the social structure in order to make sense of who we are. These examples offer an illustration of the ways in which personal relationships may be seen to be subject to change, in different ways through social, economic and technological factors and in the relationship between private and public spheres.

Summary

- New communication technologies create new opportunities for creativity in presenting and representing identities.
- Virtual identities still draw heavily on the social world which 'real' people inhabit.
- Other technologies (e.g. reproductive technologies) create new possibilities and greater uncertainties about securing identities.
- Biological, social, political and legal aspects of identity become linked in our attempts to find our 'who we are'.

Embodied identities

If the body might not offer quite so much security about 'who we are' as commonsense thinking might infer, what alternatives are there for reconceptualising the idea that our identities might be rooted in our biology, in the bodies we inhabit? Bodies are central to the idea of who we are and form the limits to the self. We live through our bodies (Woodward, 2009) but new technologies are blurring the boundaries between humans and machines. This is illustrated in sport in the highly contentious regulation of the Paralympics, where the advantages of technologies to facilitate athleticism in disabled athletes might be seen as enhancing performance unfairly.

We could reconsider how far changing technologies might constitute new spaces in which negotiations might take place in cyberspace. In the twenty-first century machines make the differences between people and machines ambiguous. Anne Balsamo argues that virtual reality offers the possibility of constructing realities free from the determination of body-based 'real' identities. Cyberspace is a body-free environment where you can be a woman or a man, no matter which label you carry in other spaces of your life. People can create avatars and conduct relationships without ever meeting physically and construct themselves through a whole series of such relationships. How can new technologies open up new ways of thinking about identity?

Cyborg thinking

Donna Haraway, writing in the US, offered the **cyborg** as a concept that challenges traditional constraining opposites, like natural/social, mind/body, human/machine, human/animal, and breaks down the boundary categorisations. The cyborg offers a new way of thinking about difference and a new way of conceptualising the relationship between human beings and technoscience, people and machines. Haraway argues that in the late twentieth century there was a breakdown in distinctions between animals and people, between humans and machines and

Plate 2.3
Oscar Pistorius of South
Africa runs for his victory of
the Men's 400m T44 final at
the Beijing 2008 Paralympics

Source: © PA Photos

between science and fiction. This can be used to construct the concept of the cyborg, which bridges the gap between human and animal and human and machine. For Haraway developments in scientific culture have made it impossible to make clear distinctions any more.

> By the late twentieth century . . . the boundary between human and animal, is thoroughly breached . . . Nothing really convincingly settles the separation of human and animal . . . Biology and evolutionary theory over the last two centuries have simultaneously . . . reduced the line between humans and animals to a faint trace re-etched in ideological struggle or professional disputes between life and social sciences . . .
>
> Late twentieth century machines have made thoroughly ambiguous the difference between natural and artificial, mind and body, self-developing and eternally designed, and many other distinctions that used to apply to organisms and machines. Our machines are disturbingly lively, and we ourselves frighteningly inert . . .
>
> . . . the certainty of what counts as nature – a source of insight and a promise of innocence – is undermined, probably fatally.
>
> Machines are quintessentially microelectronic devices: they are everywhere and they are invisible.
>
> (Haraway, 1985, in 2000: 52–53)

Haraway goes on to suggest some new ways of thinking, where the term on the left is replaced by that on the right:

Representation	Simulation
Eugenics	Population control
Hygiene	Stress management
Reproduction	Replication
Scientific management in home, factory	Global factory/ electronic cottage
Family/market/factory	Women in the integrated circuit
Family wage	Comparable worth
Public/private	Cyborg citizenship
Nature/culture	Fields of difference
Sex	Genetic engineering

Some of these visions of a brave new world might already be looking a bit out of date, and Haraway may seem to be over-optimistic about what she sees as the future. However, she is using the idea of the cyborg, not only to challenge the division between animals and humans and between humans and machines, but also to confront many such opposites. Marking out one's identity frequently involves establishing the idea of 'us' and 'them': not just differences but oppositions. So what is the cyborg and how is it manifest? The word is a bit scary and conjures up images of science fiction or of monsters. We are more familiar with cyborgs in science fiction and on the Internet, although it is clearly present in the applications of technoscience, for example reproductive technologies.

Reproduction is an area of human life that may seem to offer the greatest, most essential certainties, yet the advent of reproductive technologies mentioned above subverts even the certainty of motherhood. One woman may provide the uterus and nurture for nine months, another the egg, another the social care once the child is born, one man may provide the sperm and another the social care of the child. Conception may involve two people who never meet, don't even know each other's names and never meet the child or children that ensue.

Within political theory and feminist thinking Donna Haraway's work, especially her *A Cyborg Manifesto* (1985), is the most famous introduction to the possibilities of the cyborg. She argues that cyborg thinking breaks down traditional barriers. Instead of thinking of human beings and machines as separate and distinct, we would benefit from understanding the combination of the two. Robbie Davis-Floyd (Davis-Floyd and Dumit 1998) takes up Haraway's claim the 'we are all cyborgs now', listing the myriad ways in which body and machine merge, specifically in examples of childbirth, as well as in everyday examples of our use of computers, even wearing glasses and the synthesis of the bodies of those with disabilities with the technoscience which facilitates daily life. She cites the example of Stephen Hawking, whose active and important contributions to astrophysics are made possible through human–machine symbiosis. Instead of separating the body, which was equated with failure following illness and impairment, from machine, signifying technological success and outside control, we could benefit from thinking across the boundaries of natural = body = agency on the one side and machine = culture, on the other. Cyborgs give people control, and this merging of body and machine enables us to exercise control and agency. Haraway seeks to avoid the idea that machines are alien and that they necessarily take away our control over our own lives: they are part of us and we are part of them.

ACTIVITY

Can you think of ways in which the idea of the cyborg operates in your own life? Many people wear glasses but it goes further than this! What about those polarisations between what is 'natural' and what is mechanical and by impli-cation 'unnatural'? The machine component may include any technological or scientific intervention.

COMMENT

We have already mentioned some of the ways in which technology and more specifically machines such as computers can facilitate daily life for people with a range of disabilities. New technologies provide ease and speed of communication which liberate people, for example who might be housebound or otherwise constrained. Increasingly, what constitutes the 'natural' is unclear. There are other ways in which some activities and ways of acting are seen as natural. Think of the range of products in the supermarket that purport to be natural. The example of parenting discussed above is a rich area for instances of what is natural and what is not. Haraway also offers examples on a wider scale that indicate some of the benefits of cyborg thinking. One relates to infant feeding, another aspect of maternal identities which is distinguished by oppositions of the natural versus the technoscientific and cultural. She uses this example to illustrate the weakness of an oppositional view, to show the division between 'good mothers' and 'bad mothers' and between natural and technological (unnatural). Haraway (1997) focuses on infant mortality rates in developing countries and uses the work of Nancy Scheper-Hughes (1992) in Brazil, where breastfeeding declined drastically at the end of the twentieth century. She asks why poor women stop breastfeeding. Rather than thinking through the opposition of either promoting breastfeeding as natural, or improving bottled formula cow's milk to make it more like breast milk, Haraway argues that we do not have to take sides. She suggests that breastfeeding is practice and culture, just as technoscience is practice and culture; the body is historical, natural, technical, discursive and material. The cyborg combines all of these elements. A cyborg solution is to employ technoscience to advance not only ways of feeding infants but to support mothers, technically, materially and through how they are represented and given voice to provide them with the possibility to choose, to choose to breastfeed their infants even. This illustrates the agency of the cyborg; the choice is not between women on the one hand and technoscience on the other; a combination of the two can embody agency in women as mothers. Haraway is very optimistic and sees cyborg thinking and cyborgs as making it possible to include women who have been denied rights to mother children, such as post-menopausal women, socially excluded women, minority ethnic women and lesbian women. This can be illustrated through the challenge which cyborg thinking offers to what constitutes the 'natural'. Frequently, in talking about motherhood, the natural is invoked. This often elides with the normal and the morally approved, for example in access to reproductive technologies, to adoption, access to children after divorce or relationship breakdown, or even whose children are taken into care and whose are not. Once the oppositions are broken down it becomes much more difficult to appeal to one side as right and the other as wrong.

The cyborg overcomes the limitations of opposites, such as nature/culture, public/private. The mixture of technology and biology of cyborg thinking suggests all sorts of new possibilities, especially for those who have been dispossessed and excluded, the developing world in relation to the developed world, women in relation to men. In a set of unequal opposites cyborg thinking offers the chance for the powerless to challenge the hierarchy. The cyborg, through its amalgamation of human and machine, presents a unity between body and machine which can be united under one idea of 'I', that is, the subject who makes decisions and acts. However, in spite of Haraway's concern to amalgamate socialist, feminist and technoscientific thinking there are still some uncomfortable questions about the cyborg and its representations. Who has the power to construct the cyborg and to benefit from its challenges? How does this kind of thinking give more choice to people who lack material resources? While cyborg thinking seeks to resolve some of the limitations of the division between the natural and the social and mind and body, it still does not address the material, economic divisions between people. It is also the case that it does not compensate for the constraints of physical impairment, although technological advances can offer considerable help to people with disabilities and present them with more choices. A major contribution of cyborg thinking is its challenge to rigid oppositions and the way it encompasses technological advance to rethink the role of the body in shaping identities. Cyborg thinking may have little impact on material circumstances and in particular on the economic conditions under which identities are forged.

Summary

- Identity is embodied and our sense of who we are is closely tied to the bodies we inhabit.
- Although the body might appear to offer some certainties about identity, the natural and the social, our bodies and the societies in which we live are interrelated and cannot be simply disentangled.

- Social, political, cultural and legal matters are all involved in the production and experience of embodied identity.
- Even cyberspace, where it might seem possible to present a disembodied identity, relies on both 'real' bodies and the social and cultural meanings that are attached to them, for example as women, men, black, white and disabled people.
- Cyborg thinking offers one challenge to the idea that there are distinct separations between simple opposites, such as body and machine.

Buying and selling: material identities

Our understanding of who we are and the ways in which we represent ourselves to others are clearly influenced by our material circumstances. These material circumstances include a whole range of social divisions, such as where we live, access to employment and especially our access to financial resources and what may be called our social class position. The contemporary social sciences focus less on class as the social division which is the key determinant of life chances and identity than was the case in the past. This is discussed in more detail in Chapter 4, but in this section I want to look at some of the arguments about the extent to which identities are shaped and influenced by the interrelated processes of production and consumption and the impact of material circumstances upon identity.

Consuming identity

Can you buy an identity off the peg? Do people know who you are by the clothes you wear and the possessions you display, or maybe more significantly by the possessions you don't display because you don't have them? How important are patterns of consumption in indicating who we are? Pasi Falk has argued that identity in modern times is increasingly a consuming self. People in the West, most specifically those with some degree of affluence and access to spending power, are familiar with the notion of 'retail therapy' and the idea that when the going gets tough, the tough go shopping. Anthony Giddens has argued that patterns of consumption and lifestyle are increasingly important.

> In modern life the notion of life style takes on a particular significance. The more tradition loses its hold, and the more daily life is reconstituted in terms of the dialectical interplay of the local and the global, the more individuals are forced to negotiate lifestyle choices among a range of options.
>
> (Giddens, 1991: 5)

Although Giddens acknowledges the structural factors of **capitalist** production, he underplays its inequalities. The options for many people across the globe and even within affluent Western countries are not between lifestyle products but about how they can manage to sustain daily life. It is only possible to construct the self through lifestyle choices and patterns of conspicuous consumption if one has the resources so to do. Poverty and inequality offer significant counter-arguments to the claim that we are what we buy and that consuming identities afford greater agency to those who buy into identity positions through the consumption of goods and services. There are clearly material constraints to some of these arguments. However, the development of consumption theories and the higher profile given to consumption in economic systems in shaping and providing a means of securing and shaping identities is largely intended to counter the underplaying of cultural factors in earlier accounts that prioritised **production** and the economic base of social relations and divisions. There are, however, other limitations to the claim that we are free to manage lifestyle identities and in the process to exercise autonomy through consumption. How do we make decisions about which lifestyles to buy into? Other approaches to the phenomena implicated in consumption patterns are more aware of the ways in which consumers are constrained, not only through lack of resources. Such views emphasise the influence that corporate **capital** is able to exercise in shaping the decisions that are made by consumers, indicating dependence and lack of autonomy among consumers. We are not simply free agents, floating through the paradise of consumption and fulfilling our desires.

Arlie Hochschild has suggested that the feminist project of increasing women's independence has been curtailed by the images that consumer cultures, for example as promulgated within the women's magazine market, use to promote the idea of women using purchasing power to please themselves (Hochschild, 1994). This view is challenged and there is also space for the exercise of some independence and autonomy within such consumer cultures, for example women's magazines (Woodward, 1997). Women are not simply the passive recipients of distorted, glamorous, lean images. They can both enjoy the images and the aspirations they express and retain some critical awareness.

Zygmunt Bauman argues that social skills have become undermined by an excessive concern with individuality and the consumption that people are compelled to engage in by the market forces of the capitalist economy in late modernity:

> Unable to cope with the challenges and problems arising from their mutual relations men and women turn to marketable goods, services and expert counsel: they need the factory produced tools to imbue their bodies with the socially meaningful 'personalities', medical or psychiatric advice to heal the wounds left by previous and future defeats, travel services to escape into unfamiliar settings which it is hoped will provide better surroundings for solution of familiar problems, or simply, factory produced noise (literal and metaphorical) to 'suspend' social time and eliminate the need to negotiate social relations.

> (Bauman, 1987: 164)

Bauman presents a more constraining view of consuming identities than some of the views that express this phenomenon as potentially liberatory and as opening up new, democratic possibilities for forming and representing identities. However, the ironic play on the assumptions and contradictions of consuming identities that has become a part of popular culture in the West is very much in line with the practices of contemporary capitalism, although consumption can no longer be reduced to a function of the capitalist economy, nor a simple outcome of the production process. As Danny Miller argues, consumption is not merely an act of buying goods, it is 'a fundamental process by which we create identity' (1997: 19). Miller sees the process of consumption as creative. Patterns are multi-faceted and diverse, but the main points of his argument are that what we buy and consume contribute to our sense of who we are and that this process is active and creative. Our identities are made up and are represented by the consumer goods we buy. Consumption is much more than the response and trigger to production; the circuit of production has to include both representation and identity. This is also an active process and consumption is not passively, or crudely, determined by what is produced and how it is marketed. Pierre Bourdieu retains a materialist class-based analysis, but incorporates **taste** as exercised by consumers in line with their class identity. Bourdieu took up the idea of the active process of consumption in his work on the ways in which the consumption of goods constitutes the expression of taste. Display of the goods we have bought has symbolic significance in demonstrating membership of a particular culture. He suggests that consumption is:

> a stage in the process of communication, that is, an act of deciphering, decoding, which presupposes practical or explicit mastery of a cipher or a code . . . taste classifies the classifier. Social subjects, classified by their classifications, distinguish themselves by the distinctions they make, between the beautiful and the ugly, the distinguished and the vulgar, in which their position in the objective classifications is expressed or betrayed.
>
> (Bourdieu, 1984: 2, 6)

Thus identities are organised by their classifications and mark themselves out by the distinctions they make. This is the way in which class differences are constructed through consumption. This critique is heavily dependent on classificatory systems, which might indicate a rigidity in the marking of identity through consumption. Bourdieu argues that, although patterns of consumption are varied and diverse, they are socially structured. In fact his main analysis was of class as the major social division, paying more limited attention to other social divisions, such as ethnicity and generation; even gender receives only limited coverage. Bourdieu retained an economically based analysis of class, which prioritises the economic structures that determine social relationships, and saw class as the main determinant of consumer behaviour (1984) which is, in Bourdieu's work, largely formed through the economic structure and the outcome of systems of production and ownership. However, consumption is at the same time material and symbolic. Consumption expresses taste and taste lifestyle, and Bourdieu's analysis signifies a shift of focus from production to consumption and on to empirically supported claims that identities are created through the process of consumption.

This process of consumption can also be linked to the body. Falk provides an analysis of the role of consumption in contemporary life with an account of the ways in which the body is involved in taking up an identity. Falk bases his analysis of consumption on the body. Thus consumption is linked to sensory experience and to pleasure, for example in his exploration of luxury and conspicuous consumption in the production of contemporary identities (1994). These identities are produced through the interrelationship between the promotion of products and advertising which target the consumer and the body on which such promotions become inscribed. Think of the myriad ways in which advertisements play on these notions of pleasure in the body – from chocolate bars to cosmetics to cars.

While Bourdieu retains a strong material base in his analysis, some of the developments within the social sciences have focused more on the discursive and representational systems through which identities are produced. A shift towards greater emphasis on agency and diversity, for example, in line with the celebration of diversity, fragmentation and pleasure, may open up possibilities for different identities to be created and acknowledged. However, the shift in emphasis from the dominance of economic systems and production in shaping identities may itself open up spaces which, while appearing more free and fluid, are equally constraining.

Summary

- Consumption plays a key role in understanding identity.
- We represent ourselves to others and understand who they are through what we buy and how we look, including the clothes we wear.
- There are different views on the impact of consumption on identity, especially between how far we can make our own choices and how far we are constrained by social factors, such as lack of resources, and by the ways in which others, including advertisers, determine what we can consume.

Where do you come from?

Where do you come from? This is often one of the first questions we ask someone when we meet him or her for the first time. Knowing where people come from gives us some idea of who they are. For example, when we are away from home, perhaps in another country, some sign that a person comes from our home country or even home town presents a point of recognition and identification, and thus an immediate point of contact. Even in a globalised culture (see Chapter 7), when all major world cities feature the labels and insignia of the same companies, Mcdonald's being not the least of these, we still identify with the place we come from and recognise something in common with those who share links with that place.

ACTIVITY

Think about where you come from. If someone asks you the question 'Where do you come from?' what do you say? What meanings does this place have for you?

COMMENT

Your response to the question may vary according to the situation in which the question is asked. When asked abroad, you may specify your country of origin or domicile, whereas nearer to home you may specify the town or village or the locality, even the street you live in, within a city. There are different meanings attached to living in the countryside or the town, or even in particular parts of a town or city. Having a particular postcode can signify certain things about you, especially in relation to your social standing, and even your credit rating!

Did you think of the place where you live? Or the place where you were born, or maybe even where your parents were born? Where we live is the outcome of several different factors. People may move across the globe for a variety of reasons, some of which result from the 'push' factors of their original home being too inhospitable, even dangerous, to the 'pull' factors of a better life, including job opportunities in another country. The twentieth century was described by John Berger as having migration as its quintessential experience (1984). It may be that the extent of migration in the contemporary world, which is not to claim that migration is in any way a new phenomenon, leads to the desire to achieve some form of stability and certainty about identity through myths of origin or claims to home. People need to be able to say that they belong, and belonging is closely linked to place, as we shall see in Chapter 6, especially in times of uncertainty. Identity linked to place also matters at particular historical moments, ranging from the extremes of wartime when we are expected to align ourselves patriotically to our own people, to state occasions and even sporting events when people come together to support their country. It is at these moments that we feel we belong to a place and a nation in particular. Benedict Anderson calls these moments of shared belonging being part of an 'imagined community' (1983). He argues that, although we may never actually come together physically with the people with whom we share a national identity, there are ritual moments – state funerals, royal weddings, and international sporting events like the men's Football World Cup – when we experience a sense of belonging which is located in relation to the country of which we are part.

Links between identity and place may arise more from the categories into which we are placed by other people rather than from those into which we place ourselves. Identity is about how I see myself and about how others see me. I may see myself as belonging to the place where I was born or I may identify more strongly with the place where I live. Certain aspects of visible difference, as were discussed at the start of this chapter, may lead others to classify me as belonging somewhere different from where I place myself. For example, black and Asian people who were born and who live in the UK may still be asked where they come from, and at the response which gives a UK location be asked again where they really come from, as if being white and being British were synonymous. 'Race' and place are also closely intertwined, as we shall see in Chapter 6. The UK is a diverse, ethnically mixed society yet there is still limited recognition of that diversity in some aspects of contemporary life.

It may also be the case that we may feel that the place where we live is relatively temporary and that it does not impact upon our identity. However, our actual place of residence provides significant clues as to who we are to a huge range of agencies, including the state. Citizenship rights, which are discussed more fully in Chapter 3, can depend on residence. For example, political and legal rights and the right to receive health care and welfare benefits all depend on residence qualifications. The possession of a passport which specifies the country of which you are a citizen means much more than access to foreign holidays and for many people may be a matter of life or death. The use of identity cards both provides entitlement for citizens through a means of securing their rights as citizens, as well as a means of surveillance through which the activities of citizens and populations can be monitored as part of the process of governance. In a climate of anxiety about terrorist activities this aspect of identity cards and the surveillance role of governance has particular resonance. At a time of change, when it is not only global corporations which cross the boundaries of nation states, but also global terrorism, there are different meanings given to citizenship. These ideas are explored more fully in Chapter 3 on citizenship and Chapter 7 on globalisation. Citizenship and the rights it affords is a crucial aspect of identity which illustrates different dimensions of identity, especially in relation to who is included and who is excluded. This is another example of identity being constructed around those who are the same and who share an identity and those who are different. In this case those who are seen as different are excluded from the benefits and advantages of those who are included.

Summary

- Identities are often located in relation to a particular place.
- Places are not only geographical but have social, political, cultural and legal meanings, all of which strongly impact upon identity.
- Place can be a factor in different aspects of identity, including national identity.

Conclusion

Changing times are marked by mobilities which mean changing identities and a shift in the importance of identity in the contemporary world. In this chapter we have defined identity as linking the personal and the social; as providing a means for individuals to fit themselves into the society in which they live. Identities can be individual and collective. In both cases, whether individuals make sense of their place in the world as individuals or as part of a group, identity has to involve social factors. Some of us have more scope for choosing our own identities than do others. For example, the materialities of social, economic and physical constraints can all cut down our options. Changes in the relationship between individuals and the wider society and between what we think of as natural and social make identity a useful and important concept for promoting our understanding of how changes take place and what matters. Identity is based on difference, on having the ability to mark oneself out as different from others; it is also about accommodating diversity. This marking of difference is often made possible through visible signs and symbols, from our external physical appearance to the clothes we wear and the flags and symbols we use to identify with a particular national or ethnic identity, which present very diverse pictures of contemporary societies.

In many respects there have been significant changes, and a discussion of identity shows the extent to which mobilities of all sorts of economic and technical developments impact upon people's sense of who they are. For example, in terms of politics and the definition of national boundaries, culture and ethnicity can take precedence over the nation state in defining identities: identities have different points of connection. The migration of people across the world and the breakup of traditional boundaries through the growth of global culture and economics have led to changes in the ways in which people think about who they are and where they belong. What are the differences between us if we all shop at the same stores and eat the same food, provided by multinational corporations? However, people still seek to hold on to their sense of connection and stability, although these points of connection are also transforming. We need to know where we come from and there is resistance to this blurring of boundaries. Sometimes the resistance is manifest in conflict and hostility, for example in conflict in inner city areas where uncertainties and inequalities have resulted in racist attacks and racial tension.

Technological change has led to faster and, some might argue, more democratic means of communication, which offer new identity positions that can be taken up. Information technologies certainly offer new ways of communicating that can transcend national boundaries. Technological advances have intervened even before birth and lead to confusion of the relationship between parent and child, casting doubt on who is the mother of a child and of the family to which people might feel they belong. We all have to deal with these uncertainties and it is often only through appealing to social, political, cultural and legal practices that we can come to terms with change. The role of the social sciences is to develop new ways of thinking in order to accommodate and understand change.

Summary

- Identity is an important concept in the contemporary world because it links individuals to the society in which they live and to each other.
- Identity is marked by difference: we are the same as those with whom we share an identity and different from those who have other identities, but this is a complex picture.
- Social, political, technological and cultural changes impact upon how people see themselves and are seen by others; new identities are formed and new allegiances challenge old certainties.
- There are changes and different sorts of connections in the relationship between individuals and the societies in which they live, but contemporary societies are often characterised by mobilities.
- Mobilities also arise from technological advances as well as migration and cultural and economic changes, which can question traditional certainties, for example those linked to the body and to place, ethnicity nation, class and gender.

Chapter 3

Citizenship and social order

Introduction

Citizenship is a big issue, especially at a time of extensive movement of peoples across the world and of social changes within countries. Contemporary interest in citizenship arises from a number of different factors. Social changes which are the result of European integration, as well as migration, mobilities and the pressure of shifting populations on welfare, health and education systems have brought issues of citizenship to the fore. Migration is a major factor in population change. For example, projections recorded in Social Trends data for the UK predict that net migration will exceed net natural changes (births and deaths) so that by 2011 net migration will account for 70 per cent of population change in the UK (*Social Trends*, 2008). Changes to the welfare state, devolution and the social rights of nation states, the advances of technoscience, especially in relation to genetics and to reproductive technologies, addressed in Chapter 2, also challenge traditional ideas about who has citizenship status. Family structures and the nature of paid work and employment patterns have changed, and sexual politics and the campaigns of identity politics, such as the women's movement and gay and lesbian rights, multicultural, ethnic minority, the disability and environmentalist movements have led to demands for recognition of the rights to citizenship of those previously excluded. All this calls for a broader understanding of citizenship, as illustrated by the requirement that UK schools teach the subject as part of the curriculum from 2002. Changing times have led to new political demands and the need for new theories of citizenship.

Citizenship is a category of inclusion and, by implication, exclusion. The category includes those identified as citizens and accords those people rights as well as placing some obligations upon them. This chapter explores what it means to be a citizen in changing times and, in particular, how theories of citizenship can cope with the changes that are transforming social and political life in the twenty-first century. Citizenship is associated with geographical location. As was argued in Chapter 2, your identity is often secured and established through an association with a place, especially when it comes to accessing rights and benefits, to the place where you currently live. A permanent address might afford some security of identification and, at the wider level, rights linked to a country of residence might be further proof that you have an identity as a citizen of that country. When you are asked for a means of identification what do you present? Identity cards were approved in the UK in 2007, instituted for foreign nationals in 2008 and for British citizens in 2009, so you may well offer an I-D card. You might try to offer a driving licence or a student card or some form of bank or credit card, but usually those asking want some proof of your identity, with a name and signature, perhaps a photograph, something exclusive to you as well as some evidence of where you live, that is officially sanctioned.

A passport, if you have one, can offer specific rights through the security of citizenship, as well as the duties that are expected of a citizen of that state. A passport allows people to travel across national borders and, perhaps more significantly, the lack of a passport denies people access to a country in which they may want to live. It is often the lack of an appropriate passport that receives more media attention in the contemporary world, especially when migration and asylum seeking lead to citizens in European countries such as the UK feeling that 'their space' is being threatened by those who do not have the right to belong and are sometimes called 'illegal immigrants'. Migration has a long history and has been interpreted, experienced and represented in different ways, ranging from hostility in the country of arrival to a welcome to much-needed new workers who can redress skills shortages. Hostility and fear of the 'other' and of outsiders may well have always been a more familiar scenario, however. Indeed, in the twenty-first-century UK, attitudes towards asylum seekers have frequently been negative. The rights of citizenship are seen as privileges and those who have them are not always keen to share them.

Citizenship does however provide a means of regulating population and of gaining an enormous amount of information. One means of governments doing this is the census, but there are all sorts of state interventions as well as those of private corporations which construct populations through their regulatory practices that are organised around the idea of citizenship. How is this done?

ACTIVITY

Make a list of all the government identifications that you currently possess (e.g. birth certificate). Which of these, if any, did you apply for yourself? List all the identification cards that you have from private corporations, such as credit cards, loyalty cards and so on.

COMMENT

Some of these documents will be a requirement of the state, such as a birth certificate; others will be benefits that you have requested yourself. All of them provide information and a means of regulating population. You are likely to have a pretty long list: birth certificate, health card, passport, National Insurance card, driving licence, marriage or civil partnership certificate, council tax registration, registration to vote; and the private sector, with bank cards, loyalty cards, mobile phone registration, store cards and so on. It is not only the government that tracks the movements of populations. Private corporations collect an enormous amount of data on individuals, which they can use for marketing purposes (Savage and Burrows, 2007). Citizenship works both ways; it provides benefits and the statement of rights, as well as rules and regulations and a means of surveillance through which populations are constructed and classified.

Summary

- Citizenship is a big issue of contemporary concern, especially at times of large-scale migration.
- Media coverage can exaggerate the apparent threat of those who do not have citizenship.
- Citizenship has legal, political, social and cultural implications.
- It concerns inclusion and exclusion.
- Citizens are also subjects.

Who is a citizen? What does citizenship mean?

Citizenship is concerned with one of the most basic questions of any society: who belongs to that society? Citizenship status is usually, and traditionally has been, granted according to one of three criteria:

1 By birth in a particular place.
2 By descent, according to blood relationship.
3 By naturalisation through recourse to law.

Citizenship also confers rights and much of the writing about citizenship has emphasised the issue of entitlement. The entitlement to paid employment goes with citizenship status. This may also be what is seen as most threatening to settled communities of white British workers who may express anxiety about the possible threat to their own entitlement to paid work posed by 'outsiders'. The right to work in a country in which one has citizenship has been a key component of the entitlements, but there are others. Much of the anxiety about the influx of asylum seekers into the UK has been fuelled by media representation of the pressure this movement of people would place upon Social Services and the provision of welfare benefits, housing, health and education. The following extract outlines the features of citizenship as expressed by one of the most influential thinkers on the subject, T.H. Marshall. He wrote about the historical development of citizenship in Britain through the nineteenth century and into the mid-twentieth century.

I have divided citizenship into three elements, civil, political and social . . .
civil rights came first, and were established in something like their modern
form before the First Reform Act in 1832. Political rights came next, and their
extension was one of the main features of the nineteenth century, although the
principle of universal citizenship was not recognised until 1918. Social rights
. . . revival began with the development of public elementary education, but
it was not until the twentieth century that they attained equal partnership with
the other two elements of citizenship . . .

Citizenship is a status bestowed on those who are full members of a
community. All who possess the status are equal with respect to the rights and
duties with which the status is endowed . . .

Citizenship requires . . . a direct sense of community membership based on
loyalty to a civilisation which is a common possession. It is a loyalty of free
men [sic] endowed with rights and protected by common law.

(Marshall, [1964] 1994: 24–26)

Let us unpack this a little more. Marshall identified three components of citizenship.
The first is civil. What does that include? Civil rights are those that are guaranteed
through the legal system, that is, through the lawcourts. The law defends the person
and the property of the citizen, and provides a means through which individuals
can seek to protect themselves through both criminal and, in the case of individuals,
civil law. Civil rights are essential to individual freedoms and cannot be denied by
individuals or by the state. As we saw in Chapter 2, the law is invoked to protect
and assure the rights of individuals at very early stages in their biographies. With
the developments in reproductive technologies which create some uncertainties
about the rights of the person, this can be relevant even before birth. Marshall
locates civil citizenship as the earliest form of citizenship in modern Western
societies, involving a move from feudal society where status was based on family
and class to an individual, uniform status of citizenship. Political citizenship gives
us the right to participate in activities involving political power, most obviously
and most commonly by voting, although holding political office is another aspect
of this participation. The 1832 Reform Act gave British men the right to vote.
Women did not achieve comparable status until 1928, by being granted the right
to vote at 21. In 1918 only women over 30 years of age were allowed the vote.
There is political significance in Marshall's reference to the loyalty of 'free men'.
Having the right to a free vote may be a right that is not universally practised, for
example in the UK, but the possession of this right is an essential component of
political citizenship. To take the debate into more recent times, for example, the
turnout at the 1997 General Election, which returned the first Labour government
led by Tony Blair, was the lowest since 1935. In spite of the attempts of this and
subsequent Labour governments to involve more people in an active democracy
by creating devolved institutions in Scotland, Wales, Northern Ireland and London,
strengthening individuals' rights through the Human Rights Act and abolishing the
majority of hereditary peers in the House of Lords, matters did not improve.

In 2001, only 59.1 per cent of people voted in the General Election, which returned the second Blair government. This was the lowest level since 1918 (British Social Attitudes, 2002: 199–200). Ironically, or maybe sadly, more people apparently voted in the Series 3 *Big Brother* evictions than at the election. There are, of course, many other ways of participating in political life at a broader level, using a more inclusive and wide definition of politics and political life. Political protests have taken place across a spectrum from anti-globalisation protesters at the 2007 G8 Summit in northern Germany, massive protests against the Iraq War, demonstrations against the Israeli invasion of Gaza in 2008 and 2009, to the coalition of farmers and lorry drivers protesting about fuel prices in 2000 and the Countryside Alliance marches in 2001 and 2002.

Finally, social citizenship is the right to enjoy a reasonable, appropriate standard of living, that is, one which is possible through access to education and welfare systems. Social citizenship involves addressing some of the problems of inequality in modern society. Access to welfare systems, such as health, social insurance, unemployment and child benefits and housing, redress some of the inequalities which necessarily arise in a society based on a capitalist mode of production. Access to education for all provides the means of securing equal opportunities and possibilities of improvement for those who are otherwise disadvantaged and without the means of advancement. In Marshall's account, in order to enjoy 'full citizenship' the concept needs to include all three of these aspects.

Marshall acknowledged the inequality between people especially in terms of economic inequality, and focused his discussion on social class. As we saw in Chapter 3, class is a very important aspect of social divisions. However, class intersects with other divisions and other differences between people. Marshall's account gives very little acknowledgement of the different experiences of women and men and still less to other aspects of difference, such as ethnicity, race, sexuality and disability. However, many of the differences which so characterise, for example, the contemporary UK, could not have been foreseen by Marshall. Devolution, multi-culturalism, changing patterns of family life and women's greater participation in the labour market have all had enormous impact in much more recent years. Class is used in a number of different ways within the social sciences and the further discussion of these different approaches shown in Chapter 4. Class is used as a structure of social division, a means of distinguishing groups of people according to their social and economic position within society. Class may be based on the work you do, your resources, your status and social standing or your relationship to the means of production in a given society, for example as an owner of a factory or workplace and an employer of others, or as someone who works for wages. The economic inequality of capitalist societies, based on the pursuit of profit, might, as Marshall argued, be redressed through the rights of social citizenship, for example through equal rights to education and welfare, regardless of class position and financial standing.

Could we apply Marshall's account to the more recent example of asylum seekers? They clearly lack citizenship rights, for example civil, political or social rights. Until granted legal citizenship they do not have the right to vote, to participate fully in political life or to gain access to all the benefits to which British citizens can claim rights. Their situation also highlights the importance of access to paid work which is not detailed in Marshall's account. Being unable to undertake paid work, or only to do so under 'illegal' circumstances compounds the inequity of their position and they have little scope for appeal to civil rights as defined within Marshall's definition. It is difficult to explain their position in terms of class alone since they experience a specific form of inequality, as people who do not 'belong' in the country to which they have fled. However, although class is still a significant factor in relation to the kind of work which asylum seekers may be able to undertake, it is still the case that even highly skilled people are compelled to engage in low-skilled work in this context.

Summary

- Citizenship confers rights.
- Citizenship is closely linked to place, birth and law.
- Marshall's theory of citizenship stresses civil, political and social rights.
- Marshall acknowledges class differences which citizenship can help redress.
- A focus on equality can overlook important differences such as race and ethnicity, gender, sexuality and disability, by concentrating only on class.

Weighing up the argument

I have suggested that there may be gaps in Marshall's account of citizenship and that we might pose questions about his definition of citizenship. Before going on to look at other accounts, I would like to consider some strategies for evaluating an account such as Marshall's.

One of the key skills in the social sciences is evaluating theories, weighing up an argument and either supporting its claims or countering them and pointing to their weaknesses. We do something like this in our daily lives in the discussions we have with friends, colleagues and family, but the whole process is more formalised and substantial when conducted within the social sciences. Even in our daily exchanges it is rarely enough just to claim something is right because you think it is. You usually have to offer some support in order to stand your ground and win the argument. What kind of criteria do social scientists use to evaluate an argument? First, there needs to be some supporting evidence, or evidence with which to counter the claims of the argument. An assertion without any supporting evidence is likely to be very weak. Second, the argument needs to cover all the situations to which it lays claim. If it claims to cover all the people in a category then it cannot be sustained if there are gaps and several examples of people to whom it does not apply, or if it is full of exceptions. It is important to pose the question 'What's missing?' when confronted with an argument. What does the argument *not* cover? Third, the argument needs to make sense. The conclusion needs to follow from the first claims or initial premises. Can we apply these criteria to Marshall's argument about citizenship?

How useful is Marshall's account and what weaknesses might there be in his approach? His analysis has been very influential, especially within the discipline of sociology, although there have been many recent critiques which have pointed to problems. First, in relation to evidence, Marshall used historical evidence, largely located within the context of Britain. We might want to suggest that changing times present different forms of evidence, which might challenge the claims of a universal category of citizenship. In a changing world, we need to develop new theories and explanations to cope with the transformations that are taking place. Evidence from a very particular culture and history might not fit every instance. Second, is everyone included? Marshall refers to 'men' which has been the custom in the social sciences until fairly recently, where the word 'men' was used to include women. However, Marshall's 'men' do not include women. Women are missed out; they did not get the vote on a par with men until 1928. Women's rights to full citizenship in the past, and in some cases in the present, have also been severely curtailed by their lack of access to paid work and the benefits that can accompany full-time paid work. Nor does Marshall's category of 'men' include differences among men, except for social class differences. Third, we might want to raise questions about the assumptions at the outset that citizenship means the same thing to everyone. Marshall's basic premise is that it means full involvement in the community resulting from equal treatment. If people are not the same at the start, treating them equally, that is, the same, may not lead to equal outcomes. There are inequalities other than class that could be included and that might change what is important. Gender is one; women's access to civil rights might be different from men's because of their role in reproduction and involvement in child care and more interrupted involvement in the labour market. The French justice minister Rachida Dati's return to her desk, five days after a Caesarean section in 2009, is beyond the possibilities of most human embodied selves. (Although it was her refusal to name the father of her child that attracted more media attention than her superwoman return to work (*Guardian*, 8 January 2009: 21)). Disability is another factor that might challenge the universal claims of the initial premise. In order for them to participate fully in social and political life there needs to be recognition of the specific needs of people with disabilities and some understanding of difference, especially in the ways in which social organisation and the physical structure, for example of the workplace, can operate against full participation. Ethnicity may also be a factor that brings in other aspects of difference not embraced by Marshall's theory of citizenship, which suggests a homogeneous society to start with. Failure to recognise the different cultural practices of different groups of people can lead to exclusion from political and social life.

Summary

There are three questions we can usefully pose in order to weigh up an argument. We will come back to these questions when we have looked at some different accounts of citizenship.

- What is the evidence which supports the claim being made?
- Does the claim cover all the situations and people involved or are there circumstances and people left out?
- Do the conclusions follow from the initial premise and does it make sense?

The challenge of other arguments

Another useful strategy for weighing up the strengths and weaknesses of an argument is to compare one argument with another, different approach. While Marshall's approach to citizenship stresses equal treatment of all concerned, other critiques stress the importance of difference. What are the sources of difference and diversity in contemporary society? How might these differences lead to the demand for different treatment in particular instances or is it more just and fair to treat everyone the same? In order to recognise the diversity of contemporary societies like the UK we need to accommodate *difference* among UK citizens as well as demanding *equal treatment*. Some critiques even go so far as to suggest that equal treatment, that is, treating everybody the same, may ultimately lead to an increase in disadvantage and social exclusion.

Equality of difference: race and ethnicity

ACTIVITY

Read this extract from Bhikhu Parekh's *Rethinking Multi Culturalism: Cultural Diversity and Political Theory*.
   What do these examples tell us about equal rights of citizenship?

In multicultural societies dress often becomes a site of the most heated and intransigent struggles. As a condensed and visible symbol of cultural identity it matters much to the individuals involved, but also for that very reason it arouses all manner of conscious and unconscious fears and resentments within wider society. It would not be too rash to suggest that acceptance of the diversity of dress in a multicultural society is a good indicator of whether or not the latter is at ease with itself.

In 1972, British Parliament passed a law empowering the Minister of Transport to require motor-cyclists to wear crash-helmets. When the Minister did so, Sikhs campaigned against it. One of them kept breaking the law and was fined twenty times between 1973 and 1976 for refusing to wear a crash-helmet. Sikh spokemen argued that the turban was just as safe, and that if they could fight for the British in two world wars without anyone considering their turbans unsafe, they could surely ride a motor-cycle. The law was amended in 1976 and exempted them from wearing crash-helmets.

(Parekh, 2000b: 243)

The Construction (Head Protection) Regulation 1989 requires everyone who works on a construction site to wear a safety helmet, the Employment Act 1989 exempts turban-wearing Sikhs. The 1989 Act considers that the turban offers adequate though not exactly the same protection as the helmet, and is thus an acceptable substitute for it. This means that if a turbaned Sikh were to be injured while working on a construction site due to another person's negligence, he would be entitled to claim damages for only such injuries which he would have sustained if he had been wearing a safety helmet. He goes on to cite another example with economic significance:

Many Asian women's refusal to wear uniforms in hospitals, stores and schools has led to much litigation and contradictory judgements in Britain. A Sikh woman, on qualifying as a nurse, intended to wear her traditional dress of a long shirt (quemiz) over baggy trousers (shalvar) rather than the required uniform, but was refused admission on a nursing course by her Health Authority.

(ibid.: 246)

Parekh goes on to explain that the Industrial Tribunal agreed with the woman's complaint because her dress was a cultural requirement and wearing traditional clothes did not prevent her from carrying out her duties. The Industrial Tribunal decided that asking her to replace it with a uniform was unjustified. However, this Tribunal was overruled by the Employment Appeal Tribunal, which took the opposite and much-criticised view. However, because rules about nurses' uniforms are laid down by the General Nursing Council, the council was able to intervene and decided upon more flexible rules. This meant that the Health Authority was able to offer the Sikh woman a place on the course with the agreement that as a qualified nurse her trousers should be grey and the shirt white (Parekh, 2000b).

COMMENT

These examples raise some important questions about the rights of citizenship. Are citizens entitled to be treated equally? What if equal treatment leads ultimately to exclusion and inequality? In these examples about dress and the cultural and religious demands of some groups of UK citizens, Parekh is suggesting that we can achieve a more equitable and fairer outcome by recognising difference and treating people differently. Parekh argues that in a multi-cultural society, when cultural differences are taken into account, equal treatment is likely to involve different treatment. Sometimes it may even be necessary to those who have been marginalised or ostracised by mainstream culture. The extent of the accommodation of multi-cultural needs is, however, highly contentious. How far is it necessary to go in extending additional rights to minority groups in order to promote greater inclusion and ethnic diversity? Parekh takes a reasoned middle way by arguing for the promotion of cultural diversity while accepting that the ability of any society to treat all citizens equally is necessarily limited. He goes on to cite the use of minority languages which can never be accorded equal status with the dominant language, English, in the UK. Similarly, he considers the status of holy days and suggests that while the common acceptance of Sunday in most Western societies puts Muslims, and one could suggest Jewish people, at a disadvantage as they have Friday and Saturday as their holy days, it is unlikely that there will be a complete social and cultural restructuring to accommodate diversity.

The exclusion from full citizenship rights that can result from equal treatment and which fails to accommodate different needs is not the only important feature of a citizenship that assures sameness. British society, for example, has not only failed to come to terms with cultural diversity in every case, it is also a society in which racism can be part of everyday experience. The Macpherson Report, discussed in Chapter 6, concluded that the racial violence which led to the death of Stephen Lawrence was indicative of a much wider experience of 'institutionalised racism'. This institutionalised racism is a measure of the failure of citizenship in its civil, political and social dimensions. However, although Sir William Macpherson's report stresses the existence of exclusionary practices in major British institutions, it also recommends more inclusive procedures, many of which have since been adopted in an attempt to instate a more inclusive citizenship that addresses multi-culturalism. Ethnicity and racialisation cannot be examined separately from the other dimension of difference in relation to citizenship. For example, different cultural practices relating to dress are experienced in specific ways for women and for men and may have particular, gendered meaning. Similarly, cultural practices relating to family and marriage also illustrate the ways in which gender and ethnicity cannot be separated when looking at how citizenship rights are experienced.

Summary

- Approaches to citizenship which assume cultural sameness and stress equality can marginalise ethnic differences and lead to unequal outcomes.
- Ethnicity is an important dimension of citizenship in ensuring full participation.
- A focus on ethnicity must include race and racism as factors which directly counter equal citizenship status.
- Ethnicity interrelates with other aspects of difference, including class and gender.

Equality of difference: gender and sexuality

Many accounts of citizenship have focused on the rights of men. In some instances the word 'men' has been taken to include women, as if there were no significant differences between women and men; we are all human beings. However, admirable though this emphasis on our common humanity may be, it is often men's humanity at the expense of women's, and the norm of citizenship is male. At particular times and in particular societies, 'man' does mean 'man' and women are denied equal rights, such as the right to vote and to participate fully in social life, and even rights over their own bodies and reproductive rights. The exclusion of women from the rights of citizenship has a long history and has taken different forms. At its most extreme it has meant not only exclusion from political life, through voting and taking public office, but lack of rights over their own bodies, for example reproductive rights, and over choice of sexual partners, lack of property rights, the right to take paid employment or over choice of where to live and freedom of movement in the public sphere. In the twentieth century, although women had been granted civil and political rights in most Western countries, there were still areas of exclusion, notably in accessing the social rights, for example through welfare benefits, which had been instituted to redress social inequalities; several inequalities persist into the twenty-first century.

Feminist social scientists have argued that the notion of equality which informs much understanding of citizenship and even campaigns to promote equal rights (like the suffrage movement which argued for equal rights for women on a par with men) is based on an assumption that 'equality' is gender neutral. Carole Pateman argues that the modern state, far from being gender neutral, is patriarchal. The citizenship constructed and promoted on the basis of notions of equality is thus specific to the interests more of men than of women (Pateman, 1988; Phillips, 1999). Pateman suggests that the modern welfare state, rather than promoting equality between women and men, constructs them differently because of women's association with the family and the private sphere of the home and domestic, unpaid caring work. The different roles of women and men undermine notions of equality and citizenship.

A particular aspect of the different dimensions of gendered citizenship is the changing relationship between public and private arenas, and the experience of intimate relations. The private sphere of human activity and experience has particular impact upon the gendered aspects of citizenship. The private arena of the home and of domestic life has often been taken for granted as associated with women.

Relationships with children and with family members and partners may be seen as taking place within the private space of the home and this has also led to women's exclusion from the more public sphere. The public arena of civil and political life and of paid work has been seen as separate and distinct from the private arena of the home. Feminist critiques (Eisenstein, 1981; Nicholson, 1992) have shown how this distinction has been used either to exclude women from the public world of paid work or active participation in political, social and cultural life, or to marginalise the contribution of women's caring and domestic labour in relation to the wider economy. Nicholson has pointed to the importance of exploring the public/private dualism as separations which she argues obscure the changing dynamics of gender relations (1992).

Feminist critiques arising from the Women's Liberation Movement of the 1970s focused their analyses on the identification of women as wives and mothers and on the classification of sex, personal relationships and family life as private matters (Eisenstein, 1981). Eisenstein notes the history of this separation as deriving from the classical Athenian construction of the male citizen, occupying the public arena of the marketplace and the gymnasium and the relegation of women to unacknowledged domestic labours in the household (1981: 22). It has certainly been the case that women have engaged in economically productive labour out-side the household, whether in agricultural labour or, for example, in factory production through the nineteenth century, but this work has been denied or obscured through the higher status awarded to male engagement with public life (Rothman, 1992: 128). The marginalisation of 'women's work', and indeed of women's lives, as confined to the private sphere has been noted in the classic social science texts.

Janet Woolf has argued that the presence of women in texts produced in the social sciences existed only in relation to men and in the family:

> The literature of modernity ignores the private sphere, and to that extent is silent on the subject of women's primary domain . . . the public could only be constituted as a particular set of institutions and practices on the basis of the removal of other areas of social life to the invisible arena of the private.
>
> (Woolf, 1985: 44)

If the literature of the past was silent, that of the present is exceedingly noisy, especially in the discussion of sexuality and, in popular culture, in revelations about the disclosure of the private and the personal in the most public of arenas, especially in the television and radio media.

The argument which sets up the public and the private as opposite and separate is flawed for two reasons. First, it is impossible to separate these two spheres of experience. Life in the domestic, private arena of the home is influenced and structured by social and political activities and policies which are associated with the public arena of the state and of civil life. The experience of individual households and the relationships between the people who live in them cannot be separated from the economic activities of those people and the economic organisation of the wider society in which they live. Second, it is not possible to disassociate these areas of human experience so that the private arenas of the home and of the emotional, intimate and personal life are seen as distinctive aspects of people's lives which are not carried into their experiences of the public arena, for example, of paid work.

However, the purpose of this discussion of the interrelationship between the public and the private aims to indicate the need to deconstruct some of the assumptions of the separation of spheres in order to explore the impact of the separation on the experience of citizenship.

The social and economic organisation of societies also impacts on the personal relationships which people experience, and individuals carry their own experience of the private arena, with the diversities and inequalities which may be manifest there, into the public arena of economic, social, political and cultural life.

Welfare provision has been largely based on the importance of maintaining the family as an economic unit. The views of William Beveridge, the architect of the British Welfare State, established after the Second World War in the 1940s, were that

> the great majority of married women must be regarded as occupied on work which is vital though unpaid, without which their husbands could not do their paid work and without which the nation could not continue.
>
> (Beveridge, 1942: 49)

While women's 'special role' in supporting the family and male workers in paid employment may have been acknowledged by Beveridge, the full implications of their dependency on male breadwinners was not. Elizabeth Wilson argued in the 1970s that the British postwar Welfare State was itself dependent on women's unpaid work linking the public and private arenas. Many foods and services previously provided by the family in the private arena have since transferred to the public arena. Wilson argued that it became women's responsibility to ensure that the clients of the Welfare State received those benefits (1977). However, women were not always able to access benefits themselves. For example, unemployment benefit, sickness benefit and even retirement pensions are all dependent on the contributions made when in paid work. Women, because of their unpaid caring work, have often been unable to qualify for the full rights of social citizenship because of the assumptions made by Beveridge that inequalities could be addressed by supporting men through the welfare system. As Carol Pateman argues, exclusion from the labour market prevents individuals from accessing the resources necessary to play a full part in civil society (1988). Women's greater participation in the labour market at the end of the twentieth and into the twenty-first century has had a significant impact on their inclusion as citizens.

Although there have been significant changes, for example in legislation in response to changes in the workplace, with more women doing paid work, changes in the family with more divorces and lone parents and the growth of multi-culturalism, a legacy of traditional thinking about gender and ethnicity still informs our understanding of citizenship. Diane Richardson argues that gender has been neglected in the analysis of the national development of the entitlement and obligations of citizenship. She argues that citizenship status is closely linked to heterosexual as well as male privilege, whereby the 'normal' citizen is male and heterosexual (Richardson, 2000). Richardson goes on to suggest that by this standard, lesbians, bisexuals and gay men are only 'partial' citizens. For example, same-sex relationships have not benefitted from the same entitlements, in terms of recognition, pension, inheritance and tax rights as those of heterosexual couples. Civil partnerships, however, mean an extension of rights for same-sex couples. Richardson points out that, although not all heterosexuals are privileged (for example, young single mothers are not), overall it is the middle-class, nuclear, heterosexual family that is 'held up as the model of good citizenship' (2000: 80). Focusing on the example of reproduction, she suggests that what she calls 'sexual citizenship' has two aspects. First, it removes the right of people to choose and to control the conditions under which they have children – or don't. This includes the right to terminate a pregnancy as a sexual right. Second, people have the right to choose their own, legitimate sexual partners and experience intimacy within the given legal framework. This would, of course, include same-sex relationships between adults. Sexual citizenship concerns the rights of women in particular to reproduce, and to have equal access as men in the public sphere, that is, to active political and economic lives. Throughout the twentieth century women fought to achieve equal pay, welfare benefits for children and working women as well as the right to vote. To these are added rights related to reproduction for women and to self-determination in areas of sexuality for women and men in order to attain full citizenship status.

Summary

In this section we have seen that:

- An emphasis on equality can obscure differences and lead to unequal outcomes.

- Gender differences impact upon citizenship; women have been excluded both explicitly and implicitly from full citizenship and rights.
- A focus on sexual citizenship includes differences of gender and sexuality.
- The separation of the public and private arenas has been linked to particular understandings of gender.
- The interrelationship between public and private arenas has changed over time.
- These changes and the connections between public and private are well illustrated in relation to citizenship.

Equality of difference: generation and disability

The gendered body is an important dimension of citizenship. Many of the entitlements to citizenship have assumed an able-bodied man, capable of undertaking paid work, as the embodiment of the citizen. As many of the arguments about women's exclusion from full citizenship rights have shown, the marginalisation of differences can lead to inequality and exclusion. The importance of paid work in accessing other entitlements, including sick pay, unemployment benefits and, of particular importance at a time of an increasingly ageing population, pension rights, has particular implications for women and for other groups of people who may not be able to enjoy an uninterrupted pattern of full-time paid employment.

Generation presents a significant issue at a time when, for example, in the UK the population aged over 60 exceeds that under 16, as revealed by the 2001 UK census, which indicated that the over-sixties made up 21 per cent of the UK population, while under-sixteens made up only 20 per cent (Census, 2008). This evidence of an increasingly ageing population which includes not only higher numbers of people aged 85 and over, as well as the over-sixties, has led to the expression of anxiety about the financing of pensions and health and welfare support for people of pensionable age. Concern about finance and in particular about pensions has had a strong impact at the start of the twenty-first century with turmoil in global markets and falling stock market prices. The near collapse of investments and of European insurance companies such as Equitable Life led to striking reductions in policy payouts and to the abandonment of final salary pension schemes by many companies. While most of the anxieties have been expressed in terms of economic factors, there are significant repercussions for the full participation of retired people in social and civil life. The economic recession has hit those who depend on income from savings very heavily as interest rates have fallen. The plight of pensioners has been recognised if not resolved. In 2008 the UK government even appointed the broadcaster and writer Dame Joan Bakewell as a champion of the elderly (BBC, 2009). Charities have drawn attention to the likely outcome of demographic changes in a climate of financial and economic uncertainty and flux. They have suggested that 'the changing age profile required a rethink from politicians about issues such as health and pensions, public transport, and ageism at work' (Carvel, 2002: 4). Gordon Lishman, Director General of Age Concern England, responded to the first report of the 2001 UK census by claiming that it 'will only be a crisis if we don't address the issues now and come up with imaginative, flexible policies' (ibid.).

As a result of the centrality of employment in industrialised market economies the notion of retirement from paid work has created the idea of dependency in old age. What do changing economic and demographic changes mean for citizenship? Many social scientists prefer to use the term 'life course' in the biographies of individuals. 'Life cycle' might suggest fixed points, whereas 'life course' is preferable in order to accommodate different responses to life events, like getting a job, having children, falling sick, changing jobs and retiring. Different age groups of adults will experience these events within differing social, cultural and economic circumstances, sometimes of constraint and sometimes of opportunity. Thus 'life course' links the individual to the society. Changes in the life course, especially the dependency of old age, have been recognised within the development of the social rights of citizenship. While generation impacts upon citizenship at earlier stages, for example in youth, with demands for legislation to accord young people civil and political rights, to vote, to marry and to take responsibility for their own lives, older generations have assumed more dominance on the political and economic agenda in recent years in some respects, notably in the context of financial support. The primacy of engagement in paid work in order to contribute to insurance schemes and pension funds has led to the exclusion of married women in particular. Some married women in the UK were denied pensions because, although they had undertaken paid work they had only contributed a reduced payment (the 'married women's stamp'). Thus married women were dependent on men – their husbands – for support in retirement. Entitlements to pensions are dependent on 'lifecourse interdependencies of child-care and rearing, labour market participation and unemployment' (Twine, 1994: 43). Not only is age itself an aspect of difference that has to be addressed in relation to citizenship, but generation is itself subject to differences, of gender, class, health and disability. Those who have been least able to make contributions, and who have earned low wages through their working lives, are also those who suffer most in retirement. Proposals for dealing with the apparent crises of financing pensions for a growing elderly population at a time of falling markets have to address these differences among that population. Remaining in paid work until the age of 70 assumes that people are already in paid work and that they are fit and healthy enough to continue. The current UK workforce is likely to have to work until their late sixties before taking their pensions, although somewhat perversely age-related legislation has meant that those in their early sixties in the first decade of the twenty-first century are not allowed to continue working after age 65. Fred Twine argues that, although retirement occurs at a relatively fixed point in a person's life, the 'welfare prospects for the retirement years are largely set by the interaction of the three elements of citizenship prior to retirement' (ibid.: 42). These three elements include the relationship between the individual, the government and the society, expressed through Marshall's social rights of citizenship. Twine argues that a focus on the life course aspects of interdependence permits connections between reproduction, work and retirement (1994), at a time when global networks transcend the boundaries of nation states and world markets impact upon traditional means of financing pensions and supporting those in retirement. The global economic recession, which began in 2008, affected pensions as well as mortgages and household borrowing and spending. Pensioners are vulnerable when interest rates fall and when they have to purchase annuities to fund their retirement, with very few people receiving final salary pensions. What may appear to be individual experience, located within our own personal body and biography, through ageing, may be seen as linking social economic and cultural factors operating within a transnational context.

Just as generation and gender have social aspects which impact upon full participation in citizenship, so does being able-bodied or disabled influence the experience of citizenship. Disability is another dimension which can be overlooked by the assumption that the rights of citizenship are equal, thus involving equal treatment for all.

Different models of explanation present arguments about appropriate strategies for addressing the problem of the exclusion of disabled people from full citizenship. Strategies for promoting wide inclusion, for example, are put forward by the disability movement and those engaged in identity politics and political campaigns focus on positive action and the limitations of liberal notions of equality. Equal rights have not, on the whole, led to equal participation, for women, for minority ethnic people or for people with disabilities. People with disabilities have had to take action to challenge assumptions, especially those of able-bodied people who may have assumed that they know what disabled people want and need. As Lira Abu-Habib argues:

> There is a sense among the able-bodied that disabled people need their protection. Concern with the welfare of disabled people is seen as charitable ... Achievements and successes in advocacy work on disability can be attributed in large measure to the efforts and perseverance of groups of disabled people.

> (2002: 266)

One of the ways in which it has been difficult for people with disabilities to organise to express their own needs has been the way in which disability has been constructed as an individual problem. The medical model of disability defines disability as a medical condition which might be treated to permit the individual to 'fit into' what is seen as 'normal life'. Thus the source of authority or disability was the medical profession. This model was challenged by the social model, which shifted the emphasis from the disabled person to the disabling society. Advocates of the social model recommended the full integration of people with disabilities into mainstream society. Political activists and campaigners in the disability movements of the 1960s and 1970s focused on the need to integrate into the mainstream and for the wider society to change and to recognise the needs of people with disabilities.

While there are considerable problems with approaches which see disability as individual and medical, the social model has been criticised for failing to accommodate the diversity of forms of impairment and disability (Goodley and Rapley, 2002). More recently, the argument has shifted towards fuller recognition of the different experiences of people with disabilities, while accepting the importance of the social construction of differences. The kind of access to public spaces and employment which women have begun to achieve has only recently been accorded to people with disabilities through legislation, for example through anti-discrimination laws, such as the UK Disability Discrimination Act and the US Americans with Disabilities Act. In spite of legislation changes disability is still seen

> as a bodily inadequacy or catastrophe to be compensated for with pity or good will, rather than accommodated by systematic changes based on civil rights . . . disability . . . arises from the interaction of physical differences with an environment . . . the particular . . . disabled body demands accommodation and recognition. In other words, the physical differences of using a wheelchair or being deaf, should be claimed, but not cast as lack.
>
> (Thomson, 2002: 234)

Not only does the specific experience of disability impact upon people's participation in citizenship, but some of the negative social stigmatisations of particular disabilities prevent full engagement. For example, in the case of psychiatric illness, the medical model may persist and individuals may remain stigmatised by records of illness earlier in their lives. Anne Wilson and Peter Beresford cite the example of a woman who visited her GP with migraine symptoms. Thirty-two years earlier the woman had been wrongly diagnosed as having schizophrenia as an 18-year-old. The woman describes a visit to her GP:

> As I took my prescription from her outstretched hands, and smiled my thanks, she looked down at my medical card and said in a rather interested voice, 'I see it says here that you had schizophrenia when you were eighteen'.
>   . . . In a thin voice I heard myself say, 'That was a mistaken diagnosis. I am absolutely horrified to find it's still on my medical record'.
>
> (in Wilson and Beresford, 2002: 149)

Having a 'psychiatric record' can have all sorts of negative effects in different areas of our lives in relation to employment, applying for life insurance, travelling or applying to be a foster-parent or child-minder (ibid.).

Summary

- Generation and disability present important aspects of difference with implications for citizenship rights.
- Assumptions about equality and equal treatment can lead to unequal outcomes in terms of the needs of different people, according to gender, ethnicity generation and disability.
- Differences in age and disability have often been reduced to the problems of the individual or to physical differences which obscure the importance of social meanings.
- Social, individual and embodied differences interrelate in the experiences of people in relation to gender, sexuality, ethnicity, generation and disability.

Taking action

Each of the areas which has been identified in the previous section as restricting access to participation in full, active citizenship has also been involved as the focus for action, that is, for campaigns and political movements that have sought to effect changes. The new social movements of the late 1960s and 1970s were based around the unequal power relations of gender, race, sexuality and disability. These movements strove to erode the boundary between the public and the private arenas of social life and, in the words of the women's movement, to make the case that 'the personal is political' (Woodward, 1997a). These movements and the identity politics which developed from them were not always specifically addressed to the issue of citizenship, but they sought to transform politics to promote greater recognition of those who had been excluded and ignored, for example in dominant and taken-for-granted assumptions about the 'normal' citizen. New social movements challenged the role of traditional political parties and class allegiances, and appealed to the particular identities of their supporters, for example with feminism appealing to women and the black civil rights movement appealing to black people. 'Identity politics involve claiming one's identity as a member of an oppressed or marginalized group as a political point of departure . . . Such politics involve celebration of a group's uniqueness as well as analysis of its particular oppression' (ibid.: 24).

Identity politics was concerned with both challenging the divide between public and private spheres and with making differences between groups of people visible. The social movements of the 1970s drew attention to the exclusion from politics and from representation in the public arena of women, black people, people with disabilities and gay and lesbian people. This was achieved through making visible past and current ways in which these people are oppressed and to create new political identities. Putting into the public arena and making visible past and present sources of disadvantage and the power relations which had produced these exclusions helped to create new identities which brought individuals into public view. Thus, new connections were forged between public and private spheres through collective action. In this sense the public spheres mean the places where decisions are made, and collective action ensured that those who had been marginalised or ignored were not only noticed, but legislative and social changes were made as a result of such action.

New social movements have replaced the restrictive focus upon single issues and bounded identities of identity politics, and have developed across traditional boundaries of class and party politics, even across nation states (as is argued in Chapter 7 on globalisation), but they also impact upon nation states, especially in terms of political change. The Internet has opened up massive possibilities for political networking. Some of the transnational networks of new social movements have been particularly manifest in the activities of environmentalist movements but also have a place in all the areas of concern of such organisations. Manuel Castells has made significant claims for the ways in which new social organisations have combined with new technologies to transform political action:

> dominant functions and processes in the information age are increasingly organized around networks. Networks constitute the new social morphology of our societies and the diffusion of networking logic substantially modifies the operation and outcomes in the process of production, experience, power and culture. While the networking form of social organization has existed in other times and spaces, the new information technology paradigm provides the basis for its pervasive expansion throughout the entire social structure.
>
> (Castells, 1996: 469)

The movements for social change and for broader inclusion in social participation and in all aspects of citizenship and civil life are seen as part of a wider transformation which has effected large-scale changes on political and social life across the globe. While these movements may be seen as part of a global transformation of politics, they are also indications of the effects of human agency. They may be new groupings and, in many instances, employ new technologies, but they also illustrate another key concern within the social sciences, namely the relationship between structures and human agency. Some social structures have been transformed through collective action. For example, the campaigns of the women's movement have led to legislative change in the passing of laws against sex discrimination and the promotion of equal pay. Similarly, the disability movement has achieved some success in the implementation of equal opportunities and anti-discriminatory practices through changes in the law. Thus some social structures have become transformed and re-formed as a result of human political activity.

Agency and structure

As we saw in the first part of this chapter, citizenship involves being a subject of the state; citizens' lives are routinely monitored and under surveillance by government from the cradle to the grave and even before and beyond those extremes of the human life course. Citizenship involves obeying the rules and submitting to structural forces. Citizenship also involves rights; this is one of the reasons why citizenship is so strongly desired and keenly fought over, especially by those denied access to its privileges. What are these rights?

ACTIVITY

What rights do you currently hold by virtue of your citizenship?
    Go to: http://www.direct.gov.uk/en/Governmentcitizensandrights/Your rightsandresponsibilities/DG_066860.

COMMENT

Many of these rights are classified by domestic living arrangements and by age and generation as well as being linked to the workplace and to welfare benefits. These rights are legal, political and civil. You will note that the rights listed on this government website are wide ranging and extend beyond Marshall's categories, notably to embrace different forms of domestic living. The emphasis here is upon the benefits through rights of citizenship, many of which have been won through collective action. What is included in the rights of citizenship has expanded and widened to embrace more groups within the community. The collective action which has been successful in winning these rights is sometimes called agency and is seen as another aspect of citizenship which counterbalances the responsibilities and duties of citizens and the rules and constraints of legal, political and social structures which regulate citizens as subjects.

There has also been some change in thinking about these issues, for example within the social sciences. Rather than seeing human agency on the one hand and the constraints of social and natural structures on the other, in a binary opposition, as if the two were separate and distinct, there has been a move towards focusing upon the interrelationship between the two. Social and 'natural' structures are the outcome of human activities, as well as influencing the ways in which people act and, in particular, constraining their actions. Structures such as the transformation of technologies can be liberating as well as constraining, and it is apparent that the relationship between the actions of human agents and the structures which organise and frame their lives is not a simple one, nor one where structures are only constraining and limiting. This tension between the extent to which human beings shape their own lives and experience and the extent to which they are constrained is not a new debate. It has a long history within philosophy and the social sciences. This debate frequently leads to the classification of social thinkers as favouring one side or the other of the agency/structure dualism. However, more recently the argument has focused upon the tension and balances between the two elements and the need to address both as inextricably involved in any study of human societies. Structures emerge and are classified through the activities of human beings. Even 'natural' structures are closely interconnected with human activity, either as a result of the impact of human activity upon 'nature' or through the categorisation of particular phenomena. In the case of disability this is illustrated by the ways in which people with disabilities have been disadvantaged by the organisation of the societies in which they live, by a 'disabling environment' rather than by disabled bodies. Another aspect of this which has been indicated in this chapter is the ways in which people are categorised and represented, for example in the language which is used to describe and identify them.

The relationship between agency and structure is transformed at particular historical moments, and the balance between structural changes and their trans-formation through human agency shifts. Debates about citizenship in recent years offer particularly useful examples of the impact of collective agency and of the emergence of new forms of political organisation, some of which are specific to their historical context.

Summary

- The interrelationship between agency and structure is an important element in framing debates within the social sciences, although it is expressed in different ways: citizens/subjects, activity/regulation.
- Debates about citizenship raise the issue of the tension and relationship between agency and structure as part of the explanations offered by the social sciences.
- Changes in the experience and understanding of citizenship illustrate the impact of collective action upon social structures.
- Although the structures of race, gender and disability constrain individuals and prevent their full participation in citizenship, these structures can be affected and transformed by the collective activity of the people involved.

Thinking again about evaluation

The discussion up until this point has illustrated some of the ways in which citizenship raises important issues within the social sciences and in contemporary life. The big issue of who is included and who is excluded in social life is hotly debated in terms of the causes of exclusion and definitions of what constitutes citizenship as well as what action might be taken in order to redress inequalities. We have looked at some of the different dimensions of citizenship and at some of the areas of exclusion. This has required a focus on some of the structures which constrain particular groups of people from full participation as well as some of the areas in which change has taken place, for example as a result of collective action. Since the area is clearly one of contestation how can we use this material to present some evaluation? What does the more detailed discussion of other approaches and additional evidence contribute to the assessment of the discussion of citizenship in the section 'The challenge of other arguments'? If we reconsider Marshall's definition of citizenship and his argument about equality, might the discussion in that section offer any new analysis?

ACTIVITY

Take each of the questions posed in the section 'Weighing up the argument' and reconsider the claims that citizenship is based on equality and that all citizens should be treated equally. Consider these questions in the light of the different issues raised in 'The challenge of other arguments'.

1   What is the evidence which supports the claim being made?
2   Does the claim cover all the situations and people involved or are there any people left out?
3   Do the conclusions follow from the initial premises and do they make sense?

COMMENT

1   Parekh's examples of the experience of people from the diverse ethnic groups which make up European societies like the UK suggest specific instances where equal treatment would lead to equality and exclusion. Similarly, evidence of racial violence makes it apparent that difference has to be addressed in all its manifestations in order to produce an inclusive citizenship. Other aspects of difference such as gender and generation also challenge the argument that full citizenship has to be based on equal treatment. For example, women's interrupted patterns of paid work lead to increased poverty in old age in a welfare system that is based on eligibility for a pension derived from continuous contributions made through the uninterrupted life of paid employment.

2   All of the groups of people, many of whom belong in several different categories, may be outside the norm of citizenship that the liberal approach based on equality assumes. Even Marshall's view which encompasses class differences cannot accommodate the diversity of the experience of ethnic minorities, women, gay, lesbian and bisexual people, people with disabilities and people at different points in the life course, often the elderly and retired. In the case of people with disabilities it is often the model of disability which leads to their exclusion from full citizenship. For example, the medical model of disability positions disabled people as victims and as dependants. The excesses of the social model may underplay physical problems and again overlook or

marginalise the contributions and participation of people who have some form of disability.

3   In one sense equal treatment follows logically from the assumption that everyone is equal to start with. However, even Marshall's account does not start with an equal playing field. As Marshall points out, capitalist industrialised societies are characterised by inequalities which full citizenship has to redress. Once there is the recognition of difference there has to be different treatment; that is, different policies in order to achieve fuller, more active participation in civil and political life.

Conclusion

This chapter has addressed the issue of citizenship as an example of a big issue in contemporary societies, which revolves around questions of inclusion and exclusion: that is, who participates and who is excluded or marginalised from civil, political and social life. Debates about citizenship have recently focused on rights and a discussion about equality and the advisability or not of policies that advocate equal treatment. The idea of equal treatment has been countered by the notion of difference and the need to accommodate differences such as those of ethnicity, gender, generation and disability. The idea of difference has been deployed to indicate the ways in which equal treatment fails to respond to the specific needs of particular groups. For example, one of the ways in which women have been excluded from full participation as citizens has been their absence from paid work or their interrupted working lives. This has meant that women have not been able to make the necessary contributions, for example, to receive a pension at the end of their working lives. Similarly, many women have not been able to accumulate the necessary pension fund owing to their interrupted employment patterns because of the greater likelihood that they were working part time, and thus did not have the necessary record of insurance. An approach that focuses upon difference, as well as seeking greater equality in outcomes, can address some of these issues, notably by taking on board the specific needs of hitherto marginalised groups. An understanding of difference also leads to a more thorough examination of what is considered to be the 'normal citizen'. Is this category an able-bodied, white man who is able to engage in full-time paid work throughout his adult life course? As has been suggested, frequently other aspects of citizenship have been dependent on the assumptions of who is the 'normal citizen'.

Increased mobility and migration across state boundaries as well as social, cultural, political and economic changes in families, work and everyday life and vicissitudes in national and global economies create changes. Some of the transformations of contemporary life have highlighted the importance of rethinking what it means to be a citizen, and in particular to draw attention to those who may still be denied full citizenship rights. This analysis has employed some of the structures which interact with personal experience and illustrate the ways in which human agency is both shaped by and influences social, political, cultural and economic structures. Some of the changes that have taken place in our under-standing of citizenship and in the experience of being a citizen have resulted from collective action. This is an area which has been the focus of political action both within the mainstream of party politics and of what has been called identity politics. Social movements which have developed out of those of the late 1960s, which led to demands by the women's movement, gay and lesbian rights movements, organisations promoting rights based on issues of race and ethnicity and the disability movement, have led to an expansion of citizenship rights in some areas and for certain people.

The discussion in this chapter has also focused on some of the strategies adopted within the social sciences for the evaluation of different approaches and theoretical perspectives. While in this chapter we have applied some of the criteria employed and questions posed to the example of citizenship and in particular to debates about equality and difference, these strategies have wider implications which relate to all of the big issues addressed in this book, especially in the interconnections between structure and agency and the role of collective action in effecting political changes. Citizenship offers a good example of both contemporary debates about social change and the transformation of societies in the twenty-first century and about the role of collective action in effecting change.

Chapter 4

Buying and selling

Introduction

> The great afternoon rush-hour had arrived, when the overheated machine led
> the dance of customers, extracting money from their very flesh. In the silk
> department especially there was a sense of madness . . . In the still air, where
> the stifling central heating brought out the smell of the materials, the hubbub
> was increasing, made up of all sorts of noises – the continuous trampling of
> feet, the same phrase repeated a hundred times at the counters, gold clinking
> on the brass cash-desks, besieged by a mass of purses, the baskets on wheels
> with their loads of parcels falling endlessly into the gaping cellars.
>
> (Zola, 1995: 108–109)

What is this about? It is a description of a shopping experience which has resonance
with many in the contemporary Western world. The reference to the silk department
might be a give-away of earlier times, as might the mention of gold and purses.
Nowadays it would be more likely to be ready-made designer label clothes and the
swiping of credit cards! However, Emile Zola's novel *The Ladies' Paradise*
captures a historical moment and, with the arrival of the department store, the
modernisation of commercial activities. The historical moment is the middle of the
nineteenth century when the Bon Marché department store opened in Paris. There
were parallel developments in the US and in England. Although the advent of such
large-scale shops meant the demise of traditional family stores, as recorded in the
novel, Zola's novel is a celebration of the activity of modernity and in a sense a
'hymn to modern business, a celebration of the entrepreneurial spirit' (Nelson,
1995: xi). The department store is the signifier of the promise of capitalism as
experienced in the life of the city and for the middle classes. The store is a model
for the capitalist economic system, based on the exchange of goods for profit. It is
characterised by the principles of speed of turnover, circulation, commodity
exchange and the rapid renewal of capital in the form of commodities.

The store and its surrounding arcades presented spaces for the display and sale
of commodities, dreams and desires. These commodities, which had initially
promised to fulfil desires, now created them. This is an important shift in the

process of consumption, and the links between production and consumption, which this chapter explores. The department store was first created to display products, but also to provide a space in which the fashionable public could display themselves. In a sense the commercial principle became displaced by the principle of seduction. This seduction of the consumer, notably of women as consumers, is the subject of Zola's novel. The novel covers a whole range of seduction techniques ranging from advertising, which was not a common practice in the nineteenth century, to free entry to the store, allowing customers to look without buying and to be seen, thus creating the idea and practice of shopping as a leisure activity. Prices were fixed, thus eliminating the interaction of bartering. The process of purchase became quick and impersonal. The physical layout of the store was deliberately organised to ensure that shoppers passed through the different departments, having to travel the length and breadth of the store to find what they had come to buy. The most significant mechanism of seduction described by Zola is the seduction of the spectacle with the excesses of visual pleasure, using light, space, colour (sometimes overwhelmingly white) and glass to present luxurious, exotic fabrics both within the store and in its window displays. Women are the main protagonists in the novel, although the management and ownership of the store are in men's hands. Mouret, the owner of Zola's *Ladies' Paradise*, is described by the novelist as successful in his creation of desire for the commodities for sale in his store because of his understanding of seduction, as well as of the capitalist system. On the first point, 'Mouret's sole passion was the conquest of Woman. He wanted her to be queen in his shop: he had built his temple for her in order to hold her at his mercy. His tactics were to intoxicate her with amorous attentions, to trade on her desires' (Zora, 1995: 234). There is some degree of poetic licence given that this is a fictional account, but it does convey the necessary strength of the creation of desire for goods so that they become important in satisfying desires rather than only serving a particular use function, that is, having use value. On the second point, Mouret's success resulted from his understanding of the capitalist principle of economic exchange and circulation, and his grasp of the need to use another new transport system. Improved transport through roads in the city and the development of the railway network in the nineteenth century greatly facilitated travel and the rapid circulation of goods both within the city of Paris and with the rest of the world. Thus development of a new and successful economic system is linked to technological advances. New modes of transport, the development of commodity culture and the importance of exchange value (rather than simply use value, that is, what you can do with the products you buy) all created new ways of seeing the world and new forms of interaction. It is the novel's emphasis on the links between individuals and the culture in which they live, especially its focus on desire as motivating the system of exchange, that gives it such contemporary resonance.

This brief discussion of a fictional account, but one that has been very important in exploring both the historical and more recent manifestations of consumption and shopping, has introduced a whole range of concepts that require further explanation. Fictional accounts retain their resonance in changed circumstances; for example, nineteenth-century novels that include the growth and primacy of markets in the heyday of capitalism also include the recession, the fall of great houses and financial corruption, as well as of entrepreneurial success, most marked in Charles Dickens' *Little Dorrit* (1857), which echoes the troubles of more recent times in the global economy.

The Ladies' Paradise is set against the background of the development of an economic system, namely that of capitalism, which provides the framework, albeit in a variety of guises, for much of economic life around the globe, especially following the breakup of the former USSR and the former Eastern Europe. Capitalism involves a system of wage labour, whereby people provide their labour to an employer in return for payment, wages. It also features commodity production for sale and exchange, that is, people make things to sell, not only for their own use, and, most significantly, production and exchange are carried out for profit. The motivating force behind capitalist production is the creation of profit. Capital is created through the purchase of commodities. These are raw materials, machinery and labour. The combination of these elements creates a new commodity which is then sold – that is, exchange value – for a price higher than it cost to produce, thus making a profit. Karl Marx argued that it was because labour had become a commodity and labour was exploited, and workers are paid less than the value their work creates for the capitalist, that profit is produced which creates more capital for use by the owners of the means of production. The Marxist approach was very influential in the nineteenth and first half of the twentieth centuries, but more recently the relationship between production and consumption has been seen as more complicated and the emphasis has shifted to a range of materialities. It has been suggested that Marx's view of the class system is too simplistic and that the working class has become better-off and not impoverished as Marx predicted. However, class plays a crucial part in the life chances of people in all modern societies, ranging from health, to education, and life expectancy to consumption and employment. Marxism stresses the role of production, its exploitation of workers, that is, of labour, and the way in which production determines what is made and hence what is bought, that is, consumed.

Have times changed? People in the West, especially, now live in what has been termed the 'consumer society'. Advertising and marketing are so embedded in Western cultures that it may be taken for granted that 'we are what we buy', and consumption shapes social relations and social divisions. People are marked out as different from each other according to the goods they purchase (or cannot purchase, because they lack the resources to do so), rather than societies being differentiated by the ways in which production is organised. The contemporary consumer society is one in which consumption may be seen as both the creator of affluence and the cause of its decline. This decline was also a feature of nineteenth-century capitalism; vicissitudes of markets and their collapse, even the contemporary practice of selling loans, an aspect of the twenty-first-century credit crunch, have also been addressed in the narratives of earlier times, including the novels of Charles Dickens, one of whose characters, Mr Merdle in *Little Dorrit*, made and subsequently lost his fortune doing just that. Credit crises are linked to consumption, especially in modern economies that are dependent upon maintaining high levels of consumption. The crisis which began in 2008 has been described as follows: 'Never in the field of human consumption had so much been owed by so many to so few, and with so little collateral' (Meek, 2009).

Before we look at these arguments in more detail I want to map out some of the ideas which came before these claims that there has been a massive shift towards the 'consumer society'.

Processes of production and consumption

Consumption is a big issue in contemporary society in all sorts of ways. For the past two decades this has been one of the most significant areas of interest within social science (Miller, 1997). Certainly consumption is now seen as important as production and work when thinking about how societies are defined and the kinds of social identities they produce. Social scientists began talking about a post-industrial society after many traditional industries went into decline and more jobs were created within the service sector in what is called a consumer society or culture to reflect how important issues of consumption have become.

Although most of us still think in terms of our work or career saying something important about who we are, a quick browse on any of the social networking Internet sites or lifestyle magazines in the newsagent will reveal that the question people are increasingly trying to answer more often is 'What are you into?' Issues of consumption, identity and lifestyle are inextricably linked to such a question because those are the sorts of issues that matter to many people when they think about who they are.

What we buy and how we consume things once we have bought them tells us a great deal about the society we live in as well as the people in it: social opportunities and inequalities, changes and conflicts, power and freedom.

ACTIVITY

Take a look at Figure 4.1. It provides some recent data collected by the Office of National Statistics on what households spend their money on during a typical week. A household ranges from a single person to a large, extended family group. Have a look at some of the figures and what people typically consume. The housing category does not include mortgage costs. Does any of the information surprise you?

COMMENT

People spend their money on a mixture of things. They spend money on essentials like food and clothing (though those categories can cover a wide range of different

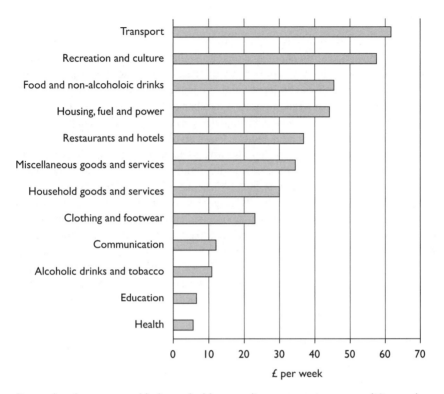

Figure 4. Average weekly household expenditure on main commodities and services, 2005–2006, UK

Source: Expenditure and Food Survey, Office for National Statistics, published 18 January 2007. http://www.statistics.gov.uk/cci/nugget.asp?id=284 (last accessed 20 November 2008

things) but also on communications, leisure and entertainment, alcohol and cigarettes. The biggest category here, though, is transport, which includes car running costs, petrol and public transport. It is unlikely that that this is all leisure travel; much of it might be associated with commuting to work. Health here might cover items like prescriptions or over-the-counter medicines and remedies. Two decades ago very few people owned a mobile phone. Now the majority of people do so and it has become a major item of weekly expenditure. Figure 4.1 provides some basic and very interesting data but it is also limited in what it can tell us. These data provide a description of broad patterns of consumption, but do not, of course, tell us why people buy what they buy. Patterns of consumption are driven by need, for basic essentials and by desire, for things that make you feel good, but most of all it is resources, or lack of them, that determine what we can and cannot buy. Purchasing power is shaped by material, economic factors, and social class is one of the concepts used in the social sciences, which accommodates these factors.

Class

The concept of class provides a very useful means of both describing and explaining inequalities, social divisions and change. Without going as far as Karl Marx and claiming that all history is the history of class struggle (see below), the notion of class has been deployed by large numbers of social scientists in the nineteenth and twentieth centuries to incorporate a number of the ways in which groups of people have both very different and unequal experiences, and different perceptions about their position in the wider society. Class involves the division of people into different groups according to their wealth, or lack of it, occupations and life chances. Factors such as sources of income, family background, education, place of residence, political affiliations and cultural tastes have all been invoked as part of the explanatory framework. However, there are key components of class, which make it such a useful tool for understanding social change. Classes are grounded in some shared material position which is linked to the work people do and how they are rewarded for their labour. Class involves an emphasis on a shared, common position which, through similarity of experience, gives rise to some commonality of perception and outlook. Class is about shared experience deriving from common conditions. Some of this commonality of interests may give rise to political action and the impetus for political organisation, for example in political parties or collective groups like trade unions or other such groups committed to action and social change. The processes of production have been given high priority in definitions of class.

As Marx wrote in the *Communist Manifesto* in 1848 of the bourgeoisie, that is, the capitalist class, whose class position derived from their ownership of the means of production: 'The bourgeoisie, during its scarce one hundred years has created more massive and colossal productive forces than have all preceding generations together' (in Feuer, 1959: 12). Times have changed and Marx could not have predicted the scale of contemporary globalisation, or its complexity. Changing times have led to different approaches to class and even challenges to the usefulness of the concept.

At certain points in the twentieth century it was claimed that class no longer mattered and other social divisions had superseded class. Such views were based on several different assumptions and different sources of evidence. For example, it was suggested that the economic basis of class differences had been eroded. The decline of heavy manufacturing industry and the increase in service sector work had led to a democratisation of the workforce, where it was no longer possible to differentiate clearly between blue- and white-collar workers. The conditions of work no longer gave rise to easily distinguishable attitudes, experience and performance. It was also claimed that political action had increasingly become organised around other areas of difference, gender, ethnicity, sexuality, disability and issues linked to the environment and the perception of risk, rather than traditional class interests. The other dimension of this debate, which we will look at in more detail later, is the argument that consumption has assumed greater importance in shaping attitudes and perceptions. This is linked to the claim that production and consumption are interrelated rather than separate and distinct, and that production should not be seen as the most important factor in shaping social divisions and inequalities.

Inequality

There has been some resurgence of interest in the concept of class, especially in explaining large-scale patterns of inequality, for example across the globe, where differences in quality of life are enormous between the rich countries of the West and parts of the developing world. Economic inequalities among countries have not only widened between the different parts of the world. They have increased within Europe, for example, and within European countries, with the spread of modern capitalism, especially since the breakup of the former USSR. According to the UN Development Programme, there has been 'The fastest rise in inequality ever. Russia now has the greatest inequality – the income share of the richest 20 per cent is 11 times that of the poorest 20 percent' (Callinicos, 2000: 2). There is also considerable inequality among UK citizens. Wealth ownership is evidence of such inequalities. The Economic and Social Research Council provides data on such inequalities (ESRC, 2008). They show that 23 per cent of wealth is owned by 1 per cent of the population. The wealthiest 10 per cent own more than half the wealth in the UK; the wealthiest 50 per cent own 94 per cent of wealth. Statistics show that the wealthy have got wealthier over the past ten years. These figures present overall wealth in the UK, which includes property, investment and unearned income, a major contributor to wealth for the top 1 per cent; for the majority of people, their occupation is their major source of income (ESRC: *Society Today*, 2008).

Evidence is often based on median weekly wages. The median is the midpoint of the distribution or spread, a halfway point with 50 per cent above this line and 50 per cent below. The ESRC reports that highest paid occupations in 2004 included medical practitioners (£1168), pilots (£1094), senior police officers (£825) and IT managers (£795). The lowest paid occupations included hairdressers (£219), bar staff (£213), check-out operators (£204) and florists (£197). Despite much media coverage suggesting high earnings, the average hourly wage for full-time male plumbers in 2003 was £10.62, less than train drivers at £15.55, sewage workers at £10.94, electricians at £11.22 and journalists at £16.83 (ESRC, 2008).

There are also differences between women's and men's earnings. Figure 4.2 charts changes in the median and mean (average) earnings according to gender. What do you notice about the differences in the earnings of women and men? How is this changing?

Figure 4.2 shows that men earned more than women in all age groups between 1998 and 2008, although the gender pay gap (as measured by the median hourly pay excluding overtime of full-time employees) narrowed between 2006 and

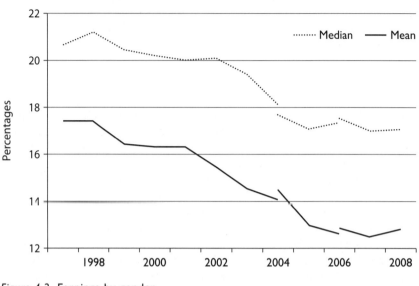

Figure 4.2 Earnings by gender
Source: Social Trends (2008)

2007 to its lowest value since records began. The gap between women's median hourly pay and men's was 12.6 per cent, compared with a gap of 12.8 per cent recorded in April 2006. The median hourly rate for men went up 2.8 per cent to £11.96, while the rate for women increased by 3.1 per cent to £10. This appears to be a significant improvement, but there are other factors to take into account, such as the availability of work and the kind of work that people are able to undertake; women work shorter hours than men on average. *Social Trends* reports that, on the internationally comparable measure based on mean earnings, women's average hourly pay, excluding overtime, was 17.2 per cent less than men's pay, showing a decrease on the comparable figure of 17.5 per cent for 2006 (*Social Trends*, 2008). In 2007, median weekly earnings of full-time employees for women of £394 were 21 per cent less than those for men (£498), unchanged from 2006.

Other factors impinge upon earnings in retirement for the older age group and it is worth noting that there are more women than men in the over-eighty categories. Ownership of wealth is another indicator of inequality within a society. What does Figure 4.3 tell us about the distribution of wealth in Britain in the late 1990s? How even is the distribution of wealth? What might this tell us about inequality?

Household net wealth in the UK more than doubled in real terms between 1987 and 2006. This may well account for increased spending. These data pre-date the economic crises of 2008 however. Wealth is less evenly distributed than income.

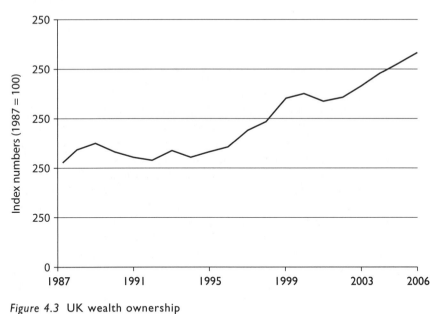

Figure 4.3 UK wealth ownership
Source: Social Trends (2008)

It is difficult to assess the wealth of individuals, especially as the assets of the very rich can be most diffusely spread and are not simple to measure. However, there has been little change in the estimation that 1 per cent of individuals owned between one-fifth and one-quarter of the total wealth. Perhaps more alarmingly, at the other end of the scale 50 per cent of the population shared only 6 per cent of the total wealth. While not being definitive, this does paint a picture of an inegalitarian society, with considerable inequity in the distribution of wealth and resources.

One of the most common ways of identifying inequality and more specifically poverty in any society is to consider the situation of children. Child poverty is an important indicator of inequality. For Britain the evidence suggests that there has been an increase in child poverty over the past three decades. This is measured by household income, for example if the household in which children are living has an income below the average wage. Many children live in 'workless households', with over two million (17.6 per cent) in households where no adults are in work. In Muslim households this is even higher, with more than one-third of children living in households where no adult is in work (HMSO Census, National Statistics Online, 2003).

If consumption is a major driver of economic and social prosperity the continuance of inequalities presents a problem in contemporary societies. Inequalities are complex, and different factors such as gender, generation and ethnicity all contribute to the persistence of significant inequalities. Social scientists offer a range of different approaches to explain the causes of inequality.

Marx and class

The history of all hitherto existing society is the history of class struggles. Free man and slave patrician and plebeian, lord and serf, guild master and journeyman, in a word, oppressor and oppressed, stood in constant opposition to one another, carried on an uninterrupted, now hidden, now open fight, a fight that each time ended in either a revolutionary re-constitution of society at large or in the common ruin of the contending classes . . .

Our epoch, the epoch of the bourgeoisie, possesses, however this distinctive feature: it has simplified class antagonisms. Society as a whole is more and more splitting into two great hostile camps, into two great classes directly facing each other; bourgeoisie and proletariat . . .

The bourgeoisie cannot exist without constantly revolutionizing the means of production, and thereby the relations of production, and with them the whole relations of society . . .

The need of a constantly expanding market for its products chases the bourgeoisie over the whole surface of the globe . . . by the rapid movement of all instruments of production, by the immensely facilitated means of communication, draws all . . . nations into civilization.

(Marx and Engels, in Feuer, 1959: 7–11)

'The essential condition for the existence of the bourgeois class . . . is the formation and augmentation of capital; the condition for capital is wage labour' (ibid.: 19).

This quotation from the Communist Manifesto by Kark Marx (1818–1883) and Friedrich Engels (1820–1895) makes a strong statement about the primacy of social class. Indeed, for Marx class was the motivating force behind social change and the primary social division. Class position derived from people's relationship to the means of production, as owners or as reduced to selling their labour. Thus production is more important than consumption and the particular form of production in any society determines social relations. In a capitalist society this means that ownership of capital and commodity production creates two main classes: the bourgeoisie who own the means of production and the proletariat who sell their labour for a wage. While there may be more complex social divisions which may cross class boundaries, class and the socio-economic positions it shapes remains a key factor in shaping experience and social relations. Marx's focus was on inequality. He emphasised the material aspects of inequality. This inequality, he argued, would become more polarised as capitalism developed. The proletariat, he predicted, would become ever more impoverished. Class-consciousness was also very important to Marx's argument, which concentrated on the working class or proletariat becoming sufficiently aware of its collective class predicament as a class 'for itself', ultimately to take action to overthrow the dominance of the bourgeoisie and the capitalist system.

Weber and class

> We may speak of a 'class' when (1) a number of people have in common a specific causal component of their life chances, in so far as (2) this component is represented exclusively by accompanying interests in the possession of goods and opportunities for income, and (3) is represented under the conditions of the commodity or labour markets.
>
> (in Gerth and Mills, 1948: 181)

Thus Max Weber (1864–1920) sees class situation as reflecting life chances that are themselves determined by the market and by people's position in relation to the market. The sorts of factors that would shape life chances would be ownership of property, skills and education. Whereas Marx identified two main classes set in conflict against each other, Weber paints a broader picture, listing these groups as social classes:

- the working class
- the petty bourgeoisie, for example small shopkeepers
- technicians, specialists and lower management
- the classes privileged through property and education, that is, those who occupy the top positions and are at the top of the class hierarchy.

Weber lays no claim to the importance or existence of class-consciousness. He presents an argument which distinguishes between class, status and party, but acknowledges that the three elements interrelate and overlap. Economic class and social class are not necessarily linked. It is possible to have status, for example in relation to occupation, without the job carrying economic ranking. In many ways Weber's account of social classes is not so very different from Marx's, especially in terms of describing classes in a capitalist society. He identifies similar areas of difference between socio-economic groups. However, whereas Marx's two classes are defined *in relation* to each other, the bourgeoisie cannot exist without the proletariat and vice versa; Weber's classes exist as a hierarchy.

Weber both concentrates on market position, including the paid work which people do, and adds other dimension to this explanation of social divisions and stratification. One of these is status which may or may not align with occupational hierarchies. Status brings in a more complex picture of social divisions, although it may still be more descriptive than explanatory in its contribution to the debate.

Summing up: differences between Marx and Weber

For Marx, class is grounded in the exploitation and domination that are an essential part of the relations of *production*, whereas for Weber class reflects life chances in the market.

Marx's definition of class is based on the relationship of different groups of people to the means of production and to each other. Thus it is a relational explanation, whereas Weber's account is based on a description of hierarchies that are shaped by life chances and market relations.

Marx gives priority to class as the most influential aspect of historical development. For Marx, class conflict motivates historical change, whereas for Weber, it is not the prime motivator of change.

For Marx, class action is inevitable, whereas for Weber, class is only one aspect of society which may present a possible motivation for action and change but the link is neither inevitable nor the only factor to consider.

Although Weber incorporates status into his analysis of social divisions, production still plays a key role in the creation of class in many accounts. There is also a separation of production and consumption and a greater emphasis on production, but times have changed.

Consumer society?

ACTIVITY

Read the following short extract from a newspaper article about a London store opening of the fashion chain Zara. The chain has been very successful, with 1,500 stores worldwide in 2008. Zara is worn by the cognoscenti, what Caroline Roux, in her article, along with many fashion journalists, calls the 'fashionista'. The Zara shops specialise in supplying designer clothes at high street prices. The clothes are worn by media celebrities and fashion journalists as well as by thousands of fashion- and budget-conscious shoppers. They bring together high fashion (Bond Street) with popular high street (Oxford Street). The company's Spanish owner, Amancio Ortega of Inditex group, occupies the number 8 spot on the Forbes' billionaire list, with an estimated $20.1bn fortune. He is the richest man in Spain, but keeps a very low profile. The company is enormously successful in spite of spending very little on advertising, with its marketing budget only 4 per cent of overall expenditure.

> What it has done is plug a gap in the market with a desirable product: high fashion for middle-class urban women . . .
> Zara's largest European store – a 3,000sq m temple to consumption – opened in Oxford Street and Bond Street, its locations rather conveniently summing up Zara's knack for offering high-style clothes at high-street prices . . . The building was completely concealed beneath hoardings with

no indication of who was about to launch themselves into the Oxford Street melee. Rumours abounded. By the time the store was ready, the Zara faithful had spread the word.

Within minutes of the doors opening, the tills were ringing and shoppers leaving laden with easily identifiable navy paper bags . . .

The speed at which Zara translates catwalk styles into high-street products is the key to its success. It can do this because it controls manufacturing more closely than any of its competitors . . . by producing 50% of its product in-house.

If a style doesn't sell well within a week, it is withdrawn.

(Roux, 2002: 6)

What parallels are there with the extract from *The Ladies' Paradise* at the start of this chapter? How does the Zara phenomenon illustrate the claim that consumption shapes experience and social relations?

What might be missing in this account?

COMMENT

In many ways this account, written in the twenty-first century, has resonance with Zola's fictional narrative written one and half centuries earlier. The emphasis is still upon profit, whether it is tills ringing or gold clinking. The profit machine is in motion. Some of the marketing strategies are the same and the new Zara store is described exotically as a 'temple to consumption' very like the Ladies' Paradise department store. The contemporary article mirrors the excitement surrounding the promotion of these products in much the same way that Zola conjures up the advent of department stores in the nineteenth century.

Interestingly, in the twenty-first century this was a relatively new venture which, while generating massive profits, does not devote much resource to advertising per se. However, there are other strategies all linked to promotion. The publicity accorded media stars and fashion icons, all of whom admit publicity to wearing Zara, is a less direct strategy. It is none the less very much part of the product promotion strategy. Similarly, the shrouded building in Oxford Street lends very public mystique and fuel for the rumours and mystery which contribute to the excitement associated with the product.

While the goods may be at 'high street prices', not everyone is included in this fashion bonanza. It is exclusive culturally and to some extent economically. What is missing is exclusion and inequality. The gap in the market it purports to fill is to cater for 'middle-class urban women'. This is an already somewhat privileged group of consumers. The cost of Zara products is low compared with designer goods, but not compared with the clothes from charity shops or the really cheap items that are possibly more within the spending power of the poorest groups of women. Low cost, however, allows for high turnover for the company and for its fashion-conscious consumers, whose wardrobes can be frequently renewed to fit in with the demands of contemporary culture.

The company has developed a series of very effective strategies which respond to contemporary patterns of consumption. Speed is of the essence in the fast-changing climate of fashion, as the Zara company acknowledges by translating catwalk styles into accessible high street products more quickly than its competitors. The company also retains its competitive edge by controlling its production at its own factories rather than tendering to other suppliers.

The production and consumption processes are clearly closely interconnected. Production is geared to the needs and demands of consumers within the market for fashionable clothes at reasonable prices. This company has found its moment and has carved out a more profitable, substantial niche in the market. Its fashions are represented through the association with attractive media celebrities as well as with the culture of cool in everyday life. Buying into this culture and the identities it constructs becomes possible for consumers, who are able to purchase affordable fashion, which none the less connotes a style that might be associated with affluence.

This notion of the interrelationships between different points in the processes of production and consumption draws upon an idea indicated by Richard Johnson, and developed by Paul Du Gay and colleagues in the 'circuit of culture' (1997). This 'circuit' illustrates five moments in the process of production of cultural texts and artefacts, like fashion. Figure 4.4 shows how the circuit operates and how the processes interrelate.

This model is useful for indicating stages or moments in the process of the manufacture and exchange of products. The circuit also gives primacy to the cultural production of meanings about products. Culture is implicated in the whole process. Representation involves the ways in which meanings are presented, through images, language and practices. This is a moment in the circuit that has

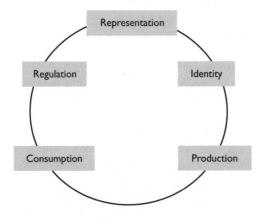

Figure 4.4 The circuit of culture
Source: Du Gay *et al.* (1997: 3)

particular resonance with the world of fashion. Fashion is intrinsically and necessarily the product of representational systems, which convey and create meanings about what is in and what is out, and which are the 'must-haves' of the moment. Representations include the images in magazines, on television, through popular culture, especially images of celebrities, as well as the fashion channel, films and the Internet. Identities are the subject positions into which people who buy the product are recruited. Fashion creates its desirable and desiring subjects through representational systems. The fashion industry depends on consumers buying into the identities which it promotes by buying its products. Production involves the raw materials, labour, time machines and technologies that combine in the creation of artefacts and services. In the fashion industry this involves new technologies in the creation of new styles, fabrics and designs. Fashion depends heavily on change and on the idea of the 'new'. New approaches are implicated at all levels, in the representations deployed, the identities constructed, and in the processes and technologies of production. Consumption refers to the exchange and services and the point at which they are purchased and consumed. This is the point at which the consumers are recruited into the identities by buying the product and we find out if the new technologies and the strategies used to promote the product have worked. Regulation involves the ways in which the public and private spheres of life are linked in the governance and control of production and consumption. This operates in myriad ways. Some involve the regulation of employment in the industry. Fashion is an industry with a long history of outworking, homeworking and the exploitation of low-paid workers both within countries like the UK and in different parts of the world where wages are low. There is also regulation of the fabrics used, including fur and animal products, and of the ways in which these can be promoted. In some of the glossy, more upmarket magazines, there has been considerable controversy over the representation of models in states of undress, smoking cigarettes and at one time displaying what was called 'heroin chic' through emaciated bodies and darkened eyes. The representation of fashion is implicated in a range of moral discourses about what is acceptable and what is not, especially in the context of its appeal for an ever-younger market. Regulations of styles, practices and processes are all involved in deciding what it is acceptable to wear, when and by whom.

What is most important for our purposes here is the interrelationship between production and consumption. This is partly what challenges more traditional views of the primacy of production and the idea that production shaped consumption.

How far have we moved the other way to the extent of claiming that consumption is dominant? Steve Spittle suggests that 'We seem to have less interest in wider social issues and more interest in the consumption-based lifestyles offered to us by television and commercial markets' (2002: 58).

Spittle is writing about television programming and the preference of viewers for consumption-based 'make-over' shows and consumer entertainment over news and documentary viewing. However, the point remains: consumption rules. Do you agree with this claim?

There is empirical evidence of increased consumer spending in affluent Western countries. In the West, household expenditure has soared in recent years and there is massive spending on a wide range of consumer goods. UK household expenditure increased by two and a half times between 1971 and 2006 (*Social Trends*, 2008: 79). This would certainly support the argument that there has been a massive expansion in consumer goods and in their purchase. Much of this spending is made using credit cards.

Look at the information below from the UK payments association, APACS, which gives details of the use of credit and debit cards in the UK in 2007. The information is adapted from an APACS press release in 2007 which describes spending trends in 2006. Has this form of transaction increased?

Plastic cards in the UK and how we used them in 2007

- In 2007, there were 165.4 million payment cards in issue – 67.3 million credit cards, 5.7 million charge cards and 71.6 million debit cards, 20.2 million ATM-only cards and 0.5 million cheque guarantee cards.
- There are 41.7 million personal debit card holders, representing 84% of the adult population.
- The average number of cards per person was 2.4 credit cards and 1.6 debit cards.
- Spending on plastic cards in the UK amounted to £354.2 billion in 2006, which comprised £221 billion on debit cards, and £133.2 billion on credit and charge cards.
- Internet card payments have risen nearly four-fold over the last five years, to £34 billion.
- There were 4.9 billion debit card purchases in 2007, an increase of 9% on 2006, with an average transaction value of £45.
- There were 1.9 billion purchases made on credit and charge cards in the UK, giving an average transaction value of £63.22.

(APACS, 2007)

APACS notes a trend towards the greater use of debit cards, accounting for 70 per cent of the purchases made in the UK in the first half of 2006. Actual spending in June on debit cards reached £16.2 billion and credit card spending amounted to £10.2 billion; we now spend much more on our debit cards than on our credit cards, whereas prior to 2003, monthly spending on plastic had been roughly equally split between debit and credit cards. Some 543 million purchases were made on plastic in June 2006 (377 million on debit cards and 166 million on credit cards), an increase of 4.9 per cent on June 2005. Of these purchases, two-thirds took place on the high street, with the strongest contribution in the food and drink and household sectors, reflecting the warm weather and the impact of the World Cup.

This kind of evidence does highlight some of the patterns of consumer spending and the practices that are implicated in the 'consumer society'. Even if people are spending less on credit cards than before, they are still spending large amounts using debit cards. Does an expansion in consumption necessarily mean that we live in a consumer society, or that consumption largely takes place for its own sake, or for lifestyle reasons rather than for the immediate *use* of the goods purchased? As we saw in Figure 4.1, much of UK consumer spending is on housing and cars. Entertainment forms a significant proportion of consumer spending with IT and media equipment high on the list (*Social Trends*, 2008: 6.1). Consumers are certainly very active in that there is a great deal of consuming going on! Consumption is seen to drive the global economy. The government's reaction to the 2008 economic recession was to promote spending, although consumers were more reticent; as earlier evidence showed, consumers were already using their credit cards more cautiously. However, this does not necessarily mean that consumers are exercising a great deal of choice and autonomy. Consumers may also have been resisting government pressure to spend their way out of a recession that they had already spent their way into. It is possible for consumption to be shaped by forces outside the consumer's control. How far do consumers resist the pressure from producers who may attempt to foist upon them products that are unwelcome? Clearly some products fail, yet considerable effort is put into their promotion. Consumers are not passive dupes and exercise considerable control through their own actions in buying or rejecting goods and services. However, if we look at the wider arena, there is also resistance to globalisation through anti-globalisation movements and green politics and campaigns against the massive environmental destruction that has arisen from the huge increase in consumption worldwide. Some of the challenges, especially in the context of globalisation, are explored in Chapter 7.

Different approaches to the consumer society

Steve Spittle argues that market-based consumption dominates affluent Western countries like the UK. Everywhere we look there is information about consumer products, in all media, in the street and on the Internet. Kalle Lasn suggests that advertising and marketing are so deeply embedded in our culture now that it is hard to imagine a time when product placement and network logo and 'burns' and 'bugs' weren't everywhere you looked, when our lifestyles and culture weren't predicated on consumption. But that pre-marketing era was not so long ago: only two generations (2000: 421–422).

This move to a consumer society is seen here as a relatively recent phenomenon, but it has become one that is taken for granted in the West. It has become part of 'who we are' and what we expect. Much television programming focuses largely on the promotion of products and services, not only through frequent advertising on the commercial channels, but also through some of the most popular programmes. Make-over programmes, whether of our houses, our gardens, our bodies or our psyches and relationships, all advocate the need to be constantly changing and re-forming. We are exhorted to review ourselves and our lives; who we are as indicated by what we own, what we do and how we do it. The constant re-production of ourselves, our homes and our gardens requires knowledge, products and services and especially the knowledge of which products to employ in this ongoing quest.

This kind of approach reflects some of the postmodernist views of the consumer society. Such approaches stress the importance of representational systems. The commodity, that is, the goods produced for sale through the combination of raw materials, machinery, technologies and labour, has been replaced by the 'commodity sign'. This means that what the commodity stands for, what it represents and how it is represented have overtaken its use value. Things are not bought to be used only, but for what they represent. So, Zara fashions mean cool, streetwise chic, Coke means freedom and energy. You will be able to think of many other examples. The message is usually stated either explicitly or by association in the advertisements for the products. These associations are not only deployed to persuade us to buy the product; they become the product and this is what we are buying into. In this sense the system is based not on the desire for material goods as much as for the meanings associated with them and the different meanings between products. Consumer goods have thus become the source of meaning in society, rather than other identifications, for example with the community within which we live, our families, religious groups or work-based affiliations. This argument as put forward by writers such as Jean Baudrillard:

> What is sociologically significant for us, and what marks our era under the sign of consumption, is precisely the generalised reorganisation of this primary level in a system of signs which appears to be . . . the specific mode of our era.
>
> (1988: 47)

However, this may be an overstatement, especially of the symbolic aspects of consumption. Postmodernism lays a heavy emphasis on the role of the symbolic and upon how commodities and artefacts are represented with its stress on signs. We are certainly bombarded with signs in our everyday lives, but the influence of these signs and their dominance in constructing meaning in our lives and in social relations can be overstated. As we saw in Chapter 2, Pierre Bourdieu incorporates an analysis of taste and consumption into a class-based critique of social relations. He retains a material base and the notion of constraints and limitations, for example in the autonomy of consumers. As Bourdieu argues, although patterns of consumption form part of communications and classificatory systems, they are also deeply embedded in social structures of class, in particular. He argued that social class was the main determinant of consumption (1986) which clearly provides a material antidote to the excesses of some postmodernist accounts, which see the symbolic as the only relevant factor. Bourdieu argues that consumption is linked to social differentiation because 'taste classifies the classifier', that is, what you buy classifies you (1986). 'Social subjects, classified by their classifications, distinguish themselves by the distinctions they make, between the beautiful and the ugly, the distinguished and the vulgar, in which their position in the objective classification is expressed or betrayed' (ibid.: 6). For Bourdieu, consumption is symbolic but it is also material. People's capacity to consume these goods refers to their material social position, including, most importantly, their financial resources, and what he calls their cultural capital. Cultural capital includes what we have learned, for example from our parents and from our education, the sort of people we are (1986).

Zygmunt Bauman also suggests a more constraining view of the free market consumer, picking and choosing an identity off the peg. He also points to the tendency in postmodernist approaches not to distinguish between different aspects of consumption. It may not be that there has been such a radical shift from the dominance of production to that of consumption in shaping our lives and experiences, but that contemporary life is characterised by a new form of consumption. As Bauman argues:

> The distinctive mark of the consumer society and its consumerist culture is not, however, consumption as such; not even the elevated and fast rising volume of consumption. What sets the members of consumer society apart from their ancestors is the emancipation of consumption from its past instrumentality that used to draw its limits – the demise of 'norms' and the new plasticity of 'needs', setting consumption free from functional bonds and absolving it from the need to justify itself by reference to anything but its own pleasurability.
>
> (Bauman, 2001: 12–13)

Bauman suggests that what has changed is the nature of consumption, and what makes current patterns of consumption significant is the move towards an emphasis on the pleasure as well as the functional dimensions of consumption. As anthropologists like Daniel Miller have pointed out, the consumption of goods has never been a purely functional activity and there is no sudden new departure into a realm of meaning which has hitherto been absent from human experience. Miller's argument is that objects and artefacts are not only imbued with meanings by those who use them but indicate their own material culture, that is, a set of meanings which lies in the object, rather than merely being attributed to it by its users. Miller is critical of some of the postmodernist and sociological views of recent years.

> Sociologists, in particular, almost inevitably write about consumption as though contemporary society were a decline from some earlier state in which our main relationship to objects was constructed through some form of utility or need . . . it is extremely hard to find evidence for merely functional or utilitarian relations to material culture in any non-industrial society.
>
> (Miller, 1997: 26)

Summary

- Previous approaches within the social sciences that stressed the separate stages of production and consumption have been challenged by more recent views which see the two as interrelated.
- The circuit of culture usefully maps out the ways different moments in cultural production and consumption interconnect.
- There has been a trend towards an emphasis on consumption rather than production as the key determinant of experience and of social relations.
- Postmodernism gives high priority to symbols and to representational systems, seeing consumption as the main practice and area of experience shaping identities and social relations in the contemporary world.
- This view is challenged, for example by more material approaches, some of which have developed out of the ideas of Bourdieu by focusing on the impact of taste and the links between class and taste as expressed through patterns of consumption,
- The material culture approach to consumption (explored in more detail in Chapter 5) of the anthropologist Daniel Miller also challenges the notion that the creation of meaning through consumption is a new phenomenon.

Where is power?

In the above discussion there has been a tension between approaches to consumption which emphasise its importance as an expression of consumer choice and autonomy and the constraints which consumers experience. For example, the Marxist view of class focuses on material inequalities and the greater power enjoyed by the capitalist class over the exploited working class because of the bourgeoisie's ownership of the means of production. In this case it is the capitalist class, the bourgeoisie, and the pursuit of profit that is required by the system, which determines what is produced, rather than any control that consumers themselves might exercise. In a theory which is based on the primacy of the production process, ownership accords considerably more power to the group of owners than to those who sell their labour for a wage. Marx did argue that the power of the proletariat lay in its collective class position and its potential and realisable power to overthrow the capitalist system, but this power was difficult to exercise within that economic system. An understanding of power and its operations lies at the heart of any study of inequality and has some relevance for exploring the debates about the consumer society. Does power lie in the hands of the producers or in those of the consumers? What do we mean by power? Does power operate from the top down or are all human relations affected by some operations of power, even in everyday exchanges? Do we associate it with people in power? Do we only think of power as involving a hierarchy?

ACTIVITY

Stop for a moment and think of two examples, either from your personal experience of from something that you have read about or seen or heard, where you think power is being exercised. This could be when you saw someone being compelled or you were perhaps even persuaded to act in a way which was not your preference. Are there any examples in your own role as a consumer or in the experiences of other people? Perhaps you can think of an example of buying something which you did not really want to buy. Is power too strong a word in this case?

COMMENT

There may be some very obvious cases of pressure being exerted on the international scale, involving the military or within a state, or involving the police. You may have thought of examples of violence and the overt, explicit exercise of power. If you focused on the context of consumption, the exercise of power is likely to have been much less obvious. Perhaps a smooth-talking assistant persuaded you to buy something which was not really what you wanted. Maybe advertising was a force you could not resist, although most of us are unlikely to admit to that one. Advertising and fashion are extremely powerful in shaping our perception of what we want to buy. Conversely, advertising may indicate how undesirable some items are. They may be associated with unacceptable, old-fashioned styles, which we are persuaded to avoid at all costs. Maybe you thought of some of the more sinister ways in which power is exercised over us as consumers. For example, CCTV (closed circuit television) acts as a surveillance device monitoring our progress through the shopping malls and precincts and inside shops. This is both a benefit and a constraint. CCTV is used to protect members of the public and store and property owners from criminal activity, but it also creates an environment in which everyone is constantly being watched. Surveillance is a form of control, although it is difficult to identify the source of power. Who exactly is it who is exercising power here? You may feel that somebody is watching your every move but it is difficult to attribute agency to the camera. Another form of control in the context of consumption is the banks and credit-rating agencies. You may recall the process of verification which many stores use in order to assess whether or not your cheque or credit card will be honoured. If you attempt to purchase items on credit the sales assistant will probably seek proof of your credit-worthiness from an agency. There are more material constraints, of course. You may have insufficient resources to make any purchases. You may not be able to buy into the consumer society because you have lost your job or are unable to work. Here the operation of power shifts beyond the local, perhaps to global economic forces. Your experience may be local and personal but the power that you lack has been exercised way outside your control, for example in the decision of an international company to close its plant in your home town so that you lose your job.

Some of the suggestions I have made may seem surprising and you may have thought that persuasion is different from power. Power may be more associated with coercion or force. However, if we are persuaded to do something that it was not our intention to do, even if we were not entirely conscious of this happening, it is likely that there has been some exercise of power, albeit indirectly. Many of the examples in the context of consumption illustrate this indirect operation of power, even at the level of the unconscious, for example in the case of advertisements.

How can we conceptualise power? What is involved? There has to be some notion of a relationship, whereby one side is not able to do what they want and another side is able to exercise some control, whether these are conscious processes for both parties or not. Power may involve authority. Those with expertise may have authority which we lack because of lack of the relevant expert knowledge.

Power can be *direct*. Power can be exercised over others. Some people may have power on the basis of expertise, or superior resources or brute force. Others may be subjected to power because they lack these resources.

Power can be *indirect*. We may not notice what is going on. This is quite likely in the context of consumption. We may not purchase goods or services owing to the unconscious meanings they carry (albeit arising from representations including advertisements) rather than from a conscious process, for example where we know that someone else is telling us what to do.

Common-sense notions of power, maybe as revealed in the above activity, are that it operates from the top down and that it may even involve coercion. The sociologist Max Weber argued that power is the probability that a person will be able to realise his (it was less likely to be hers in Weber's analysis) objectives even against opposition from others (in Gerth and Mills, 1948). This is not to say that Weber's analysis did not address gender, rather that he recognised women's lack of power in patriarchal societies. Weber is accredited with developing an analysis of patriarchy as one source of traditional authority. This concept has been very useful to subsequent feminist critiques, as a means of focusing upon some of the ways in which men exercise power over women.

Weber's initial definition of power is very broad, but he went on to be more specific. The main focus of Weber's theory of power was the power of the state over its people, rather than the exercise of power in everyday exchanges between people. He included domination, where people obey commands, and developed the idea of different strategies upon which the legitimacy of power depended, which he called 'ideal types' of legitimacy. He argued that power was the fundamental concept of social divisions, of which class, status and party were different dimensions. Class, as explained above, is the outcome of your position in the marketplace and your economic position, for example based on your occupation, thus covering economic power. Status involves the esteem in which you are held by others, thus covering social power, and party includes political affiliations, which mean political power. Power is thus the probability of people, as individuals or in groups, carrying out their will, even when opposed by others. In Weber's account, power largely operates in a top-down way. It is organised through a series of rules and regulations imposed by those in authority. It may not involve coercion, and is most often based on a chain of command, with authority being invested in those in the hierarchy who persuade others to comply with the rules through reasoned appeals to common sense and rationality. Weber's argument was developed to counter some of the oversimplifications of the nineteenth-century Marxist view, which could be read as overemphasising economic power. He wanted to develop a more complex understanding of some of the ways in which power could be seen as operating in industrialised, capitalist societies, and to focus upon its operation in modern bureaucracies. Weber's approach permits some understanding of intention as well as conflict. His definition allows for someone, some agent or group of agents, to be carrying out their will. However, within institutions, whether public or private, Weber saw power as dependent upon an individual's position within the organisation. It does seem to imply that those who are subordinate could resist the power which is exercised over them, but the understanding of power involved here seems largely to be in the category of the more direct exercise of power, even if it can be challenged.

Other explanations of the operation of power provide more focus on the ways in which power might be more diffuse. It might be operating even in situations where there appear to be no conflict, or even a chain of command or specific source of authority. In the examples of persuasion that might be part of the experience of consumption, it is very difficult to state the source of power or even of authority. Are we in any way coerced, or even explicitly persuaded to buy the goods, for example fashion items, which we say that we want (whether or not we need them)? Michel Foucault suggests that power is everywhere. As Foucault argues, power is not something that is acquired, seized or shared, something that one holds on to or allows to slip away; power is exercised from innumerable points in the interplay of non-egalitarian and mobile relationship.

> Relations of power are not in a position of exteriority with respect to other relationships (economic processes, knowledge relationships, sexual relations) but are immanent in the latter . . .
>
> Power comes from below . . . in the machinery of production, in families, limited groups and institutions, are the basis for wide-ranging effects . . .
>
> Power relations are both intentional and nonsubjective . . . But this does not mean it results from choice or decision of an individual subject . . .
>
> Where there is power there is resistance . . . one is always 'inside' power, there is no 'escaping' it, there is no absolute outside where it is concerned.
>
> (Foucault, 1980: 94–95)

Foucault's writing is quite difficult to follow and his argument is quite radical. He sees power as operating in all situations. We are all involved. He also claims that there is no 'exteriority' to it. This means that there is no source of power outside the way it is exercised. For example, the Marxist argument claims that the source of power lies in economic conditions. Access to ownership of the means of production gives power to one class. It is possible to locate the source of power in these economic relations.

For Foucault, power operates at multiple points and it works through **discourse**. His use of the term is different from that in the common currency of everyday exchanges. He defines a discourse as involving all the practices, ideas and ways of thinking about something through which meanings are produced (1980). A discourse presents a way of constructing meanings which organises and influences what we do and how we see ourselves. A discourse is a set of knowledges and practices that create their own truth. A discourse is 'true' if it is taken to be true, not by virtue of being proved to be true or false in relation to something outside itself. Foucault cites the particular example of sexuality and sexual identities in his *History of Sexuality* (1978). What is the 'truth' about sexuality? In the case of sexual identities, meanings about sexuality do not derive from biology or from the mind, or from the bodies we inhabit, but from the ways in which we describe, talk about and practise those feelings and activities which are categorised as sexual. For example, heterosexuality or homosexuality are not the result of having neither a particular sort of body, nor a particular sort of mind. They result from the way in which the society, through the knowledge, such as that produced by medical sources, the state through legislation, welfare and education systems, organise and classify what people do and what they feel and think. It is the process of categorisation which creates the discourse. For example, areas of expertise and authority, rather than depending on traditional hierarchies as in Weber's account, in Foucault's, present their own sets of meanings and truths.

Foucault extended his historical analysis of power to explore some of the ways in which discourses operate through subjects, that is, how people are positioned by discourses *and* how they position themselves. A discourse not only makes it possible to think some things, it closes down other possibilities, so that we do not even consider some actions and thoughts.

Foucault moved on from an emphasis on discourse as producing particular kinds of subjects to argue that subjects also produce themselves, through particular practices. Foucault's examples often relate to the history of sexuality and the ways in which different practices and identities have been possible, 'put into discourse', at different times. For example, he looked at the historical construction of sexual identities from fifth-century Athens to show men in ancient Greece engaged in different relationships with women and with other men, and the customs that permitted some practices and outlawed others. He claimed that what he called 'technologies of the self' enabled individuals to do things 'by their own means or with the help of others . . . so as to transform themselves in order to attain a certain state of happiness, purity, wisdom, perfection or immortality' (Foucault, 1988: 18).

What is important about this argument is the way in which it puts people into discourse and allows the idea that practices and representations do not just operate outside us, shaping what we do, but we are also involved in the processes. To apply this notion of 'technologies of the self' to more recent practices of consumption we could look at the ways in which meanings are produced through certain discourses, for example within popular culture, and at the practices through which people produce themselves. These practices include shopping and spectatorship, the contemporary practice of spending quite extended periods of time 'at the shops', looking at the clothes and styles adopted by celebrities, engaging in discussion with friends and family and reading popular magazines. In the case of other areas of consumption the consumer seeks out different areas of expertise, perhaps more authoritative sources, from the Internet or even specialist literature, for example, in the case of food and health products. Current representations of what it is possible to wear and what is appropriate in different situations and what is valued create what it is possible to think and possible to do. We can only think of particular items as desirable, for example designer labels, because these meanings are created by contemporary discourses of fashion. They do not enter our heads. Domination works through self-control. We regulate ourselves in many situations, rather than being coerced.

The notion of discourse may seem very well suited to our fashion and shopping example. In an ever-changing field like fashion it is more obvious that knowledge about what is acceptable and desirable is *produced*, rather than deriving from some external source. Fashion clothing is itself a discursive field. Consumers make purchases within this area of consumption according to the knowledge they have derived from magazines and popular culture and the influences of their peers. However, what constitutes a fashionable item may well be dictated by the producer. The Marxist emphasis on production would indeed have centred on the power exercised over consumers by the dominance of the producer and the capitalist class in shaping the practices of consumers. Foucault's more diffuse conception of power sees it operating at several different sites and not coming from one source. However, it may be more difficult to identify how meanings are produced through discourses when they are somewhat enmeshed and diffuse.

Summary

- An understanding of power and how it operates is crucial to the investigations of social scientists.
- Critiques of power take different positions about the sources of power and about how it operates.
- Weber's approach to the operation of power, based on hierarchies of authority in institutions, has been very influential.
- Marxist critiques stress the economic basis of power.
- The Marxist approach has been challenged by approaches which place greater emphasis on how power operates than on its *sources*.

- Foucault's historical critique has stressed the diffuse nature of power and the mechanisms through which it operates.
- A major division lies between a view of power as top down as in Weber's account, and as diffuse and everywhere as in Foucault's.
- Another tension is between those approaches which see power as having an *external* source, outside its manifestations, as in the economic structure of society in the Marxist account, or as being *produced* by the practices, words and ideas through which it is manifest, as in Foucault's view based on discourse.

Conclusion

This chapter has introduced some of the contemporary debates about consumption, especially the current focus on consumption itself and the idea of a 'consumer society', in order to explore different understandings of this phenomenon. The idea of consumption and the relationship between production and consumption has been used to introduce some of the wider debates within the social sciences about social divisions and inequalities and the operation of power. The contemporary notion that consumption has replaced production as the main influence upon and indicator of social divisions requires further consideration of material differences and other sources of inequality.

The explosion of consumption in the West especially, and the discussion of its implications, have led to the development of different theories, many of which have moved away from the notion that production is the key moment in the process. I have included some discussion of Marxist critiques for two reasons. The first is to provide some of the background to the move from a theory which gives priority to production to theories which provide higher status to consumption. We need to have some idea of what the theories of consumption are challenging and where they come from. Second, the Marxist emphasis on the economic base of society and the inequalities that arise from class-based social divisions provide an important counter-argument to the excesses of postmodernism. Marx's analysis necessarily brings in the issue of class divisions and the inequalities that arise from the production process. This critique also highlights some of the constraints upon consumption that are experienced by the less affluent. This approach challenges the postmodernist stress on style and the shift from the material to the representational, but also shows where some of the arguments are coming from.

Consumption cannot be adequately explained through a deterministic view of production and it has been suggested in this chapter that it is not possible to disentangle the processes of production and consumption. Nor is it possible to eliminate the impact of cultural processes from all the moments that are involved in the relationship between production and consumption. The 'turn to culture' in the social sciences has permitted a more extensive exploration of the ways in which meanings are produced, and this is well illustrated in an examination of the phenomenon of the 'consumer society'. As was apparent in the, albeit fictional, example with which this chapter opened, the whole process of exchange is dependent on the meanings as well as the material goods that are consumed. The cultural significance of goods is not a new phenomenon, as Daniel Miller argues, but it has assumed greater importance in the contemporary Western world owing to the intensity and scale of consumption.

Class has received less attention in recent years within the social sciences, but the material base of social divisions still plays an important part and operates along with other sources of inequality. Other analyses of class, which focus more upon market position and the status that can be attached to some social groupings, may have more resonance in the 'consumer society'. The concept of class also invokes the operation of power.

This chapter has briefly mapped out some of the developments and tensions in different approaches to an understanding of power. There has been a move away from a focus upon the sources of power to a concentration upon the mechanisms of power; upon how it works rather than where it comes from. Foucault's work has been important in some branches of the social sciences in offering detailed analyses of the operations of power in myriad ways at multiple different sites. However, although Foucault's insights into the workings of discourses have many applications within this field of consumption, for example in exploring how meanings are produced into which consuming subjects are drawn, his account lacks exploration of sources of power outside these discourses.

Buying and selling is a vital part of social, economic, cultural and political life, and the discussion in this chapter has indicated some of the ways in which the issues arising have been explored within the social sciences. Consumption is much more than going shopping!

Chapter 5

We live in a material world

Introduction

The first four chapters of this book have covered a range of different aspects of social life and social relations, highlighting some of the changes that have taken place, both in everyday life and in the ways in which social scientists provide explanations. Some transformations appear to have resulted from the collective actions of human beings, but these actions are always effected in a material context; in relation to other human beings, other organic forms of life and the objects that make up the material environment and the material conditions in which social life is experienced. For example, the discussion of identity in Chapter 2 showed that people's presentation of themselves in everyday life is closely linked to materialities, including the objects and artefacts to which we relate: the clothes we wear, the objects we possess and use and the material bodies we inhabit. People buy into particular identities and are recruited into identity positions in relation to objects of consumption, such as the clothes they wear. Clothes are not only signifiers of meaning about the sort of people we are, they also have value and material status in themselves as objects of consumption. Citizenship has been increasingly linked to consumption, for example through the idea that citizens have rights as consumers, although citizenship can also be marked by inequities which have material outcomes as well as sources. As Chapter 3 showed, the equalities and inequalities which create and deny citizenship rights are also material as well as involving symbolic representations and discursive regimes, such as the law.

Chapter 4 explored the importance of consumption as one of the big issues in the contemporary world. Consumption is an area which demonstrates well the importance of addressing materialities, especially the material economy which informs and shapes patterns of production and consumption and the materiality of the objects consumed. Marketing is often based on attempts to recruit consumers into the identities they may associate with particular products, which are themselves constitutive of these identities and are part of a changing landscape of consumption. The emphasis on the importance of objects has been translated into a particular theoretical approach which has been called material culture, and which will be explored further in this chapter. Chapter 5 looks at some different aspects of consumption and emphasises the extent to which we live in a material world. The material things we encounter, interact with, use and buy are cultural and social as well as material, and impact upon social relations as part of the changes taking place in the contemporary world.

As we have seen, contemporary global economies are based on consumption. Indeed, the recent 'credit crunch' which hit global markets, national governments, communities, households and individuals alike in the latter part of 2008 was in many ways focused upon consumption. Governments invested huge amounts in the world banking system in order to maintain levels of credit so that banks would go on lending and consumers would continue to buy things. If levels of consumption fell it was perceived that companies would go out of business and the crisis would deepen. This is one aspect of consumption, which demonstrates how far economies have become dependent on the spiralling levels of consumption, which, however, have other material consequences. The importance of recognising that we live in a material world dominated by markets that promote ever-increasing consumption of goods and services is illustrated by the waste that accompanies these patterns of consumption. Buying more and more new things and the built-in obsolescence of so many items means that the more we buy the more we have to throw away. If people are throwing more things away where are we going to put them and who is going to deal with all this rubbish?

Summary

- This chapter uses the example of waste as a contemporary big issue.
- The increase in waste and the problem of how to dispose of it is another side of the huge expansion of consumption in the modern world.
- Waste is used to demonstrate some of the links between the material and the social and how the two are inseparably connected.

What a load of rubbish

It may be tempting to take rubbish for granted and think that it is of no importance; what is thrown away is discarded because it is of no value. For example, household rubbish is what we throw out: we want it out of the way and out of sight. We do not want to look at it because it is one of those things that should be out of sight. It becomes offensive if it is not put where it should be; for example, if it is in the wrong place and on display instead of stowed away in a rubbish bin before being taken away in the refuse lorry.

In some ways rubbish may be thought of as the reverse of the consumption that was the subject of Chapter 4. It may be seen as the disvalued end-product of

Plate 5.1 A trip to the tip

consumption: packaging, worn-out or obsolescent fridges and computers, disposable household items, empty bottles and cans, plastic cups and uneaten food. However, like consumption and production, rubbish also involves social practices and it is a part of social life. Disposing of rubbish is just as much a social practice as consumption, but it is about matter that has its own characteristics and effects.

Even though consumption may be about display and making things visible, and waste seems to be about disposal and making things invisible, both involve social practices. Dealing with rubbish is local and global; each of us has to deal with it routinely as part of everyday life and the disposal of waste is a huge problem for governance and at local and global levels, especially in relation to the toxic waste and dangerous substances that make up the waste products of industrial production processes as well as household consumption.

The refuse lorry and its contents might be invisible to householders (although probably not inaudible if they are in their homes), but collecting household waste from the street and disposing of it has to be organised and funded. This involves the local authority and local refuse disposal workers; and this in turn involves issues of local politics, local taxation and funding priorities. It also involves a chain of disposal activities that might extend around the world and back again. Big business is involved, too, as local authority activities are tendered out to private contractors.

In this chapter waste is made visible by studying it as a material part of social life and as part of wider social practices. In the process it will become apparent that issues of rubbish and waste have plenty to tell us about the society we live in and the interrelationship between people and objects, the animate and the inanimate and the material things that impact upon social life.

From consumption to rubbish: the UK example

Waste disposal in the UK is part of a global problem, which is particularly prevalent in post-industrial, consumer-led countries in the twenty-first century. The problem of waste is a problem of affluence. People in the UK have more things than ever before; not all of them necessities, although what constitutes a necessity is changing. In the 1950s and 1960s a television was a luxury; it is now a necessity. Table 5.1 gives an indication of how household spending has shifted over the past 50 years from a higher proportion of household income being spent on food and fuel to a situation where leisure services and luxuries take up a much bigger part of expenditure.

What does this table tell us about changing patterns of consumption?

For both 1957 and 2009 Table 5.1 shows the proportion of total income spent on various categories of goods and services. The proportion of total income spent

Table 5.1 Household expenditure in 1957 and 2006

1957		2006	
Commodity or service[1]	*Percentage of total expenditure*	*Commodity or service*[1]	*Percentage of total expenditure*
Housing	9	Housing (net)[2]	19
Fuel, light and power	6	Fuel and power	3
Food	33	Food and non-alcoholic drinks	15
Alcoholic drinks	3	Alcoholic drinks	3
Tobacco	6	Tobacco	1
Clothing and footwear	10	Clothing and footwear	5
Durable household goods	8	Household goods	8
Other goods	7	Household services	6
Transport and vehicles	8	Personal goods and services	4
Services	9	Motoring	14
		Fares and other travel costs	2
		Leisure goods	4
		Leisure services	15
All	100%	All	100%

Notes
1   The categories in 1957 and 2006 are not exactly the same.
2   Excludes mortgage interest payments.

Source: Adapted from *Family Spending* (2007 edn, published January 2008, Table A, p. 3).

on 'food' was 33 per cent in 1957 whereas by 2006 the proportion spent on 'food and non-alcoholic drinks' was down to 15 per cent. Food is clearly a necessity so the proportion spent on food more than halved over the 50-year period. This raises questions too about what constituted food in this category. There has been a significant move from staple foods like bread and potatoes towards a greater range of fruit, meat, dairy products and vegetables and, what is most important for our purposes, more prepacked, prepared meals. Fruit and vegetables flown in from Kenya and ready meals all involve a great deal of protective packaging. The proportion spent on clothing and footwear also halved, from 10 per cent to 5 per cent. A category that increased is that of 'services'. Adding together household services, personal goods and services, and leisure services, in 2006 comes to 25 per cent. In 1957, only 9 per cent of income was spent on services.

Housing increased as a proportion of total expenditure, from 9 per cent to 19 per cent. This may have been because more people moved from living in rented accommodation to buying their own homes. House prices were high and increasing relative to incomes in 2006, and many households were financially stretched in repaying their mortgage. Tobacco expenditure fell from 6 per cent to 1 per cent and the proportion spent on transport doubled from 8 per cent to 16 per cent.

These changes are quite striking and demonstrate the extent of change and one of the key factors creating the problem of waste.

Waste disposal in the UK

It has become vital that all nations and transnational bodies like the European Union formulate and implement policies to deal with the enormity of the problem of what to do about the waste that mass consumption generates. This is not, of course, only a problem of household waste; industry and commerce also generate vast quantities of waste through the production process.

Unfortunately the UK does not have a very good reputation for recycling, so much so that the UK has been called 'the dustbin of Europe'. In 2006/7 the UK dumped the same amount of rubbish in landfill sites as the 18 EU countries with the lowest landfill rates, even though the UK's population is half the size of those countries combined (Waste Online, 2009).

There has been growing pressure in the UK to increase recycling. By 2007 the recycling rate in the UK was about 27 per cent recycling of municipal waste, compared with about 32 per cent in the USA and best-practice rates in Europe (Austria and the Netherlands) of more than 60 per cent (*Economist Technology Quarterly*, 2007: 22). Faced with the prospect of financial penalties for not recycling more, many local councils brought in new measures to encourage households to separate their rubbish so that more of it could be recycled. The environmental emphasis on waste became: reduce, reuse and recycle, with the addition of recover value from it.

Rubbish may be put into landfill sites or incinerated. However, landfill sites are reaching capacity and also cause pollution; and incineration directly causes pollution. Putting household rubbish out for collection seems to be a way of moving the material from one place to another, but complete disposal is hard to achieve. Disposal often means just moving the rubbish along or creating further pollution, the effects of which inevitably return. Recycling is therefore more environmentally sustainable, but reducing consumption and waste in the first place would be even better environmentally. The logical extension of reducing waste is the notion of 'zero waste'. This would transform both production and consumption as product design would have to be aimed not only at a product for consumption but a product that involves zero waste all along the processes of production and consumption.

A local story

The disposal of rubbish can be highly contentious at a local level, as has been seen to be the case in the UK with recent shifts in council policies for refuse collection and the changing practices for schedules and routines of collection. Households are now expected to sort out their rubbish and store it in different containers, which are then collected by different agencies on different days; bins may only be emptied fortnightly; only certain weights are acceptable and if your bin is too heavy it will not be emptied. Council employees may even look through dustbins to check contents, which would be an unpleasant job for those expected to undertake it as well as being seen by some householders as an invasion of privacy.

ACTIVITY

As you read this account of the problem of waste disposal in the UK in 2008 think about these questions:

- What are the main problems associated with getting rid of rubbish for households?
- What is it about the particular material of waste which makes it so contentious?
- What sorts of values are being expressed in this story? Does the discussion use normative language, that is, about what ought to be the case? How far is this an example of changing times?

THE PROBLEM OF RUBBISH RAGE

'Britain is at war over rubbish. Exasperated householders are attacking refuse collectors and stealing neighbours' bins' (Henley, 2008: 5). This may be somewhat extreme but this observation highlights the problems that have been created by the growth in waste material and the need for new policies and practices to deal with the problem. As the director of the UK Waste Resources Action Programme, the government chief advisory body on the issue, describes the situation:

We're moving away from an easy, familiar system where we just slung everything into a sack and once a week someone came and took it away for us – we neither knew nor cared where – to one where we actually have to do something. Some people will always find that difficult whatever the reason.

(in Henley, 2008: 6)

Jon Henley cites these examples of what he calls 'rubbish rage' when angry householders have protested at what they perceive to be unfair treatment (Henley, 2008):

In one county the local council is rationing households to one approved free bin bag a week; extra ones have to be paid for at 25p each.

Another county council has employed snoopers to sift through residents' rubbish, in a 'gross invasion of privacy' according to an opposition local councillor.

A woman in Bolton was fined £275 for putting her bin out a day before the collection day, a man in Cumbria was fined £225 because his bin was too full and a war veteran was charged £70 for putting his rubbish in the wrong colour bag.

An 80-year-old woman in Lancashire had to drag her bin half a mile down a steep hill for collection.

Residents in another city are complaining of rat infestation and the offensive smell of rotting material, because bins are only emptied every two weeks.

COMMENT

The main problems associated with getting rid of rubbish, for households and for local government, are due to the fact that there has been a huge increase in the amount of material which is thrown away. Quantity is one factor. The nature of the material is another. Much of this material is itself not organic – vegetables or foodstuffs that would decompose – and recycling requires technologies and investment. Landfill sites are unsustainable owing to the nature of the material that has been deposited in them. In order to sort out what can and what cannot be recycled or disposed of at landfill sites local councils have to ask householders to sort out their rubbish into different containers. The matter which does rot creates its own problems, such as smell, vermin infestations and concomitant health risks.

These stories also include the values systems of those involved; the practical considerations are influenced by an increased awareness of environmental problems and eco politics. There are also the values that are implicit in the ideas of the protesting householders, many of whom expect their rubbish to become invisible and to be dealt with by the local council as it always has been in the past. Rubbish is seen as the council's responsibility and not the householder's, although this is somewhat contradictory in that when the council staff check what is in the bins they are accused of invading the privacy of the householder. The particular examples in this case study are emotive, for example in their inclusion of a 'war veteran', the relevance of which is not very clear except insofar as he would be representative of a particular value system and the voice of 'Middle England'. Another, more material example is the 80-year-old woman who is obviously being unfairly treated in the expectation that a person of physical frailty should be expected to take her own bin such a distance. The example has emotional appeal, as do the references to the dangers of squalid infestations that collections every fortnight instead of every week may entail. Individuals in these examples see themselves as unjustly treated because they pay their council taxes and resent making further contributions, suggesting that, although most people realise the enormity of the problem of waste, some people have failed to register the scale of the problem. Councils are not seen as having a legitimate educative role by these protestors.

In this sense it is clear that the scale of the problem and the nature of the material are indicative of changing times, but so is the mismatch between value systems, with some householders not realising the nature of the problem and some agents of government failing to deal with the social aspects of the problem which is so closely linked to its material dimensions. This example highlights other sorts of values too; namely the value of the waste products themselves, or their lack of value.

Summary

- Rubbish is taken for granted and treated as if it were invisible, but it presents a big problem.
- The problem is one that exists at the level of households, localities and on a global scale.
- The material of waste has been transformed from objects which people need and desire to material that they reject and want others, notably the government, to deal with.
- Rubbish also has its own material qualities, showing that it is material, economic, cultural and social.

Waste as disvalued

Waste is something that apparently has no value; it is disvalued. It is what nobody wants, so it is worthless and has zero value. This seems straightforward, but 'value' is a social term as the example of waste disposal in the contemporary world shows.

Items do not have a particular value only by virtue of their physical properties. Items have value because people value them; or rather values are imputed to items by people who value them. People formulate their values within a social context. To say that items 'have value' is a convenient shorthand, but it is liable to suggest that values only inhere in items, rather than that items are treated as valuable in particular social contexts. 'Waste' therefore has a social dimension. In this sense it is socially constituted.

The social dimension of the language of 'waste' and 'rubbish' can become very complicated. For example, the notion of 'value' itself is used differently. Sometimes it refers to norms or to ideas about what is right or wrong. For example, to live according to your values is to live in a way that is consistent with what you think is right. Sometimes 'value' refers to the esteem that something has – or rather to the esteem with which it is endowed by people in particular circumstances. For example, a person who espouses environmentally friendly principles and recycles their rubbish might be said to be making a 'valuable' contribution to the local community and to society at large. Someone who dumps their discarded television in the hedgerow would be seen as acting according to a very different, socially unacceptable set of values. Sometimes value refers to price, so that items of high value are those with a high price. In this sense valuable means expensive.

Thus there are different senses of value. Sometimes value may be used subjectively as expressed by the claim that 'those may be your values, but they aren't mine'. This statement suggests that there is an assumption that people may disagree about the values they hold. This raises questions of how a society lives out the different values of its members. For example, is it possible or desirable to tolerate a wide range of conflicting values or should there be some core values to which a society is committed and which all members of that society accept? Can there be social as well as individual values? On other occasions the notion of value may seem to be objective, as in the value of an object which is translated into its market cost; that is, how much we might have paid for it. However, the distinction between subjective and objective starts to get muddied. For example, social values might take on an objective character if they are widely accepted. However, objective values may not be so concrete. For example, the market price of a particular kind of house might be £190,000, yet the price charged in different areas and at different times may vary. Different shops sell their products at different prices too. This suggests that the notion of the market price is an abstract conception of price that might not actually be charged in any particular transaction. On the other hand the market value of a good might be entirely dependent on the situation and has to be seen as specific to time and place. Once price is pinned down to what particular buyers and sellers are transacting at, there may be a range of prices on offer. For some items there may be a bargaining element as well. Sometimes too the different senses are inextricably intertwined so that what is valuable carries normative as well as financial ones. This even applies to rubbish. The cost of recycling may be too high to be cost-effective, but there are strong normative reasons for continuing to promote such an environmentally desirable practice.

At face value rubbish would appear to be worthless. It is not esteemed or cared about. It may even be despised or found offensive. It may thus elicit feelings of disgust. Thus the language used to refer to waste and rubbish might be emotive, that is, to do with feelings: bins full of rotting rubbish are 'disgusting'. The language used is often normative, that is, concerned with norms or what ought to be done: 'you ought to put your rubbish out regularly to be collected' or 'you ought to sort out your rubbish and recycle as much as possible'; or economic (in this case to do with prices: 'my old computer has no value now so there's no point in trying to sell it on eBay as no one would give me anything for it'). The language of rubbish and waste can also combine these different senses. A focus on values demonstrates the difficulty of trying to separate objective and subjective ideas and to suggest that what is the case can be made distinct from what people think ought to be the case. Economic value cannot be completely separated from the value that is given to a product or good, or even to rubbish by people, that is, their social value and the nature of the material itself.

Materialities take different forms, and the material is bound up with the social and with the values that are expressed in the example of waste disposal that is the focus of this chapter. Descriptive and normative accounts also combine in an analysis of the problem in terms of material inequalities in the wider arena. There may be unequal sets of practices, for example, between different regions and cities, but the problem of waste is global and also demonstrates a whole range of inequalities.

Summary

- Making waste visible means addressing the question of value: the lack of any value people place upon it and the value it has in terms of cost and the values of the people who have to deal with it.
- A discussion of waste can be descriptive and normative; sometimes the two are combined.

Inequalities and material effects

One of the great challenges of the twenty-first century is to come to grips with the environmental implications of mass consumerism. The current scale of production and consumption is environmentally unsustainable. Rising affluence in many parts of the world means that the degree of sustainability is declining. Rising waste is a part of this problem and highlights different dimensions of the problem of what to do about waste.

However, there is not an entirely uniform picture of increasing affluence, even within relatively wealthy states like the UK.

Table 5.2 Real incomes for three income[1] groups, 1979 to 2005/2006, UK/Great Britain[2]

	Poorest 10%	*Median*	*Richest 10%*
1979	130.4	230.9	407.9
1988–1989	135.3	280.5	561.1
1998–1999	153.7	312.8	650.7
2005–2006	181.0	361.8	733.9
% increase			
1979–2005/6	39%	57%	80%

Notes
1   £ per week adjusted to 2005–2006 prices.
2   Data for 1998/1999 for Great Britain only.

Source: Adapted from *Social Trends* (2008, Figure 5.1, p. 71).

ACTIVITY

Look at Table 5.2 and think about the following questions:

- Which income group gained the highest increase in earnings over the period 1979 to 2005/2006?
- What does this tell you about income inequality over this period?

The government statistics collected annually in the publication *Social Trends*, which has been cited several times in this book, provide information about earnings which shows how incomes have risen in the UK over recent years. The incomes of some groups have risen much more sharply than others, as was shown in Table 5.1. Table 5.2 provides information about the income levels of three categories of people, the poorest 10 per cent, the median (the income in the middle of the range at 50 per cent) and the richest 10 per cent. These data use 'real incomes', that is, earnings adjusted for inflation, in this case using 2005 to 2006 prices.

COMMENT

There have been increases across all income groups over the period, suggesting an increase in overall affluence, but it is striking that the richest 10 per cent have gone up by 80 per cent on average. The category that has benefited the least from so-called rising levels of affluence is the poorest 10 per cent. The UK is more affluent but some people are much more affluent than others. These data suggest that income inequality increased during this period and that, although there are significant transformations taking place, there are also instances of continuity, especially in terms of inequalities. Inequalities are much wider, however, in the global arena, for example between different parts of the world.

Across the world, environmental pollution that arises from mass consumption and the increased levels of production that it entails tends to be caused by rich countries, but the countries that suffer the most are poor countries. These poor countries are less able to defend themselves against the effects of global warming in the form, for example, of rising sea levels, irregular weather patterns and increased rate of natural disasters, all of which can threaten homes, harvests and livelihoods.

This has huge implications for issues of equity and for what is fair or just, across generations and across countries. The analysis of the material impact of waste creation and disposal suggests that current generations are not bearing the full social costs arising from their lifestyle. The cost is being passed on to future generations who will inherit a world that is more polluted and less able to provide them with resources. The environmental implications of mass consumerism together with the problems of disposing of all the rubbish have thus brought a new urgency to issues of rubbish and waste in the twenty-first century.

Those who challenge the trend of the promotion of mass consumption and commodification of goods, like Freegans (2009), espouse a life of non-consumerism, foraging for what they need in the generous wastefulness of modern consumerism. Environmentalists urge people to reduce, reuse and recycle. They also urge large-scale governmental and intergovernmental action. The reason for this is that the scale of material that is generated by production and consumption means that the environmental effects of affluent lifestyles have very unequal impacts on the material environment and on social relations. Individual initiatives that are dependent upon the market system of neoliberal governance that aims to govern 'from a distance' may deliver results that are both too little and too late. As many countries become more affluent, the environmental problems will only get worse, presenting a dilemma that is political, ethical and material.

Summary

- Waste illustrates social inequalities that are material.
- The increase in consumption due to increased affluence has led to the massive growth of waste and the need for waste disposal but this increase in affluence is very uneven; even within the UK the poor have not benefited as much as the rich.
- Waste disposal also illustrates global inequalities across time and space.

Material culture

In this chapter I have stressed that rubbish, although disvalued and regarded as worthless, is both particular in its materiality, that is, it has specific qualities and characteristics, and it has material consequences because as matter it is not separate from social life; it is a growing part of social life.

Social scientists have developed theories of material culture as part of a range of different approaches which seek to explore and explain some of the ways in which material things are central to an understanding of social life. These approaches do not belong to any particular discipline but have been used across many disciplines and may be seen as interdisciplinary or transdisciplinary. So what is distinctive about material culture and how might it help us to explain the big issue with which this chapter has been concerned?

First, objects and things matter as part of social and cultural life. Thus in explaining social life we have to take account of objects As Daniel Miller has argued:

> Academic study of the specific nature of the material artefact produced in society has been remarkably neglected . . . This lack of concern with the artefact appears to have emerged simultaneously with the quantitative rise in the production and mass distribution of material goods.
>
> (Miller, 1997: 3)

The more things our societies make, the less concerned we seem to be with the specific nature of these things in themselves as well as the significance of what they symbolise. Things matter because they are part of social life; we use them and we have to deal with them when we no longer need them, because they and we are part of the environment upon which things as well as people have impact.

Objects are also seen to be part of social life, to the extent that they have social lives. This may look a bit odd but it means that objects can change in how they are used and understood as societies change. In this way objects have a trajectory whereby their meaning, for example for consumers, changes over time. Items that are purchased and then become obsolete, unusable or just out of fashion change from being a commodity that is purchased and is the object of desire to something that is then used to becoming rubbish, waste that has no value for the consumer who no longer wants or needs the object. This applies to rubbish itself which also undergoes change, in that material things are reclassified, for example, as recyclable. Some objects that are discarded are reappropriated by others (like Freegans) who reuse material that has been thrown away, or recategorised, for example by local councils who create different categories into which householders must sort their rubbish. At the point of purchase objects are commodities which have a cash value, but once purchased they have the value they are given by the consumer as a member of a particular society or culture when they are 'subjectified' (Miller, 1997).

Igor Kopytkoff suggests that objects move in and out of commodity status and uses the example of art to explain the process. For example, a work of art is a commodity when it enters the market for sale. The work is displayed in an auctioneer's room for sale, but once it has been purchased, it is not just a commodity to be exchanged in the marketplace, it becomes once more a piece of art and may again be displayed by its new owner and assessed in terms of its aesthetic qualities. For example, an iconic piece of modern art like Tracey Emin's *My Bed*, which, perhaps ironically, includes a range of objects, some of which might otherwise be classified as rubbish (including 'empty booze bottles' and 'fag ends' according to the Saatchi website (Saatchi, 2009)) beyond the point of sale becomes a work of art and debate focuses on its artistic qualities rather than on its commodity value.

The cultural impact of things has been acknowledged in anthropology. This has relevance for the concerns of this chapter also in terms of how objects change according to their location, in time and space, for example arguments by the anthropologist Mary Douglas that dirt is matter 'out of place': it is in the wrong place (1966). For example, soil is in the right place in a field or in a garden but in the wrong place on the kitchen floor. Similarly, rubbish was once in the right place in our homes, a black and white television in the 1950s, but with the advent of colour television the black and white set was in the wrong place. As the start of this chapter suggested, some of the material which we throw away is seen as rubbish because it is in the wrong place and the values that are sometimes imputed to rubbish, such as that it is messy or even disgusting, is because it is in the wrong place, on the street, rotting in the bin, rather than at the tip. Thus a material culture approach addresses the materiality of objects and incorporates an understanding of particular things with their symbolic meaning and offers one approach to understanding change.

Summary

- A material culture approach claims that material things are social.
- Objects have meanings and are part of social life; meanings are not only created through symbols.
- Objects change, for example from being commodities to being things in themselves.
- Material culture offers an interdisciplinary approach to change that places objects at the centre of social life.

Conclusion

This chapter has used the example of rubbish to illustrate a contemporary problem that has enormous impact upon social life now and will have in the future that is indicative of the speed of change in the world today. Waste disposal is a relatively new but extremely pressing problem that cannot remain invisible as many would like their rubbish to be. Although people might hope that their rubbish would disappear, the more consumers buy and use, the more waste there is and the more difficult it is to find ways of dealing with it.

The problem is not one that is evenly and equally represented or experienced. There are material inequalities that extend across the globe and across time that are created by the problems of waste disposal.

The problem has been expressed in terms of values and politics, especially in terms of possible solutions, but it has been used in this chapter to highlight the importance of materialities and the necessity of addressing the interconnections between the material, the social and the cultural. Rubbish may be perceived as having no value, but it is material in its effects and in its impact upon social relations and global politics. Value in all its different interpretations is nevertheless an important part of the process of understanding materiality. Values include the ideas people have about norms and what ought to be the case and the monetary value, the cost of things. An emphasis upon materialities offers a useful way of countering an excessive stress on symbols and representations and upon cultural meanings, and locates the big issues within their material context and of providing a way of understanding what things mean and what they represent and their material place in the world.

A material culture approach has been used to demonstrate that objects and things, even when they are unwanted and apparently have no value, have their own life stories and social life. Objects change in their uses and the meanings that they carry, and rubbish is an excellent example of some of the transformations that objects undergo. The problem of waste is also a particularly good example of a big issue in the consumer societies that are spreading across the globe. The problem of waste disposal will not be solved or reduced by straitened financial times and economic crises which reduce spending power and consumption, because rubbish is a material presence in the contemporary world.

Chapter 6

Mobilities

Place and race

Introduction

Where do you come from? As was suggested in Chapter 2, this is a question frequently asked when we meet someone for the first time in order to gain some idea of who they are, of their identity. Even if lifestyle and patterns of consumption have become central to people's sense of who they are, especially how they present themselves to others, place invokes a strong sense of connection and attachment. Place, especially one's place of origin, is an important part of knowing who we are. Individuals want to know where they were born, where they come from, as well as who their parents are. It may well be that we are trying to gain some understanding of who someone else is by locating them in relation to a particular place. Knowing where someone lives gives us all sorts of clues as to their identity. It is often through place that we position people, not only as individuals, but this is also how governments and official agencies situate us, according to our address or place of birth. Patterns of consumption are notably classified by postcode. Place, especially the place where we were born or the place where we live, may offer some security in a world which is characterised by mobility and movement, even movement across nations and continents. However, in a climate of insecurity, attachments to place are problematic, especially for some migrant peoples. Responses to the question 'where do you come from?' may not be so simple. This is the answer given by the athlete Zaf Shah: 'I'm a Bradfordian, a Yorkshireman and I'm British.'

Shah seems quite certain about his identity as British, but he is also from a particular region; he is from Yorkshire. Shah applied for dual nationality and preferred to represent Pakistan in international competitive sport, however. Although his father fought in the British army, he came from Kashmir. 'I am hungry to show the world that Asians can compete at the highest level and do well' (in Arnot, 2002: 2). This is a complicated story. It is not so easy to read off who we are from where we come from, nor is it easy to decide which place is the most important. Different places have different meanings. However, Shah's story is a particular story which links specific places: Kashmir in Pakistan where his father came from, and Yorkshire, the particular region in which Bradford, the town in the

UK where he lives, is situated. Shah offers a specific brand of Britishness that has different strands. Indeed, he is suggesting that he wants to retain his identity in relation to his parents' country of origin. Shah was a promising cricketer in his teens but, in spite of being praised at the highest levels, he was not selected to play for his home county cricket club, Yorkshire. His experience of rejection is described by Chris Arnot as 'tasting the bitterness that many British-born Asian sportsmen and women have felt before (ibid.: 2). Shah changed his sport and did achieve considerable success. What is not stated explicitly in this story is the power relations of empire and of a colonial past that are part of the story of who Shah is. There is the implication in Arnot's account that not being selected to play cricket for his country may have been the result of some kind of racialised prejudice. It may be for a political reason, that is, he wants to show that athletes from Kashmir can be successful at the highest levels, that Shah chooses dual nationality and to compete as an athlete for Pakistan and not for England, even though he sees himself as British. Place is deeply implicated in people's histories and of the routes which they, their families and the people with whom they identify have travelled. Why is place important? In this chapter I want to suggest that it is important for two main reasons. First, place matters because it locates people. Place provides us with an identity that is associated with not only the place where we currently live, but with the different places with which we have been associated. This is especially important at a time in history when there is large-scale movement of people across the globe, whether for economic or political and social reasons. Place can offer some sense of security, either in relation to the place which has been left, perhaps the 'real', 'true' home, or the place where people currently live and which perhaps provides safety from a place where there was considerable danger, as in the case of asylum seekers. Place can provide a sense of attachment. Places are themselves the site of change, in that the people who live in a place can create changes. Second, place, especially the place where we live, provides insight into the ways in which a society is ordered and organised. The places where we live provide information about who we are, how we live.

Summary

- Place is important in shaping experience and social relations.
- We know ourselves through the places where we live and the place we have come from.
- Others place us in relation to our home and where we come from.
- Places change as different people form connections to those places.

Mobilities and diaspora

Increasingly more and more people have different places associated with their own biographies. The movement of people across the globe is not, of course, a new phenomenon, but through the twentieth and into the twenty-first centuries there has been extensive migration, resulting from war, economic and environmental disasters, the movement of markets and the overall impact of globalisation. People move across countries and continents, as well as within their own country of birth, for a whole range of reasons including the need to find employment. In such circumstances it becomes more difficult to fix one place as being of primary importance. In such times it may be more useful to look at the different places that are associated with people and the routes they have travelled, rather than fixing one place as the source of connection.

Diaspora

One way of looking at migration is thinking about the places people have come from as well as where they now live. The artistic director of Britain's oldest Asian theatre company Jatinder Verma is asked about his 2002 epic production of the play *Journey to the West*, the story of the migration of Asian people from East Africa in 1968 and their settlement in the UK, 'Is your play about roots?' Verma replies:

> It depends how you're spelling the word ... I prefer to think of it as r-o-u-t-e-s. Roots lead backwards. Routes are more progressive, leading you to make connections with others. I'm not interested in the particular village in India where my grandfather came from. My identity is located on the road. East Africans are a real conundrum for modern anthropologists because, in some ways, we represent the future, beyond ethnicity. In a truer sense, we are world citizens. I know people who are moving on again, to America. It's as if, having taken the first step out of India, our people are perpetually on the move.
>
> (in Arnot, 2002)

Verma cites the specific example of East African Asian people and, in this short quotation, conjures up ideas of movement and routes. 'My identity is located on the road', he says. His own autobiography embodies movement. He arrived in the UK from Kenya aged 14, his own family of origin having travelled from India to East Africa years before. Verma's *Journey to the West* includes three plays, which mirror the routes he and his family have travelled. The first is set in 1901 following the first exodus from Gujarat, which began in the late nineteenth century. The second is set in 1968 and the third in the present in the twenty-first century. Verma's story is one of success and the routes that he has traversed, which make up his identity.

What does Verma mean by routes? How does this distinction between roots and routes work? The routes he talks about involve the journeys he has taken, the paths which he and other diasporic people have followed and the narratives in which they have been involved. Routes link journeys and stories, places and people. Verma's preference for routes rather than roots also attributes more mobility and more potential for change and adaptation to routes. Routes are dynamic. As he says, people who have already travelled from India to East Africa to the UK might travel elsewhere and create new opportunities and new identities. In this account routes seem to afford more potential for agency and for people taking some control over their own lives. It is this potential for change and the desire to look forward as well as back that Verma clearly finds attractive and which makes 'routes a better description than "roots"'. However, the routes he has travelled also relate to his past and provide the inspiration for the plays he has written.

These come from past experience, from the experience of diaspora, but particularly from the journeys he has travelled, the routes he has already taken. This is what informs the question to which his response is that he prefers routes to roots. Diaspora involves the dispersal of people across the globe. The term was first used to describe the movement and resettling of Jewish people around the world, but it is now used very widely to describe the identities of a range of people in the contemporary globalised world.

Diaspora covers a whole range of experiences including what has been called a myth of origin and the idea of a homeland to which the diasporic long to return and the idea that it would be possible to go back. This is not to suggest that a myth is a distortion of truth or a falsehood, but rather that, as in the sense that Roland Barthes has understood myth, as the means through which we make sense of our lives, what we think appears to be universal, even 'natural' (Barthes, 1972). Myths are like the stories we tell each other in order to make sense of who we are. Similarly, groups, communities and nations tell themselves collective stories about their identities. A myth is thus a way of making sense of the world through 'a complex system of beliefs which a society constructs in order to sustain and authenticate its own sense of being: i.e. the very fabric of its system of meaning' (Hawkes, 1988: 131). In this sense a myth becomes absorbed into culture, is taken for granted and merges with nature. It is clear that Verma has more interest and investment in the dynamics of the present and the future, and the possibilities for change than in tracing his past and his origins in an Indian village, but for other diasporic peoples, not least the Jewish diaspora, the idea of home, located in a particular place, is very powerful.

As Madan Sarup suggests,

> It is important to know where we come from. All people construct a home, all people have a place to which they feel an attachment, a belongingness. This is in contrast to some post modernist writers who stress the subject as a nomad, a wanderer, roaming from place to place. We have to understand the power and pull of home.

> (Sarup, 1996: 181)

While movement, change and the possibilities of the new might be attractive, there is also the attachment to home and of some authentic source of certainty that has appeal both for individuals and for ethnic groups and nations.

Although the notion of diaspora is very useful in describing mobilities and movement of people around the world, it cannot encompass all such peoples. There are different diasporas: forcibly displaced peoples, those expelled from their home through slavery and colonisation, and there are entrepreneurial migrants, like those Chinese people who have travelled across the world to set up businesses. The term diaspora has been stretched to include a very wide range of migrant and mobile peoples, and embraces the idea of diasporic networks and consciousness. Diasporic people may not want to return home but they retain an awareness of cultural influences and consumption practices; they may also send money home even if they have no plans to return to live there.

Not all collectivities of people, whether in ethnic groups or nations, can be located in a single place of origin. Verma acknowledges the connections to India for East African Asian people like himself, but his birthplace was in Nairobi, which was where he lived until he was 14. India may be one sort of 'home' even though it is a place where he has only ever been a visitor. Verma's idea of 'home' is like Benedict Anderson's notion that belonging to a nation, having a national identity, means being part of an 'imagined community' (1983). Verma's views indicate the importance of place, but more particularly the places and the routes we have travelled, rather than stressing the priority of roots and a single place.

Summary

- Place can provide strong feelings of attachment, for example in the myths of origin through which we try to establish a sense of home.
- Most people do not belong in only one place, so the idea of routes as the places with which we have had connections is more useful.
- Diaspora has been used by social scientists to explain mobility and connections with new places; they are dynamic and allow for change.
- The concept of diaspora may have been expanded too far and cannot adequately explain all movements of people and all migration.

Place

Identity is connected to a particular place ... by a feeling that you belong to that place. It's a place in which you feel comfortable, or at home, because part of how you define yourself is symbolized by certain qualities of that place.

(Rose 1990: 89)

Place is important in shaping our sense of who we are. Place also plays a significant part in shaping our life chances. Our life is influenced by an interaction between social and economic factors, social divisions and to a greater or lesser extent the levels of choice we may be able to exercise in the matter.

ACTIVITY

Stop for a moment and think about where you live. What factors have influenced this aspect of your life? Did you have any. choice? Has this place changed in recent years? Would you prefer to live somewhere else if you did have more choice?

COMMENT

There are a whole range of factors which you might cite. Where you live might be determined by your family circumstances, by your job, by your culture or ethnicity and your resources. You may feel you belong in a particular place, with family, friends and those who share your ethnicity. You may have been attracted to life in the city or the countryside and have made a conscious choice, or you may have moved because of your partner's work. All sorts of factors are relevant but they are likely to come into the categories of class, gender and ethnicity along with life chances shaped by culture, generation, disability and sexuality. Access to resources is a key factor in enabling us to exercise choice, and choice is likely to be exercised in different ways at different points in the life course.

Place gives meaning to and shapes social inequalities. The place where you live is important in influencing your life chances. The term 'life chances' was used by the sociologist Max Weber in his analysis of social class and status. For example, the ownership of property and goods determines a person's chances of realising their goals in society. The expression has since passed into more general use in the social sciences in relation to social mobility and equal opportunities, as mentioned in Chapter 1 in the discussion of changing places as represented in the housing estate that was the focus of the case study.

As we saw in Chapter 1, places may reflect social divisions and connections, which they also construct and shape. Where you live can have a major impact upon your life chances. Places are not simply geographical locations; the people who live there shape the places and the places influence the lives of those who inhabit them. Place may be important but there is not a simple equation between where you live and who you are. We may accord different status and weighting to different places at different times. It is also the case that others position us in relation to our understanding of place. Place can carry a complicated and even contradictory set of meanings.

The English writer Tony Parker went to Belfast in Northern Ireland in 1991 to conduct a series of interviews with different local people. Belfast is a city where place and culture, identity and nation are defining features of everyday life, especially in relation to politics and religion. As Parker observed:

> The first thing you need to know about someone as soon as you meet them – and they equally need to know about you – is whether each or both of you is Protestant or Catholic. To be 'neither' is not sufficient.
>
> (Parker, 1994: 3.4)

He goes on to illustrate how closely these identities are linked to place. He cites different examples, including visiting an estate agent to enquire about a property. It appears that the estate agent assumes that Parker is a Protestant, being English, but he attempts to find out, just to make sure. The estate agent mentions Malone Road, an area that was formerly largely Protestant but which has in recent years become mostly Catholic, to see what Parker's response will be. Lacking the specific knowledge of place that is required to pick up the clue, Parker does no more than ask about the housing on this road. The estate agent is endeavouring to find out about Parker's identity by using clues which Parker fails to read accurately. This is how we understand others and make ourselves known to them, but sometimes we lack the detailed knowledge to read the clues correctly.

Parker describes going into a chemist's shop in order to get a film processed. The assistant asks him where he would prefer to have the film sent as the shop does not process them on the premises:

> They go either to Johnson and Hunter or Collins and Sullivan, which would you prefer? . . . they both take exactly the same length of time . . . No they're the same price, there's no difference. Johnson and Hunter give you a free fillum with them – but then of course so do Collins and Sullivan too. Well it's for you to say which one you'd like sir. Really no preference? Then we'll send them to Johnson and Hunter. OK?
>
> (Parker, 1994: 10)

Parker reflects on this strange situation. If there is no difference between the two companies why does it matter? Why is he asked to choose? As he says:

> Only several weeks later did the penny suddenly drop. Johnson and Hunter are of course at once recognisable merely by their name as being Protestant. Just as Collins and Sullivan are Catholic, as surely as all but the dimmest of the dim would be expected to recognise . . . And of course, because of which she chose, apparently randomly and on reflection most certainly not, it was obvious what she was.
>
> (ibid.: 17–18)

This is a scenario rehearsed across the globe where different ethnic groups and cultures coexist, sometimes amicably, sometimes very acrimoniously. Meanings are produced through signs and symbols, names, which are in this instance linked to place. In a place that is as fraught with conflict as Northern Ireland it is not an option to remain neutral. People are expected to take up a position and to understand the codes and clues that are used to position them. Place is closely linked to the ways in which societies are divided. It is not only religion and culture which divide up communities by the places in which people live. In other situations the estate agent's strongest consideration would be whether the client had the resources to buy or rent a house in a particular place. The place where you live is closely connected to a whole range of life chances.

Place and postcodes

What do we mean by place? Place is a geographical location but it carries other meanings as well. The place where you live has different meanings. It means one thing to the people who live there and may mean other things to those who live elsewhere. As in Tony Parker's experience of Belfast, the different parts of the city mean one thing for those for whom that location is home and another for those who live in a different community. Place may be home to one group and a hostile and dangerous place for other people who live outside that place. Place carries political meanings but also meanings associated with consumption and the purchase of a whole range of goods and services. Place may be categorised according to politics, class, culture and ethnicity. There are different reasons for classifying places and for classifying people by the places in which they live. The Health Service needs evidence of the concentration of people who might be suffering particular forms of ill health and disease. Governments require data on areas of high unemployment. Neighbourhoods are categorised according to educational achievement and how many young people carry on to higher education, for example by the Department for Education and Employment and by the Higher Education Funding Council. All of these associations between people and places are linked to the policy requirements of the state but the associations go further. Public policies and state interventions are also based on assumptions about the links between particular people, places and culture, which themselves contribute to the further classification of a place as deprived or problematic. Carrying such a label may lead to additional resource allocation but it also creates meanings about a place and may make it difficult for those who live there to redefine themselves. For example, local authorities deploy census returns and other sources of official data to link places and social problems, such as crime and deviancy. The Social Exclusion Unit was established by the Labour government in 1997 in order to target places associated with social deprivation. This association of place with social exclusion and disadvantage also reflects the ways in which countries can be divided geographically and socially, with a higher concentration of poverty and inequality being experienced in specific geographical areas, as in the UK example of the 'north/south divide'.

Place is increasingly seen as concerned with lifestyle. The above examples outline lifestyles that may be associated with risk and a higher incidence of social deprivation, but there are also those places associated with social advantage and with affluence. These meanings attached to place have become increasingly important in recent times. Over the past two decades, marketing and promotional techniques were developed using systems of targeting potential customers in particular areas. This is

> based on the idea that birds of a feather flock together, it gives recognition to the fact that people with broadly similar economic, social and lifestyle characteristics tend to congregate in particular neighbourhoods and exhibit similar patterns of purchasing behaviour and outlook.
>
> (Wilson *et al.*, 1992: 202)

This kind of approach which classifies communities according to lifestyle, culture and, especially, what the people who live in them buy, represents a move away from a class-based analysis of social divisions. Instead of class-based measures of social divisions, the Henley Centre, one of Britain's leading management consultancies, argues that the most effective method of classifying people is to identify the drivers of a particular market's demand. This is followed by categorising consumers along lines which are largely based on where people live (The Henley Centre, 2009).

Postcode classifications offer descriptions of a particular postcode zone giving information such as demographics, socio-economic profile, housing, food and drink, durables, finance media, leisure and attitudes. These categories are drawn from those using systems such as those of A Classification of Residential Neighbourhoods (ACORN, 2009), which are used by companies who seek to target their direct mailings in order to ensure maximum take-up of their goods. When you collect your mail in the morning you may be surprised at the amount of 'junk mail' but, unless you have specifically requested the material, it is very likely that you have been sent this mail as a result of your postcode.

Increasingly the target places of marketing have shifted from physical places to virtual spaces, and social networking sites are used by companies to promote their products. Such sites provide much of the kind of information that is required to direct advertising, and accessing email addresses is a cheap way of focusing upon market sectors (Henley, 2009).

This use of place highlights location specifically as measured and classified by postcode or electronic address, and focuses on lifestyle. While the word has been used in the past in the social sciences, for example in sociology in Max Weber's work on social class and status, it has recently become more widely used. As the sociologist Mike Featherstone argues:

> Within contemporary consumer culture it connotes individuality, self-expression and a stylistic self-consciousness. One's body, clothes, speech, leisure pastimes, eating and drinking preference, home, car, choice of holidays, etc. are to be regarded as indicators of individuality of taste and

sense of style of the owner/consumer. In contrast to the designation of the 1950s as an era of grey conformism, a time of *mass* consumption, changes in production techniques, market segmentation and consumer demand for a wider range of products, are often regarded as making possible a greater choice (the management of which itself becomes an art form) not only for youth of the post 1960s generation, but increasingly for the middle aged and the elderly.

(Featherstone, 1991: 83)

It appears that we are all involved; even the elderly are expected to look cool and buy into 'lifestyle'. Stop and think about Stone's account of lifestyle. He emphasises choice and the agency which consumers are able to exercise. This counters some of the points made earlier about the association between place and social divisions. People are classified by the place in which they live, for example as socially deprived, without exercising any choice in the matter. What do you think might be missing from Featherstone's account?

Think of the example of social housing in Chapter 1. Those who have been forced to live in postcode areas which are classified as socially deprived because they lack the resources to live anywhere else are unlikely to be targeted by advertising and promotional material. They are also unlikely to be able to define themselves as they might wish in relation to clothes, cars and other patterns of consumption. Pierre Bourdieu used the concept of cultural capital to explain the complex ways in which socio-economic class and lifestyle interact (1986). For Bourdieu, social divisions cannot be based entirely on economic relations of power. Other elements have to be considered. Bourdieu identified four forms of capital – economic, social, cultural and symbolic. Beverley Skeggs summarises these four forms as follows:

i   *economic capital*: this includes income, wealth, inheritance and financial assets
ii *social capital*: capital generated through relationships with others, links with influential groups
iii *cultural capital*: this can exist in three forms – in an embodied state, that is in the form of long-lasting dispositions of the mind and body; in the objectified state, in the form of cultural goods; and in the institutionalized state, resulting in such things as educational qualifications . . .
iv *symbolic capital*: this is the form the different types of capital take once they are perceived as recognized and legitimate. Legitimation is the key mechanism in the conversion of power. Cultural capital has to be legitimated before it can have symbolic power. Capital has to be regarded as legitimate before it can be capitalized upon.

(Skeggs, 1997: 7)

Economic power does not necessarily guarantee what Bourdieu calls 'distinction'. Just being rich does not ensure that someone is accepted in all social circles, even

Plate 6.1 Cultural capital: getting physical

if they can afford to buy a house in a very expensive area where those in the highest social circles live. In contemporary life it seems that the economic and cultural capital of football stars and those of popular culture have been legitimated but this was not always the case. Those who live in the poorest areas are likely to lack all four forms of capital, although as Bourdieu argues these are certain forms of cultural capital which may be available. For example, in impoverished areas, people, traditionally young men, often from migrant or minority ethnic groups, may be able to access cultural capital through engaging in certain sports like boxing.

Summary

- Place shapes and reflects and reproduces life chances.
- Place is linked to lifestyle, for example in the targeting of companies seeking new markets for their products.
- Postcodes can also signify social deprivation, which may be used both to label certain places and to target support and welfare policies and resources.

Place and race

Place and **race** are connected. Think back to the example at the start of this chapter. The athlete Zaf Shah's family had lived in different places. They had moved to the UK, along with many other people from British colonial countries, after the Second World War. In the period following the war and the passing of the 1948 British Nationality Act, there was a significant increase in the numbers of people from countries of the New Commonwealth, although subsequent legislation in the 1960s and 1970s curtailed this trend. What has this got to do with race? Race is a problematic term and we will think about how it is used and the different meanings it carries in this section. Some social scientists prefer the word ethnicity. There are ways in which Shah's experience can be used to illustrate how race and place intersect, which can be deployed to introduce a fuller consideration of what we mean by race. You will recall that Shah, while seeing himself as British, competed at international levels representing Pakistan, the country his parents had left to come to settle in England. One of the reasons suggested for Shah's enthusiasm for representing Pakistan rather than England was his previous experience of rejection in his home county. He was not selected to play cricket for his county, even though he had been identified as a very promising young player. This was in a county with a relatively high proportion of people from Pakistan and India. The underlying message of Arnot's discussion above is that Shah's rejection was caused by **racist** attitudes, and that these racist attitudes were connected with place, the places Shah's family had come from, and with visible difference. This raises questions about how people identify themselves and about how they are classified by others. More and more people have mixed parentage. The UK has an increasing number of people, especially young people who are mixed race (Asthana and Smith, 2009). This is in itself contentious. Some people argue that if they are mixed race they are black, like US President Barack Obama; 'black' is part of a political statement and identification which 'mixed race' is not, although views on this vary. The words we use matter.

Thinking about the words we use

In this book I have used several different terms in order to address some of the issues here: diaspora, migration, race, ethnicity and racism. We have considered some of the strengths and weakness of the concept of diaspora, but how are the other terms used?

ACTIVITY

Look at these four words and jot down what you associate with each:

- Migrant
- Race
- Ethnicity (or ethnic)
- Racism

Think of an example for each of them, a situation in which you may use one of these words. In everyday use you may be more likely to use 'ethnic' than ethnicity, but you can choose either.

COMMENT

You might have thought of several different examples. These are words around which there may be some anxiety. Migrant is a term that frequently appears in the press, with competing meanings, not all of which are positive. Sometimes we are not sure which word to use. Should we talk about race or is ethnicity more appropriate and acceptable? Race is sometimes used to suggest some kind of biological categorisation that differentiates the human species, based on the idea that human beings can be classified into racial groups. You may have thought of examples in everyday discourse or in the media where race is used to describe black or south Asian people, as in 'race riots' in inner city areas. Race is a term with a wide range of meanings. It may invoke biology or be about visible difference, or be a catch-all expression to cover a range of differences among human beings. Ethnicity might be less in everyday use than 'ethnic', which often refers to certain kinds of food, clothes or music which are seen as outside the mainstream, belonging to 'other' cultures, perhaps even connoting certain exotic characteristics. For example, Indian food may be called 'ethnic', whereas British fish and chips, or even Mcdonald's, would not. Sometimes people use the term ethnic only to refer to people who are different from themselves, and especially to refer to non-white people and cultures, as if white people did not have an ethnicity. As the Parekh Report points out

> There is a gulf between specialist and non-specialist usage of the term 'ethnic' . . . In popular usage the term 'ethnic' implies non-western (as in 'ethnic food'), non-classical (as in 'ethnic music), non-white ('ethnic communities') or non-British (as in the late 1990s dispute about insignia on British Airways aircraft).
>
> (Parekh, 2000b: xxiii)

Racism is more clearly understood as discrimination on unfair grounds against people who belong to an identifiable group. You may have thought of examples of situations where you have experienced racism, either against yourself or observing incidences, or perhaps having read about them in the press. These are mostly common-sense everyday ways of understanding and using these terms. Language is very important in producing meanings through which we make sense of the world and the words we use matter. This is particularly apparent in discourses of race, ethnicity and racism and is well illustrated in everyday experience. What light can the further explorations of social science throw on these terms and how might they be understood as concepts in a deeper study of the society in which we live?

Who is a migrant?

There are many different ways to think about migration and the people who are called migrants. Residence or place of birth is a common tool for categorising migrants. A migrant is thus someone who lives in a different place from the one where they were born. Residence is used as the criterion in the census (Census, 2008). Movement, which includes arrivals and departures, is used to analyse migration, for example through the International Passenger Survey (2009). Another aspect of migration, which we looked at in Chapter 4, is citizenship which sometimes suggests ideas about nationality (using terms like 'nationals' and 'non-nationals') to suggest the status within the community of those who are called migrants. Citizenship also implies rights, for example to welfare benefits and social care, which are dependent on the legal status of the migrant. Ethnicity is not used to classify migrants even though a glance through the popular press might suggest that this is the major criterion. Migrant may be preferred because it is more neutral and merely describes the legal status of an individual rather than suggesting anything about their ethnicity or culture. However, in the popular media the two are often elided, but social scientists use the term descriptively as it is used within official statistics like the census.

Race

Kum-Kum Bhavnani suggests this definition of race:

> 'Race' is a concept which has no biological basis . . . All the criteria which apparently assert the reality of 'race', such as hair type, shape of face, blood group, are shown not to be discrete across human populations and genepools. In other words we are all members of the same species . . . However, the acceptance of 'race' as a scientifically valid concept has helped to create a certain type of legitimation for racism: that is, that racism comes to be seen as 'natural' and as intrinsic to 'human nature'. Given that there is no sound evidence from the natural and biological sciences to justify the supposition that the human species can be divided up into separate 'races', however, both 'race' and racism become economic, political, ideological and social expressions. In sum 'race' is not a biological category which is empirically defined. Rather, it is created and reproduced, as well as being challenged and eliminated through economic, political and ideological institutions.
>
> (Bhavnani, 1993: 31–32)

What sort of definition of race is being offered here? You will notice that Bhavnani uses 'race', putting the word in inverted commas. This is common practice in the social sciences, in order to differentiate between the use of race as a biological classificatory system, a view now largely discredited, and the use which the term has for describing and ultimately explaining social divisions and conflicts based on this aspect of difference. How does Bhavnani define 'race'? What are the key points?

- Race is not a biological category. There is no scientific evidence for this view, but it has been very influential in the past and informs contemporary views, especially those leading to racism.
- Racial divisions seem natural because they are so much part of everyday life; they are constantly represented and reproduced, for example through the media.
- Racial categories and 'race' are often based on visible differences, such as hair type and skin colour among people.
- The emphasis here is on the social construction of 'race'. 'Race' and racism are social structures. They may constrain people but there is resistance, and people can exercise agency and reject racism.

The main argument here seems to be to focus on the social construction of 'race', while acknowledging physical characteristics and differences between people, to argue that what is really important is not the differences themselves but the meanings that different societies attribute to them. These meanings often involve hierarchies and hostility, which is where racism is involved.

The Parekh Report argues that the term race is crucially important, since

> [It] refers to the reality of racism. It is unhelpful, however, to the extent that it reflects and perpetuates the belief that the human species consists of separate races. A further disadvantage is that overuse can deflect attention from culture and religious aspects of racism as distinct from those that are concerned with physical appearance. It needs often, therefore, to be complemented with other terms.
>
> This report uses the phrase 'race equality and cultural diversity', sometimes shortened to 'race and diversity', to refer to its overall area of concern. The phrase stresses that addressing racism requires not only the creation of equality but also the recognition of difference . . .
>
> The term 'racist violence' is preferred to 'racial violence', as recommended by the Stephen Lawrence Inquiry report. It alludes to the causes of such violence and to how perpetuators justify it.
>
> (Parekh, 200a: xxiv)

Ethnicity

Ethnicity is a term which includes some sharing of culture, possibly language and place. This place could be the place you come from or the place where you live. According to Avtah Brah, ethnicity and especially ethnic identities are maintained through:

a belief in common ancestry, claims to a shared history that gives shape to feelings of shared struggles and shared destinies, attachment to a homeland which may or may not coincide with the place of residence, and a sense of belonging to a group with a shared language, religion, social customs and traditions.

(Brah, 1993: 15)

Some social scientists have adopted the use of ethnicity in preference to 'race' because of the associations of 'race' with racists, biological categories that have involved the assertion of the superiority of some races over others. However, others have pointed out that ethnicity lacks a political dimension. For example, Bhikhu Parekh points out that, counter to the common-sense understanding of 'ethnic' as involving non-white or non-Western cultures, there is a more precise description of ethnicity:

For specialists, an ethnic group is one whose members have common origins, a shared sense of history, a shared culture and a sense of collective identity. All human beings belong to an ethnic group in this sense.

(Parekh, 2000a: xxi)

However, because of the risk of misunderstanding, whereby the common-sense assumptions are that ethnicity is a synonym for 'non-white' or 'non-western', the term 'ethnic' can be problematic. It also does not address the political meanings of hierarchies of ethnic groups, for example the racism that is often implicated in attributing ethnicity. While it is indeed the case that all human beings belong to some kind of ethnic group, using this term in all cases may obscure or marginalise the discrimination which is directed at some groups more than others.

However, ethnic is the term largely used in official statistics, for example in the census, in order to classify populations. You can probably think of several other situations in which you are asked to disclose your own ethnic identity, for example in job applications, where ethnic monitoring is a requirement of equal opportunities and diversity policies. Finding the right words is difficult and complicated and beset by problems, but this is not only a matter of getting the right word. The words we use not only carry existing meanings, they also create new meanings. It has been a very important aspect of what have been called 'identity politics' to use terminology that frees people from the negative associations of some of the terms used in the past. Ethnic has been used in the context of equal opportunities policies and practices in order to avoid the limitations of 'race' as involving biological categories. You may think of other examples, such as the use of 'disabled people' rather than the derogatory 'handicapped', or 'gay' as a positive, celebratory alternative to the clinical category of homosexuality. Words, along with other features of representational systems, images, practices and rituals, are important in shaping and constructing how we understand the world, and as part of political activity.

An associated term often accompanying references to ethnicity is 'minority'. You are very likely to have seen references to 'ethnic minorities' in media reports and television programmes, especially providing news coverage or drawing on the data of official statistics. Less frequently do we see or hear references to the 'ethnic majority', although a majority always haunts discussion of minorities. Although the expression 'ethnic minority', sometimes expressed in the reverse order of 'minority ethnic', is in common usage, it too is problematic. As Parekh comments:

> The term 'minority' has connotations of 'less important' or 'marginal'. In many settings it is not only insulting but also mathematically misleading or inaccurate. Furthermore it perpetuates the myth of white homogeneity – the notion that everyone who does not belong to a minority is by that token a member of a majority, in which there are no significant differences or tensions.
>
> (Parekh, 2000a: xxiii)

The claim of homogeneity applies to whiteness too. The argument here suggests that 'white' is a single category with shared ethnicity, which it clearly is not. Different groups of white people have different histories, cultures, religion and languages and adopt different positions in relation to others.

One of the routes through which meanings are produced about whiteness is through classificatory systems such as the categories to classify persons in a variety of places. The census offers one example of a site at which people are recorded as belonging to particular ethnic categories. Censuses provide a means of racial categorisation. Policy decisions are made on the basis of census data. Although people may be invited to categorise themselves, the categories provided are determined by others, by those who design the questions. The census does not just classify race, it also decides what counts. For example, Sharon Lee, using the US census, has demonstrated that census categories have suggested that any proportion of 'black', 10 per cent or 20 per cent makes the person black, rather than 90 per cent or 80 per cent white (1993). Census categories have altered in recent years, although categories of non-white people have changed more than those of white people, with changing times. In the case of the US census, some categories remained constant, notably that of 'white' at the top of the list for 200 years, since 1850 in fact. The US census changed to include Irish as whites whereas they had previously been categorised as 'black' (Warren and Twine, 1997). In the early nineteenth century Celts and other European migrants were classified as 'black' in the US but all, along with the Irish, became white by the end of the nineteenth century. Categories may be used for political purposes, for example 'black' may be used as a political category, whereas white may be seen as an assumed class without differences. In the 2001 UK census a question on religion was introduced to ascertain more information about the diversity of respondents in the 'Asian' category. However, there have been those who bear the visible difference of whiteness yet who are not classified as white. This has been the case with the Irish, who have been a key 'other' for the British. The Irish have been racialised even more than the Welsh and negatively characterised by particular stereotypical features. Roddy Doyle, in his novel and film *The Commitments*, has a character claim that the 'Irish are the blacks of Europe'. At different times people are differently classified and there may be 'degrees of whiteness'.

Racism

What do we mean by racism? What sorts of acts, thoughts, representations and practices might be so labelled? Here are some examples from *The Parekh Report*.

> He swore and shouted 'Paki', something I'm used to being called. I felt that the incident wasn't significant enough to report. In fact the police would have laughed at me . . .
>
> Two of us went shopping together, always. Two of us had to be in the house to defend the others. We used to be scared going home. We used to phone Mum and say, 'Mum, I am coming round the corner. Please look out of the window'. We had to let the family know what shops we were going to so if we were late they could go and check. Everything was really organised.
>
> I still don't feel British. Because I know we haven't been fully accepted. We still walk down the street and get called a Paki.
>
> (Parekh, 2000a: 58)

Many of the voices recorded in *The Parekh Report* speak of daily acts of racism and xenophobia, of conducting their daily routines in an atmosphere of discrimination and hostility, often taking place on the street and perpetrated by the most disadvantaged of white youths. These acts constitute some of the most explicit experiences of racism, ranging in seriousness from name-calling to actual acts of violence. Such acts are, of course against the law, but none the less do still take place. Racism also has a less direct and less immediately obvious face, which still has an enormous impact upon people's lives. It can be seen to operate in education, in employment, in the provision of welfare services and even in the criminal justice system.

The Macpherson Inquiry (1999) into the murder of the black UK teenager Stephen Lawrence gave much more public awareness of the concept previously used mostly within the social sciences, *institutional racism*. Hitherto this concept had been largely confined to academic research within the social sciences, but Sir William Macpherson brought the expression into everyday usage. His report noted that, although directly racist practices had been prohibited by antiracist legislation like the Race Relations Act and by the implementation of a range of anti-discriminatory policies, for example in education and by employers in the public and private sectors of employment, racism was still present. The only difference was that it was practised *implicitly* in the procedures and policies of many public bodies. The report's statement has been widely quoted as a definition, although Macpherson's claim was that it should provoke further discussion and not be fixed for all time. The suggested explanation was that institutional racism involved the collective failure of an organisation or institution to provide appropriate and professional service and to permit unwitting prejudice, ignorance, thoughtlessness and racist stereotyping (in Parekh, 2000: 70). The Macpherson Report suggested that

> The term institutional racism should be understood to refer to the way institutions may systematically treat or tend to treat people differently in respect of race. The addition of the word 'institutional' therefore identifies the source of the differential treatment; this lies in some sense within the organisation rather than simply with the individuals who represent it. The production of differential treatment is 'institutionalised' in the way the organisation operates.
>
> (Macpherson, 1999, para 2.2)

This concept of institutionalised racism has been criticised in many ways but it is important for a number of reasons. First, it points to the ways in which racism is socially produced and reinforced; racism is a social structure, rather than being the responsibility of individual agents and the outcome of individual acts. If it is embedded in social institutions this suggests targets and strategies for change, rather than punishing individuals only. Everyone is implicated and we all have a responsibility. Second, the concept draws upon empirical and theoretical work within the social sciences and illustrates the relationship between social science and policy. This is not only important for social scientists. It indicates the ways in which academic work supports policy making and permits the application of the findings of sustained endeavour, linking intellectual, academic work and other areas of work within the wider society. Social scientists do not live in ivory towers!

Race and gender

Another of the interconnections which it is important to suggest in exploring the impact of race, ethnicity and racism is that between race and gender. As we saw in Chapter 2 people have multiple identities. Everyone has some kind of ethnic identity along with a gender identity, others relating to work, family, friendships, sexuality, being able-bodied or having some disability, and to nation. Race and ethnicity do not exist in isolation from other areas of human experience. This is well demonstrated by a speech made in 1851 by Sojourner Truth, a woman who was born into slavery in the US. She campaigned for both the abolition of slavery and equal rights for women.

> Well, children, where there is so much racket, there must be something out of kilter, I think between the Negroes of the South and the women of the North – all talking about rights – the white men will be in a fix pretty soon. But what's

all this talking about? That man over there says that women need to be helped into carriages, and lifted over ditches, and to have the best place everywhere. Nobody helps me any best place. And ain't I a woman? Look at me! Look at my arm. I have plowed (*sic*), I have planted and I have gathered into barns. And no man could head me. And ain't I a woman? I could work as much, and eat as much as any man – when I could get it – and bear the lash as well! And ain't I a woman? I have born children and seen most of them sold into slavery, and when I cried out with a mother's grief, none but Jesus heard me. And ain't I a woman?

(in Bhavani and Coulson, 1986: 83)

Truth points out most forcefully in this powerful speech that she is no less a woman because she belongs to a group of people who are oppressed on grounds of race too. It is the legacy of slavery and of colonialism that has informed the development of black feminist approaches to social divisions and inequality. Such critiques have stressed the need to look at the ways in which gender and race operate together in shaping experience. Black feminists have argued that feminist politics needs to take on board the specific experiences of different women, rather than assuming that there is a single category 'woman' with shared history and shared experiences of oppression. There are differences in culture, in family, in religion, in place and in history, all of which make for particular experiences about which it is not possible to generalise on the basis of gender. For example, whereas the women's movement in the West has argued strongly for free access to contraception and abortion in order to control their fertility, for many black women control of their fertility would have a different emphasis. They would stress the need to be able to have children and in some instances to have access to fertility treatment, which on occasion they have been denied. Race, class and gender are all significant influences and operate together. Not only do we need to acknowledge all these different factors, we also need to include specific circumstances and histories.

Race and nation

There are times when race is also widely enmeshed with the experience of nation. For example, at the beginning of this chapter we considered the question of how being black, or more specifically south Asian and British, is possible. The experience of racism can militate against feelings of inclusion and of being part of the nation where you currently live. One of the examples of the voices quoted in *The Parekh Report* cited the failure of belonging, saying that he did not feel 'British'. What we mean by Britain and 'the British people' is, however, deeply problematical. Most modern nations consist of diverse and disparate people. 'The British people' is the result of a series of conquests, Celtic, Roman, Saxon, Viking and Norman. The UK presents a mixture of peoples and a mix of cultures. There are issues of naming involved too. Britain usually refers to England, Scotland and Wales, whereas the UK includes these three and Northern Ireland.

What do we mean by a nation? For example, in the UK, which is a nation state, England, Scotland and Wales are usually thought of as nations. Some people would consider Ireland, the whole land mass and its people a nation, whereas others, notably Ulster Protestants, would strongly contest this. Nation is a contested term. Nation states have external, fixed demarcated borders and some uniformity of law that is recognised as such. A nation has a named people who recognise their shared identity which is the outcome of a shared history, culture and of belonging to a homeland. In this context we are focusing on the idea of a nation and the question of how race and nation interconnect. The nation is also a cultural community and brings together the political nation state and the culture of the nation. Does having a national culture mean that there is a unified culture? There may indeed be a tendency to attempt to achieve some sort of unity. It may be this unity that actually creates the feelings of exclusion expressed by some of the people quoted in *The Parekh Report*, excludes them. The anthropologist and philosopher Ernest Gellner argues that all modern societies require the development of a common culture and language or they will disintegrate. As he argues:

> culture is now the necessary shared medium, the life-blood, or perhaps rather the minimal shared atmosphere, within which alone the members of the society can breathe and survive and produce. For a given society it must be one in which they can all breathe and speak and produce; so it must be the same culture.
>
> (Gellner, 1983: 37–38)

This view seems to undermine the notion of an inclusive national culture which encompasses diversity and embraces differences among its people. It does foreground the importance of culture and the combination of the political and cultural aspects of nation, which are useful for exploring some of the ways in which people may feel that they are excluded as well as the reasons why others feel that they belong.

The nation as 'imagined community'

The political scientist and historian Benedict Anderson sees the nation as an 'imagined community'.

> It is imagined because the members of even the smallest nation will never know most of their fellow members, meet them, or even hear of them . . . The nation is imagined as limited because even the largest of them, encompassing perhaps a billion living human beings, has finite, if elastic, boundaries beyond which lie other nations . . . it is imagined as a community, because, regardless of actual inequality and exploitation that may prevail . . . the nation is always conceived as a deep horizontal comradeship.
>
> (Anderson, [1983] 2000: 6–7)

This draws attention to some of the processes that are involved in the construction of nation. How do we imagine ourselves as belonging to a nation? A nation has to be thought of in relation to other nations. We belong to one nation and not to another. According to Anderson, modern nations arose historically from the emergence of new communication media, like printing and the free market activities of capitalist enterprise (1983). New communications systems allowed people to imagine themselves more easily. People are aware of the signifiers of their own nation, the flag, the shared culture and the rituals that are associated with a particular nation. These are the ways in which a nation produces meanings about the culture of a nation that is shared.

Rituals

Rituals play a crucial part in sustaining the collective memory and reinstating notions of the nation. Such rituals may have religious and secular aspects. As Emile Durkheim argued, despite differences in content there are few functional differences between religious, national and secular rituals and ceremonies because their aims and outcomes are remarkably similar (1915). This has been especially marked in England and Wales, where the monarch is both head of state and head of the Anglican Church and the Church of England in Wales, whereby as the established church, it still plays a significant role in rituals ranging from state events such as the Opening of Parliament and state funerals to memorial and commemorative events. Secular occasions such as the Football Association Cup Final may even employ quasi-religious songs and hymns and serve a very similar function in bringing people together for moments of shared national identification. Drawing on the language of religion and the history of the state, rituals serve to confirm and establish notions of a British way of life and national identity. Such rituals, especially those that involve the state and its dignitaries as well as the monarch, often draw on historical narratives and the authority of archaic practices, historic costumes and often the use of Latin phrases to lend the status of the past and of past glories to current re-enactments. The military may also be involved. For example, Remembrance Sunday constructs a particular view of belonging to the nation which invokes a military past where the identity of the nation is closely linked to military endeavours and associations of self-sacrifice and heroism. The state funeral provides a site for the enactment of the glorious past of the individual who has died in the context of the nation's past. This was particularly well represented at the funeral of Winston Churchill, the British wartime leader during the Second World War, who died in 1965. On this occasion the military had a very dominant presence, and even though this point may be seen as marking the end of Empire there was a parade of dignitaries and officers of state signifying the past that was. This was a traditional funeral, attended by dignitaries of state, Commonwealth and other world political leaders, the monarchy and the aristocracy. Thousands of people lined the streets, largely deferentially, as British subjects. The funeral of Diana, Princess of Wales, in 1997, was in many ways very different.

As one observer remarked, people were there as 'British citizens', rather than as British subjects as at Churchill's funeral (Woodward, 2000b). This suggests more active involvement and even control over the shaping of events, rather than being a passive spectator. Diana's funeral saw a break with protocol, the flag at half mast at Buckingham Palace, the Queen responding to the 'people's' demands and the presence of a more diverse range of people, including media stars and Diana's friends. Whereas in 1965, the global presence at Churchill's funeral was that of political leaders, and the largely elderly, white, male colonial order, by 1997 there appeared to be a more diverse, inclusive representation. In 1997 the state ritual involved the expression of emotions and the presence of numerous media stars with the popular singer Elton John singing at the funeral service itself in Westminster Abbey, yet many of the traditional rituals of state were maintained (Woodward, 2000b). By 1997, the British nation could be seen to have been reconstructed as more diverse, more inclusive with some representation of women and minority ethnic people.

Such rituals offer defining moments in the story of the nation through rituals of particular practices, incorporating dignitaries and heroes (even newly constructed popular heroes, as in the case of Diana's funeral). They retell the nation's history in specific ways that re-present dramatic accounts of national identity, and thus compound people's investment, both in a particular narrative and in a specific story of the nation's 'real' and shared past.

Another aspect of the process of inclusion and exclusion, which positions people as 'us' and 'them' and more especially of the insiders and the outsiders, is explored in Edward Said's influential work on the Western colonialisation of Asian societies, *Orientalism* (1978). In this book Said explores the ways in which representations and discourses of colonised peoples as 'Other', and thus as different or inferior, are an integral part of political economic colonialism. His claim is that representational systems in the West produced the idea that the diverse nations of the Near and Far East can be grouped together as the same, into a single civilisation, namely 'the Orient'. Thus the 'Orient' becomes the binary opposite to the West, the 'Occident', against which the Orient is defined as backward, despotic and undeveloped as well as mysterious and exotic. Said's argument was that the 'Orient' was not discovered but *made* (1978). He argued that

> a very large mass of writers, among them poets, novelists, philosophers, political theorists, economists and imperial administrators, have accepted the basic distinction between East and West as the starting point for elaborate theories, stories, novels, social descriptions and political accounts concerning the Orient, its people, customs, 'mind', destiny and so on.
>
> (in Bayoumi, and Rubin, 2001: 69)

In *Orientalism*, Said's aim was to use Michel Foucault's idea of discourse, based on the meanings that are produced through discursive fields, to unpack this whole thought system and to expose its power relations and structures, in order to challenge the dominance of Western thought. Said shows how deeply implicated are the practices and representational systems through which such knowledge is produced in the interplay of power between West and East. The identities so produced through these processes are polarised, as are the 'Orient' and the 'Occident'.

How does this connect with race and nation? For example, Said's concept of 'the Orient' as 'other' and outside' shows how different people within the nation, for example within Britain, are excluded from the culture of the nation. It illustrates not only *who* is excluded, for example peoples who are associated with colonised countries and 'the Orient, but also *how*', for example through the construction of the nation's culture, its rituals, practices and imaginings. Where is race in the imaging and imagining of nationhood and what is the role of race in the shared histories which characterise nations? In countries in the Western world such as the UK, the histories that are implicated in the construction of the nation involve some aspect of colonialism. Contemporary examples also demonstrate other insecurities in the post-9/11 world of fear of constructed outsiders. Migrant people are also subject to suspicion as 'whiteness' comes under scrutiny as the site of anxieties and insecurities in a changing world. Think of the examples that have been cited in this chapter in relation to Britishness. The imagined community may not encompass the full diversity of the nation's history. The stories that are told about 'we British' may be a predominantly white story and exclude the histories of people from Africa, the Caribbean and south Asia, for example.

As Paul Gilroy has argued, in exploring ideas about race and racism and the nation and belonging,

> We increasingly face a racism which avoids being recognised as such because it is able to line up 'race' with nationhood, patriotism and nationalism. A racism which is taken a necessary distance from crude ideas of biological inferiority and superiority now seeks to present an imaginary definition of the nation as a unified *cultural* community. It constructs and defends an image of national culture – homogeneous in its whiteness yet precarious and perpetually vulnerable to attack from enemies within and without . . . This is a racism that answers the social and political turbulence of crisis and crisis management by the recovery of national greatness in the imagination. Its dream-like construction of our sceptered isle as an ethnically purified one provides special comfort against the ravages of [national] decline.
>
> (Gilroy, 1992: 87)

However, the contemporary UK is very much a multi-cultural society in the sense that it includes a wide range of ethnic groups. For example, empirical evidence indicates the presence of considerable diversity in the UK population.

The 2001 census showed that about one person in 14 in the UK was from an ethnic minority. It also indicates the age categories, showing that there is still a relatively low proportion of minority ethnic people in the older age categories. Increasing numbers of people of different ethnicities mean that the UK is a multi-ethnic society (Census, 2008). The evidence in terms of population points to diversity as does the migration of numbers of people from European countries in the first part of the twenty-first century, although some of these, for example Polish people, may well return to Poland as the economic recession deepens. However, numbers do not give any clue as to the extent to which minority ethnic people feel that they belong, in the sense of identifying with being British. The continuance of racists acts, including acts of extreme violence as well as the acts of discrimination that minority ethnic people have to suffer, militate against full participation and the multi-cultural society which the UK might appear to have become. At one level there is a celebration of multi-cultural Britishness, for example in sport, music and art and even in political life. There are increasing opportunities for the expression of diversity and for full participation in all aspects of contemporary life, including the culture of the nation. At different historical moments there may be greater inclusion in national identities expressed through being British or by being English or Welsh or Scottish for minority ethnic people.

One of the moments at which we belong to the 'imagined community' of the nation is during sporting competitions at an international level. The men's Football World Cup is a good example of a secular coming-together of the nation, when huge numbers of English people support the English team. Paul Gilroy suggests that the St George's flag may offer a more positive symbol of inclusion than the more imperialist Union Jack (Gilroy, 2005) although the experience of the 2006 World Cup may challenge this. At the 2006 World Cup, some, albeit a few, England supporters waved the St George's flag to accompany chants of 'Ten German Bombers' and a range of racist expletives in German cities (Panorama, 2006). What's happening here? The 'Ten German Bombers' chant seems to refer to the defeat of Germany by Britain and her allies in the Second World War, but serves as a shorthand signifier of xenophobia and racism in this context. The people chanting it may not have much understanding, let alone memory of its history, but it symbolises hostility. There remain many examples of racist activity, although it rarely occurs explicitly on the terraces at British games (Woodward, 2007b); yet it does still happen in various ways and there are many parts of Europe, such as Spain, where it remains in a range of sports, even Formula One as Lewis Hamilton would testify (Times, 2008), when Spanish spectators wore black curly wigs and black make-up, disporting the slogan 'Lewis Hamilton's family'.

This is not a simple story, but translating antiracist policies into sporting practice is much more than wearing the T-shirts. Black players, although not as yet many British south Asian players, occupy leading roles in the Premiership and in the England team, but racism is still enacted on the terraces and even on the pitch. Racism still exists in the English game as the attempts to eliminate it reveal, through the evidence of campaigns like *Kick Racism Out* and *Football Unites, Racism Divides*.

The picture in Plate 6.2 shows what has become quite a regular feature of UK football: a display of antiracist credentials and commitment. Does this reflect

Plate 6.2 A banner is held up promoting the 'Kick it Out' campaign during the Soccer–Coca-Cola Football Championship, Birmingham

Source: © PA Photos

a move towards multi-culturalism? Maybe a popular mass entertainment activity (albeit largely through spectatorship rather than active participation) like football is one possible avenue towards greater inclusion and the development of antiracist strategies which could lead to a new multi-cultural Britishness. Maybe.

Summary

- Race and place are interconnected through past and present experiences.
- Place includes the places we have come from and the ways we reconstruct these places as well as the place where we live.
- Symbolic systems, rituals and language are very important. The language of race creates meanings and has material consequences. Symbols and rituals create inclusion into and exclusion from the culture of the nation.
- Race and gender interrelate and include different experiences and specific experiences of inequalities.
- Mobilities and migration create new connections with nation and impact upon experience in different ways at different times.

Conclusion

Race and place are interconnected in many ways. Place has different meanings. There are places where we live and have lived and the place where we were born. Place carries meanings related to class, ethnicity and national identity. A study of place and an exploration of the concept of place also raises issues about the degree of agency which people are able to exercise over where they live. Living where we do may be completely outside our own area of choice or we may be in a position to make our own decisions. As with migration between countries, even within the same country, there may be push-and-pull factors and some people are able to exercise much more autonomy than others. Mobility presents new connections.

The links between race and place involve the routes which we travel, the places where we have lived and, in particular, those places which have the most meaning in shaping our lives. At a time of mass and fluid, uneven migration these connections are brought to the fore. Of course, migration is not new, but it has intensified over the past century and there are relatively large numbers of people who live in a different place from the one where they were born or where their parents were born. Race is a shorthand expression for a whole range of processes. These include the process of being classified as belonging to a particular race or ethnic group. Diaspora offers one way of thinking about race ethnicity and migration, although it cannot explain all versions of migration and mobility or always situate the connections to home which many diasporic people feel.

It is also important to look at the ways in which race intersects with other aspects of social divisions such as those based on gender and nation. One of the arguments of recent theoretical critiques in the social sciences has been to focus on the ways in which different matters interrelate, rather than seeking to isolate different factors, and in this case different social structure.

These processes can usefully be called *racialisation* and *ethnicisation*. They look like unnecessarily long words, but they do have the advantage of indicating a process, something that involves change and is ongoing. Race and ethnicity are not fixed, they are constantly being produced. Race is not some biological category fixed and set in our genes. It is a social process that is constantly evolving. Change is a key aspect of the politics of race. One such issue which illustrates the changing politics of race in the first decade of the twenty-first century is the possibility of transformation that is afforded by the election of the first black president of the US.

One of the major contributions of the social sciences has been, first, in exploring the empirical evidence about race and place. Second, the examination of how race and place are represented and especially the language we use to present knowledge about race has been an especially important contribution. By asking questions about what we mean by the words we use and the ways in which we construct knowledge about race we are able to reveal some of the power structures which underpin our ideas and practices.

The social sciences have largely stressed the importance of materialities: the social, economic, political and cultural production of meanings about race. These are what have been most influential and useful in influencing policies and strategies, in particular to combat the negative impact of racism and to develop new ways of thinking about diversity and difference which can accommodate and welcome change.

Chapter 7

Globalisation

Opportunities and inequalities

Introduction

Globalisation has become a familiar term in recent years. It may even have become a commonplace and overused term for a whole range of diverse developments in politics, economics and culture, where the term is broadly used to cover the growing connections between societies worldwide. The impact of global networks takes different forms. At one level it seems as if we live in a world where globalisation has become part of everyday life. In almost any major world city you can see the familiar yellow M signalling the presence of a McDonald's fast food outlet. The high streets and shopping malls of most major towns and cities across the world look very similar with the same franchises and a uniform display of chain stores. Globalisation may be seen as focusing on the marketplace and the availability of goods around the world. Brands such as McDonald's have global status because of their market availability. This is an availability that is the result of the successful promotion of US products across the globe. This has extended to parts of the world that it was previously thought the US market could not reach, for example Russia, China, and the states of what was formerly Eastern Europe. Terms such as 'McDonaldification' and Disneyfication' have been coined to describe, albeit somewhat simplistically, this marketing phenomenon. Latin America and Africa have been brought into the global economic networks, most notably through agribusiness and land purchase in recent years. In the field of marketing and consumption, branding has been a particular feature of US international activity which has been taken up in other parts of the world, for example in Europe and Japan. The whole process has become much more sophisticated, as Naomi Klein argues, taking a critical stance on global marketing, in her book *No Logo*. Klein argues that it is no longer possible to identify the signs of US-dominated marketing and we are presented with a cultural mix, what she calls a 'market masala'. This 'masala' involves a cultural mix, for example in advertisements targeted at young people in the 'teen market' of black and white 'Rasta braids, pink hair, henna hand painting, piercing and tattoos, a few national flags . . . Cantonese and Arabic lettering and a sprinkling of English words' (2001: 120). Klein claims that this kaleidoscope represents a new departure in globalised markets:

Today the buzzword in global marketing isn't selling America to the world, but bringing a kind of market masala to everyone in the world . . . a bilingual mix of North and South, some Latin, some R & B, all couched in global party lyrics. This ethnic-food-court approach creates a One World placeness, a global mall where corporations are able to sell a single product in numerous countries without triggering the old cries of 'Coca-Colonization' . . . By embodying corporate identities that are radically individualistic and per-petually new, the brands attempt to inoculate themselves against accusations that they are in fact selling sameness.

(2001: 117–118)

There is evidence of shared, globally comprehensible culture, through television, especially MTV, broadcast in 83 countries in the late 1990s (ibid.: 120), films, the news media and the Internet. There is not only the food and drink that originate in the US, like McDonald's and Coca-Cola, but a hybrid gastronomical culture that mixes a wide range of local cultures. In any UK city one can see a huge range of different restaurants representing myriad different cultures and the mingling of different traditions. For example, the fish and chip shop is very likely to sell pizza, spring rolls and donner kebab as well as the traditional cod or haddock and chips. 'TexMex' food, another amalgamated cross-cultural hybrid, is widely available in supermarkets. Postcolonial cooking involves the mixing of different cultures and traditions across the globe and sometimes unusual, new combinations. The Balti cooking that people consume in what may be called 'Indian restaurants' in the UK was derived from a UK city, Birmingham, and not the Indian subcon-tinent. Not only is there a plethora of restaurants and small catering services for different cultural tastes and traditions, but supermarkets stock goods from all over the world and the ingredients to prepare dishes that originate from diverse cultures. Migration, for example across Europe, means that even small towns show a new international diversity. The movement of people, for example from Poland and other parts of Europe to the UK, means that a huge range of languages are represented in UK schools and small local shops offer a new range of goods. The pet shop is now a Polish deli. There were two last year, but one of them now sells computer parts.

It is, however, possible to exaggerate the extent of this influence. This small town had many more Polish shops, several of which have now closed as the economic recession bites and migrants return to the countries they left. The twenty-first century is marked by such mobilities, rather than being a one-way movement or the dominance of a single culture. The local appropriation of global products also shapes how they are used (Sassatelli, 2007). It is in the local context that goods such as Coca-Cola and Big Macs are consumed. However, 'the local appropriations of global commodities may alter their meanings and images, but may leave global commodity flows which sustain them somewhat unchanged' (Sassatelli, 2007: 115–116). Diversity does extend to a whole range of cultural and artistic practices and experiences. Popular music draws upon an extensive and very mixed repertoire

Plate 7.1 An ordinary street in a small town in the UK

of traditions to produce new manifestations of fusion music and world music, although there is also a dominance of techno rhythms that masquerade as innovatory and diverse. The most exciting of contemporary art forms draw upon traditions and techniques that cross continents, times and experiences.

There has been an explosion of communication technologies such as television and radio broadcasting and the Internet. The Internet provides very fast communication across the globe with an immediacy that has been hitherto unknown. Call centres receiving queries from people in the UK might be located in Glasgow or in Calcutta. Communication by electronic mail greatly facilitates the transmission of information about markets. Financial markets cover the globe and communicate and operate across national boundaries. In many cases the huge multinational companies not only dominate local markets but also their powers cross the borders of nation states.

Not only do US and other producers reach global markets and draw on the raw material from across the globe, the production process has been moved to occupy diverse global sites. For example, Japanese car manufacturers relocated a great deal of their manufacture to the UK in the 1980s, but have subsequently closed many plants, including the Nissan factory in Sunderland, UK, in 2009. A market slump or boom in one part of the world can send repercussions across the globe with which not only nations are unable to deal; they impact upon the global economy. Even within the West, a crisis on Wall Street or in US-based multi-national companies or banks (e.g. Lehman Brothers in 2008), can mean pensions are at risk, or endowment policies will fail to provide the monies required to pay off the mortgages on people's homes in the UK. (I have used the term 'the West' as a shorthand term of reference for the advanced, industrialised countries including North America, Europe and Australia and New Zealand, but I am aware that the word is deeply problematic. To use 'the West' may suggest opposition to something which might be called 'the East', as Edward Said has pointed out. Thus one might appear to be asserting, not only the sameness of all countries involved in each category but the superiority in all respects of that which is called 'the West' (1978). Some writers prefer to use Euro-American, which seems just as limited. My use of 'the West' is practical and avowedly limited but serves to provide a category for parts of the world that have particular eco-nomic and political histories.)

The common practice of outsourcing labour across the globe or to migrant workers in Europe, for example, creates low-cost goods that boost consumption, but at times of economic recession it highlights global inequalities and exposes the exploitation of those who make the goods. For example, the popular, cheap, or 'value' in market terms, fashion chain Primark has been shown to use TNS knitwear which supplies a range of outlets including 20,000 garments a week to Primark. TNS has been revealed to employ child labour for its Primark garments and to pay Pakistani, Indian and Afghan immigrants £3 an hour for a 12-hour day and a seven-day week (White, 2009).

Global climate changes impact upon everyone, not the least upon those in less developed and less affluent regions of the world, who have least resource with which to cope with the devastation of floods, drought or earthquakes which might result from climate change. Many of these changes, which most dramatically impact about the poorer parts of the world, have been initiated by some of the excessive patterns of energy consumption in the West. Globalisation in this context may be seen to have significantly negative effects upon people across the world.

Globalisation is subject to considerable debate within the social sciences and because of its impact upon our daily lives. As Anthony Giddens stressed in the introduction to his 1999 Reith lectures, many of the effects of globalisation were positive. He claimed that globalisation

> also influences everyday life as much as it does events happening on a world scale . . . in parts of the world women are staking claim to greater autonomy than in the past and are entering the labour force in large numbers. Such aspects of globalisation are at least as important as those happening in the global market-place. They contribute to the stresses and strains affecting traditional ways of life and cultures in most regions of the world . . . other traditions, such as those affecting religion, are also experiencing major transformations.
>
> (Giddens, 2002: 4)

Giddens was accentuating the positive aspects at this point and putting forward a view that is less persuasive in 2009, at a time of global economic recession and in a world beset by the insecurities arising from the perceived and actual fear of terrorism. The debate within the social sciences is focused around the arguments about the extent to which globalisation has been taken as far as supporters of the globalisation thesis contend. The other important dimension of this debate is the tension between those who see globalisation as largely beneficial and who see its transformative characteristics as far outweighing any of its disadvantages on the one hand, and those who point to its most destructive, largely Western-led dominance on the other. The tension is between the opportunities of global expansion and the inequalities that global networks can reproduce (Chua, 2003). Amy Chua argues that pro-market reforms promoted by international companies in developing countries are carried out to benefit elite groups in those countries and to reinforce the inequalities and exploitation experienced by the majority population. Global inequalities have a long history, and globalisation may not be such a new set of phenomena as some might argue, although global networks have re-formed and changed in recent years, which makes the concept of globalisation an important one in the social sciences.

At some moments the impact of what may be called globalisation is much more alarming than at others. The merging of cultures, for example in relation to food, dress and music and improved communication and transport systems, may seem to offer exciting possibilities for new developments and new experiences. However, interconnections between societies can also illustrate the wide differences and inequalities that exist alongside the apparently more anodyne and even positive aspects of globalisation. This can be demonstrated in one of the experiences of the twenty-first century that involved the meeting of very different worlds.

Summary

- Globalisation involves complex connections between different countries, their economies and cultures, across the world.
- Globalisation is an important term in the social sciences which impacts upon our daily lives and has been used to focus on global inequalities and conflicts as well as new opportunities and greater democratisation through the spread of neoliberal governance across the world.
- This impact ranges from the relatively mundane everyday merging of different cultures to significant, often destructive events on the world scale.
- Globalisation involves economic, social, political and cultural aspects of life.
- There are different views on the impact of globalisation, as positive or negative, and even on the extent of its impact.

Different worlds

ACTIVITY

Look at Plates 7.2 and 7.3. What do they mean to you? What can the events recorded here tell us about globalisation?

COMMENT

There are many different responses to the images presented here. In many parts of the world the first image will be very familiar, as it has been reproduced so many times to signify the shock that this invasion of the US heartland provoked. The photographic image and the date of the event became symbolic of the US experience, so much so that the event is known by the US way of recording the date, 9/11, with the month preceding the day. The second image taken in 2008 on the anniversary of 9/11 purports to represent a hopeful future, with lights replacing the destroyed towers.

It is a scene of unthinkable destruction, in a world where we are familiar with such scenes of devastation, but in 'other' parts of the world, not in the US and not in New York. On 11 September 2001, with the destruction of the Twin Towers of the World Trade Center in New York and of part of the Pentagon in

Plate 7.2 9/11: Plumes of smoke pour from the World Trade Center towers in New York

Source: © PA Photos

Plate 7.3 A new global agenda? Twin towers of light from the Tribute in Light
converge over the spire of Trinity Church in Lower Manhattan

Source: © PA Photos

Washington, DC the United States was plunged into a state of war against an enemy who could not be immediately identified. More alarming even than the devastation and destruction of life on US soil was the immediate uncertainty about who had committed the atrocity and thus the uncertainty about what action should be taken. What was certain was that the US, its way of life and what it embodied, had been attacked. It was a shocking reminder that everyone is vulnerable to acts of terrorism, even in the most powerful, most protected and most affluent of countries. The second image represents the possibilities of rebuilding and reconstruction, although in the intervening years between the two photographs there was considerable further, global damage.

In some ways these images challenge the notion that we live in a globalised world. We live in a world marked by inequalities and conflict, which is experienced even at the heart of one of the world's most affluent and most powerful nations. This attack has been followed by others at different sites across the globe. However, the attack did involve a significant crossing of borders of **nation states**. The occasion achieved such iconic status because it involved such a hostile attack on US territory and because of the actions of the Bush administrations that followed in the invasion of Iraq and bombings of Afghanistan. Not since the Japanese bombing of Pearl Harbor, with which the events of 9/11 were compared, had the US been so attacked. 9/11 was clearly about one world clashing with another, but not about the attack by one **nation** on another. At first the US was very unsure about the identity of its enemy. No nation state had declared war upon the US either formally or by the implications of its actions, as in the case of Pearl Harbor. This was made clear by the US President in his first address to the American people on 15 September 2001, when George W. Bush described the conflict in the following terms:

> This is a conflict without battlefields or beachheads, a conflict with opponents who believe they are invisible . . . Those who make war against the United States have chosen their own destruction . . . We are planning a broad and sustained campaign to secure our country and eradicate the evil of terrorism.
>
> (*Observer*, 16 September 2001: 3)

This was an enemy of the US who seemed to be invisible because it was not an enemy associated with a particular state or even a group of states. The enemy was identified as terrorism, and what is called terrorism crosses the boundaries of the nation state. Al Qa'eda, the terrorist organisation later seen as responsible for the attacks on the World Trade Center and the Pentagon, was characterised by its transnational networks. Transnational networks are a feature of such terrorist groups, which operate outside and across the boundaries of nations, employing a diverse range of networks, all of which are heavily dependent on new technologies and Internet communication, as well as drawing on traditional religious affiliations and loyalties. There is no simple opposition between the hi-tech West and the low-tech 'outsiders', terrorists or guerrilla fighters. There are complex interconnections between these different worlds. The technologies, many of which may have been generated and financed in the West, especially in the US, are utilised across national boundaries. The pilots who flew the planes involved on 11 September were trained in the West, even in the US, just as those responsible for the bombs of 7/7 in London were educated in Britain, although the flow of ideas and ideologies which constituted their political education was more international. The separation between the different worlds is complex. However, there are marked distinctions between the access to resources and overall levels of poverty and affluence in these different worlds. Giddens argued that the greatest dangers to the advanced industrial nations, like the US, came not from other such nations but from

> failed or collapsing states, together with the fears and hatreds such situations engender . . . Countries struggling against poverty, bearing the long-term impact of colonialism and the Cold War, or both, and where government lacks legitimacy, are breeding grounds for resentment and despair. They can become havens for transnational networks, which as the rise of Al-Queda showed, can provide a very real source of threat to the integrity of nations.
>
> (Giddens, 2002: xiv)

Globalisation may be read as the ever-increasing dominance of Western, in particular US, economic, political and cultural systems across the world. Such an attack as that of 11 September 2001 may also be seen as a response to aspects of globalisation and the perceived threat to non-Western traditions of religion, culture and politics. The desperation of terrorism may be seen in response to the ever-increasing influence of Western economics and thought, especially of Western secularisation, and the desperate need to assert their own values in a globalised world. Global stakes are high, and however far-reaching the political, economic and cultural mix may seem to be global, the world is still characterised by oppositions, especially those based on inclusion and exclusion. The events of 11 September illustrate some of the underlying conflicts and inequalities in the experience of globalisation. The key questions relate to whose culture, whose way of life is dominant. Who has power and who is threatened?

The outcome of Western, especially US, responses to 9/11 was a reinstatement of nationally based hostilities which could be challenged by the more optimistic image of the lights soaring in the sky (Plate 7.3), but were still based on the assertion of the dominance of some nations and an introspective approach. More material hope comes from political transformation and the promise that was offered in the inaugural speech of the 44th president of the US, Barack Obama, in stating that he would close the Guantánamo Bay detention centre within a year and promote peace rather than retribution and 'a new way forward with Muslim countries' rather than a 'war on terrorism'. On his first day in the White House Obama proposed different strategies to deal with international relations and the impact of globalisation: peace talks and negotiation rather than the assertion of superior strength and force (Obama, 2009), pointing to a future of nation building.

Plate 7.4
US President Barack
Obama speaks to
the audience at the
Neighborhood
Inaugural Ball,
20 January 2009

Source: © PA Photos

Summary

The example of 9/11 illustrates some aspects of globalisation:

- Globalisation involves conflict as well as consensus in the inter-connections between countries that are taking place across the globe.
- Cultural globalisation through the flow of commodities may sometimes obscure the conflicts and inequalities upon which they are based.
- Globalisation is characterised by a crossing of the boundaries of nation states.
- New media technologies and communication systems play a crucial part in the processes of globalisation.

- The transmission of visual images and reports of people's experience was conveyed at speed and almost universally, thus giving particular meaning to certain events like 9/11.
- Globalisation may be seen as bringing together very different worlds and as highlighting the inequalities between them.
- Globalisation may involve conflict and inequality as well as consensus and new opportunities, and highlights the different political strategies that might be adopted to deal with the power relations that are involved.
- There are different views on the impact of globalisation and on its outcomes, especially in relation to the inequalities that may result.

Globalisation

The impact and extent of globalisation are strongly contested, but it clearly has a part to play in the movement of peoples and the disruption that took place in the twentieth century. I have already suggested some of the main features of globalisation: the crossing of national boundaries by financial concerns, political, social and cultural systems, the interconnection between states and the impact of new technologies. What else can we add to define globalisation? Given that there is considerable disagreement, what areas of agreement might there be? Globalisation involves:

- A complex process whereby connections between people in different places across the globe are becoming faster and more closely linked.
- Movement of people, goods and services and information across the globe, characterised by range, intensity and speed.
- An explosion of global trade with the development of new communications and deregulation of markets and, especially within OECD (Organization for Economic Cooperation and Development) states, a vast expansion in exports, employment and technology investment, controlled by multinational corporations.
- The reduction of the sovereignty of nation states, although there has been an increase in the formation of new nation states, for example following the breakup of the USSR.
- New relationships between the local and the global are being developed through new networks.
- Global migrations including flows of refugees and asylum seekers on a massive scale.
- Environmental crises on a larger scale than ever before experienced, and a much greater perception of risk than in the past.

Globalisation is frequently categorised by different dimensions, such as economic and political processes, social relations, the role of technology or its environmental impact. Discussion of globalisation has often focused on the growth of economic globalisation and the demise of the importance of the nation state and of local cultures in the face of global culture, and on the role of new technologies in opening up possibilities for change. At the basis of this issue are questions about the all-encompassing forces of globalisation. The scale and scope of the different phenomena associated with globalisation suggest that there are imbalances of power and that there might be a much stronger weighting in favour of the agency and control of some parts of the world and on the part of some protagonists. Some debates have focused on the imbalance between the local and the global. David Held posits an alternative to the extremes of the globalists who see globalisation as imposing enormous economic and political changes, and the opposing, more traditionalist view which argues that far from being a massive new phenomenon, globalisation has a long history, and recent changes have not completely under-mined nation state powers. Indeed, although recent acts of terrorism have not been committed in the name of any nation state, it is nation states that have been the target of retaliation, for example, Iraq and Afghanistan. There are also peoples who fight for recognition of their own nation; in Chechnya, the Basque country and in Kashmir, groups are struggling to gain autonomy. The Palestinians are desperate for a secure national identity that would strengthen them against the power of the neighbouring nation state of Israel. The debate has shifted more into a discussion of the question of security and insecurity and of the inequalities that are highlighted by globalisation.

The outcomes of globalisation are neither fixed nor clear. It is a phenomenon that can be harnessed. Thus globalisation offers opportunities for

> redefining the role and functions of national government, emphasizing its potential strategic co-ordinating role – the intelligent state or the competition state – as opposed to the interventionist, redistributive state of the post-war era . . . [and] stress investment in human capital and technical skills – to make national economies more competitive – as against the provision of 'passive' welfare benefits.
>
> (Held *et al.*, 1999: 250)

The views of positive globalists like Thomas Friedman (1999), who has argued that the era of globalisation has been one of peace, because the economic links have led to greater overall prosperity, which has created strong interests for all in the development of those relationships, have been disrupted by political events during the past decade. Such views suggested that poorer countries benefit particularly from increasing efficiency of markets, which has been another outcome of globalisation. The American Foreign Policy Association produced a study which concluded that, using the criteria of information technology, finance, trade, politics, travel and personal communication, the world's most globalised countries have achieved greater income equality than their less globalised counterparts (Foreign Policy Association, 2002).

This approach is countered by the more negative views of globalisation taken by the opposing view. For example, J. K. Gallbraith (1999) has argued that the forces of competition, deregulation and privatisation have been disastrous for the world's poorest people. This perspective is supported by feminist critiques, some of which are discussed in more detail below. For example, Jill Steans has commented that 'the least unionized and poorest paid of all workers, women have been particularly vulnerable to the market policies which have continued to characterize global economic restructuring in the 1990s' (2000: 368).

Globalisation and the technologies associated with it necessarily involve the crossing of national boundaries. This means that there is increasingly a transnational dimension to economic, social, political and cultural life. Anthony Giddens has stressed the plurality of globalisation and its multi-dimensional processes. What he describes in his 1999 Reith Lectures as a 'Runaway World' involves both the erosion of traditional boundaries as well as the increasingly interdependent aspects of globalisation. He stresses the ways in which the world has become a single social system as a result of growing ties of interdependence with social, political and economic connections cross-cutting borders between countries and impacting on those living within them. Giddens (1999) acknowledges some of the inequities involved in these processes, but argues against the claim that globalisation means Americanisation and everyone becoming the same, and for an optimistic approach, which stresses the creation of new opportunities and developments. He claims that processes involved in globalisation open up opportunities more than they impose particularly dominant Western US cultural practices and systems.

While globalisation is clearly multi-faceted, some facets have been given greater emphasis than others and those such as race, ethnicity and gender, which are implicated in unequal relationships and contribute more to debates within development studies, have been subsumed or marginalised in the mainstream of globalisation (Adam 2002). Saskia Sassen has argued that gender and race are key components in the global political economy. For example, she shows how, in the global cities (1998, 2006), most of the daily servicing jobs in the financial sectors are carried out by women, immigrants and people from minority ethnic groups, often all three in the same person, since they are, of course, overlapping groups. This work is an integral part of globalising processes, although they are not always recognised as such.

The rapid transmission of information across the globe and the spread of corporations, economic systems and cultures across national boundaries open up new networks and opportunities, as well as new means of expansion, dominance and exploitation. Time and space merge through the use of the Internet and even the telephone, where call centres dealing with customers' queries about their accounts may be based thousands of miles from the customers who call them. In this sense space and time are shrinking. Information technologies facilitate very rapid communications across the globe and people can be physically transported in journeys that cover extensive distances in a very short time. Cultural products, films, music and television programmes are transmitted across the globe so that they are no longer the cultural property of one place. The key question now is not so much what period in chronological time do we find ourselves, nor in what geographical space, but in what time–space (Bauman and May, 2001). The elision of time and space is a transforming feature of globalisation. However, the compression of time and space may, at times, be overemphasised to underplay material and economic inequalities that are still experienced by many people across the globe. Time in this relationship is the speed of communication, not human experience of daily life. Images and information may be transmitted very fast, but this does not necessarily alter people's experience of birth, life and death, nor the experience of poverty through that life course.

Manual Castells (1997) has argued that the concept of the **network** is crucial to the global process of interconnection, for example, through communications networks such as those of information technologies. He suggests that the speed and efficiency of contemporary global communications networks create new power relationships. Networks provide a new material basis that can shape social structures themselves. According to Castells (1996), the power of globally networked financial flows takes precedence over the flows of power. The 9/11 example illustrates some of the more sinister operations that are possible for global networks. Al Qa'eda is a global network combining human resources, most likely men, machines, technology, training and other financial networks deployed to finance terrorist activities. Terrorist movements like Al Qa'eda are a network that appears to have no boundaries, no specific beginning (or end). Castells is writing about a wider range of networks, however. These are networks that involve money, the global media, the Internet and social movements, itinerant people as well as terrorist organisations. These include the global networks of corporations like McDonald's, which cross space and time, overcoming regional and national boundaries, through the production and consumption of their products (all of which are the same). There is some fluidity in the operations of such networks in that they cross the boundaries of nation states and the specific cultures associated with particular regions, although the products so promoted may show a striking uniformity. Network theories may also overemphasise the universal processes that are involved. There are significant differences between the experiences of different people. There are regional, cultural and ethnic differences, all of which illustrate some of the inequities that are involved in the operation of global networks.

One significant area of difference, which is often overlooked by network theorists, is that of gender. For example, women's experience of the networked society in developing countries is not the same as men's. If women are employed at all by transnational corporations, they are likely to be employed in the most vulnerable posts and at the lowest levels of remuneration. In addition, as Barbara Adam argues, for women in developing countries, 'when the torrent of networked financial flows rushes past you in a parallel universe, you may be thrown off balance by the accompanying waves, but for the rest of your life the established flows of power continue to reign supreme' (2002: 8). The point is not only that globalisation involves uneven development and inequality, but that inequalities are experienced differently by different people, and much of the globalisation literature has omitted one of the most strongly experienced areas of difference, namely gender (Visvanathan *et al.*, 1997).

Not everyone has equal access to the most powerful new technologies, although there may be some cultural democracy in the availability of new products and entertainment worldwide. **Culture** is a term that has a variety of meanings and applications, including the distinction between 'high' and 'low 'culture. This distinction was somewhat value laden, with those activities, practices and representational systems classified as 'high' culture being more highly valued than those classed as 'low'. This was the sort of distinction that might have claimed that opera was 'high' culture and football was 'low'. This was a dichotomy that was challenged by the 'cultural turn' in the 'social sciences (Hall, 1997). My use here involves more of the anthropological understanding of culture, which includes all that characterises the way of life of a group of people, whether this is a community, a nation or any other social group. Anthropology is concerned with finding out about how particular groups of people make sense of their lives and the symbols and practices they deploy that may be distinctive to them and characteristic of their way of life. Culture includes all the ways we have of making sense and of making meanings. This understanding of culture may also appear to stress shared meanings and the ways in which people who share a culture might have a common set of understandings about the world, or more specifically the community, they live in.

Summary

- Different approaches to globalisation can hold positive views which stress the opportunities, or a more negative approach which stresses inequalities, or present a middle line which highlights the uneven nature of global networks.
- An emphasis on opportunities, especially of commercial benefits, sees everyone gaining from expansion which could also lead to the expansion of democracy and neoliberal governance.
- Those who stress inequalities point to the further exploitation resulting from globalisation.
- Global networks and flows operate differently for different groups of people.

Cultural globalisation: a sporting diversion

Men's football offers a useful case study of globalised culture that might appear to present a positive view of the accessibility of global culture. Football might seem to be a very popular activity in which people across the world can participate especially as spectators of the game and as fans of the big clubs. Indeed, so popular is men's football that it may be seen as recruiting more followers than any other activity or even belief (Goldblatt, 2006). The game is truly cosmopolitan, as illustrated by the World Cup with the financial investment, politics and passion it evokes. The credit crunch may be biting in 2009, but the transfer fee offered in 2009 for AC Milan superstar Kaká to Manchester City, the richest club in the Premiership, owned by Sheikh Mansour bin Zayed, the brother of the ruler of Abu Dhabi, the biggest of the United Arab Emirates with an estimated family fortune of $1 trillion (£555 billion), was reputedly €110,000,000. The player's refusal to move, even for a promised massive personal salary, does not alter the magnitude of the sums involved. However, it is at club level that the deepest passions might be implicated, especially involving the mass of popular support. Football makes money for elites and for its top celebrity players, but it is also an enormously popular sport among ordinary people, women and men, in the communities where they live (Woodward, 2007b). Club football also goes global, and not only through participating in international competitions. Clubs like Chelsea, Manchester United, Arsenal and Liverpool at the top of the English Premiership have an enormous worldwide fan base as well as a very large proportion of foreign players. For example, spectators at the African National Cup may be seen wearing the team strip, even though the club does not play in this competition. Increasingly, African players like Emmanuel Adebayor, the Arsenal striker of Nigerian descent, from Togo, and Didier Drogba of the Ivory Coast and Chelsea (still at the time of writing) also play for these clubs, providing a double interest: local heroes and the glamour of the Premiership as a global spectacle.

The democratisation of global networks makes it possible for almost anyone around the world, provided they have access, to watch these clubs on satellite television and indeed to identify themselves as supporters of the club, and, if they have the resources, to purchase versions of the club strip. However, there are wide discrepancies between those who view and those who decide what is to be seen, and those who buy into the culture and those who make profits from communications networks.

So powerful are these networks that it is probably unlikely that anyone reading this will have no idea what these Premiership football teams and the whole commercial synergy that accompanies them are. Men's football offers a particularly good example of the globalisation of culture, economics and politics, with the development of the men's game growing out of the relative autonomy of nation states' regulation and control of their own football associations. More countries belong to FIFA, the world football organising body, than to any other international body. The English game, in spite of the relative lack of success by the national team, which is still living nostalgically off the glory of the 1966 World Cup victory, plays a significant global role especially through the dominance of Premiership clubs, with their associated cultural synergies, although, increasingly, club loyalties supersede those to the nation.

Men's football has huge capital investment, and remains cash rich from satellite television with enormous global media coverage, which has built on and massively extended grass-roots support. Recent crises are unlikely to have much negative impact on the really big clubs, although competitive balance is very likely to mean that smaller clubs will be unable to survive, so much is the game dominated by the top five. In 1998, men's football's global appeal was indicated by the entry of 173 nations in the World Cup that year (Armstrong and Giulianotti, 1999) and over 200 in 2006 (Goldblatt, 2006). The 'World Cup' means the men's competition. It is only the Women's World Cup that is gendered in the naming, another indication of the ways in which globalisation can appear to be gender neutral and conceal the very different and unequal experiences of women and men in the processes involved. Women's football suffers from the dominance of men's football and its occupation of the mass cultural media stage.

Summary

- Football is a global sport with massive participation which makes it truly a globalised cultural activity, involving a range of technologies and media.
- Economic dimensions of globalisation include financial investment, the enormous profits generated by the game, the huge transfer charges for celebrity players, and the synergy of products associated with the game, especially the big clubs.
- Political aspects indicate the crossing of national boundaries; the big clubs all have a large number of players of different nationalities and a governing body that crosses the boundaries of individual nation states.
- Football is a mass involvement phenomenon.
- Football, like other global activities and cultures, involves inequalities and exclusions, for example related to gender.
- Global sport offers opportunities but also highlights massive inequalities.

Movement of people: migration

Not only does globalisation facilitate the transmission of culture across the globe, it is also characterised by the movement of peoples that is also a key feature of globalisation. Migration is not, of course, a new phenomenon but it has become an important part of the notion of movement of ideas, resources and people which go to make up globalisation. Why do people migrate? The movements of peoples and itinerant communities were features of ancient societies. There is some overstatement in the claim that migration is a recent phenomenon. Migration not only has a long history, it has different dimensions. Incentives to migrate often take the form of economic forces. People move across the globe in order to do paid work, either because they have no such work where they currently live or because they want to improve their circumstances and seek opportunities elsewhere. People have long moved to facilitate access to food and resources. Increasingly the motivation to migrate is tied up with economic factors. It may be argued that in the modern period, i.e. since the fifteenth century, migration has been closely linked to labour power. The movement of people has been tied to economic factors on a large scale, whether that movement has been the result of coercion or has been the outcome of voluntarily made decisions: the result of 'push' or 'pull' factors. As Saskia Sassen has argued, there are reasons why people migrate. Migrations do not 'just happen: they are one outcome . . . in a more general dynamic of change' (1998: 116). Much of the recent discussion of globalisation has centred on the extent of migration across the globe and the developments that have facilitated the speed and frequency of global movements of people. Migrations have taken place across large areas and have involved both the compulsion of 'push' factors, including threats of violence and of starvation, and the draw of 'pull' factors, with economic, social and political incentives. Contemporary debates and media coverage, especially, as was illustrated in Chapters 1 and 2, about refugees seeking asylum in European countries also oversimplify the categories and the motivating factors behind migration, by separating out economic migrants from those who are classified as political refugees. 'Political' refugees, classified as deserving refuge, are set apart from economic migrants, who are deemed to be seeking advancement and not deserving of refuge, in a binary logic that underplays the complexity of the operation of 'push' and 'pull' factors and the distinctions between the political and the economic. Political and cultural factors may deny participation in economic life and this can operate in more or less traumatic ways. It has been dramatic, as in the case of the expulsion of East African Asian people from Uganda by Idi Amin, and has been accompanied by violent action, as in Afghanistan, the former Yugoslavia and, with catastrophic consequences, in Rwanda, but the interplay of different forces is not always so dramatically and publicly enacted. The interpretation of migration as motivated by either push or pull factors can underplay the different experiences among migratory peoples and overemphasise the homogeneity of any group of people who are leaving their homes to settle in another place.

As the German writer Bertolt Brecht described his own experience of exile from Nazi Germany during the years 1933 to 1948, in his poem 'Concerning the Label Emigrant',

> I always found the name false which they gave us: Emigrants.
> That means those who leave their country. But we

Did not leave, of our own free will
Choosing another land
. . .
Merely, we fled. We are driven out banned.
Not a home but an exile, shall the land be that took us in.

(in Jarvis, 2002: 80)

Migration across the globe can have negative or positive outcomes and sometimes both. Refugees are sometimes able to escape the horror of oppressive regimes in their own country and gain sanctuary in the place to which they migrate. People do achieve considerable success in their new home, but they can also meet with hostility and resentment, which may go a long way towards offsetting the relief they feel.

As Lydia Potts argues, some contemporary discussion of migration, in the context of globalisation, fails to explore the power imbalances and inequities that are involved, especially those relating to race and gender. A focus on the exploitative dimensions of migration in relation to labour yields very different understandings of the opportunities for those who migrate from more optimistic readings (1990). Potts argues that human beings as 'living labour power' have been transferred in large quantities and over long distances since the end of the fifteenth century. This period covers the enslavement of the Indians that followed the conquest of America, various forms of forced labour and forced migration in Latin America, Asia and Africa, African slavery and the coolie system used to dispatch the people of Asia all over the world. In the present day there is labour migration, the search for political asylum and the brain drain, including the exodus of academics from developing countries to the West. Potts stresses the lack of freedom for the people who were involved in these migrations. In the past, as now, the global market for labour often involves exploitation, especially along the lines of gender and race (1990).

Migration is experienced differently by women and by men, by children and by older people, and by people of different ethnic backgrounds. At many historical points it has been men who have played the major role in migration. In enforced migration, this has taken the form of the enslavement of larger numbers of men than of women or, more recently, men have left their homes to look for work before women. Migrant workers are however often assumed to be male and little attention is given to the specific circumstances of women. Migration has different meanings at particular times in history and for different groups of people. Potts's argument points to the need to question, first, the idea that migration as part of globalization is a new phenomenon, and second, to challenge the argument that migration is always from choice and is a liberatory experience for those involved.

Summary

- Migration is an important aspect of globalisation.
- Migration is not new but may be seen as having intensified over the twentieth century and in different forms in the first part of the twenty-first century.
- Migration involves complex factors (political, social, economic and cultural) which it is difficult to separate since they are interrelated.
- Different people have different experiences of migration, for example women and men and people of different generations and ethnicities.

Equality, inequality, risk and danger

The climate of insecurity which followed 9/11 and other terrorist attacks across the globe, in Bali, London, Madrid and Mumbai, may have provided an important illustration of the vulnerability of all those who inhabit this planet, including the most powerful. Terrorist attacks are certainly not confined to the powerless in their target, although it may well be the lack of power and lack of resources which prompts participation in terrorist activities. Whereas old-style terrorism involved attacks on nation states, newer forms of terrorism draw upon repertoires of globalisation. Al Qa'eda websites express hatred of the West, although they may have highlighted the US as their main enemy (Halliday, 2002). As Saskia Sassen argued, after 9/11, the rich countries discovered that they could not insulate themselves from the poor and destitute and hide behind their prosperity. Terrorism strikes at the most affluent heart of Western states (Sassen, 2001). Sassen claims that the debt and growing poverty of what she calls the South (that is, the developing world) and those countries outside the wealthy West are connected to terrorist acts such as 9/11. The growth of poverty and debt has led to large-scale migration into the ever-more-wealthy, and hence ever-more-attractive, countries of the West. Sassen describes terrorism as a 'language of last resort', through which those on the outside endeavour to make themselves heard in the rich countries of the world (2001).

It is frequently the less powerful and the poorest societies that are the victims, notably of environmental degradation and disaster, which are also features of the globalised economy. Environmental danger and risk is not entirely selective in its impact. There may also be some human agency involved in the location of environmental dangers and disasters. In her Reith lecture on poverty and globalisation in 2000, Vandana Shiva argued against complacency about the benefits of globalisation. She claimed that many of the 'natural disasters' experienced in the developing world are not natural at all, but 'man made'. She cites the example of a drought which is 'the result of mining scarce ground water in arid regions to grow thirsty cash crops for exports instead of water prudent food crops for local needs' (2002: 1). Similarly, she attributes the ecological and social disaster of the Punjab, formerly one of the most productive and prosperous agricultural areas in India, to heavy use of pesticides which have killed the pollinators. Shiva makes a strong case against a positive view of economic globalisation:

> It is women and small farmers working with biodiversity who are the primary food providers in the Third World, and contrary to the dominant assumption, their biodiversity based on small farms are more productive than the industrial monocultures. The rich diversity and sustainable systems of food production are being destroyed in the name of increasing food production . . . Planting only one crop in the entire field as a monoculture will of course increase its individual yield. Planting multiple crops in a mixture will have low yields of individual crops, but will have a high total output of food.
>
> (Shiva, 2002: 2)

Here Shiva's point is about politics as well as agricultural practice and it is impossible to disentangle the two. The political power relations to which she refers involve the tensions between the different worlds of the affluent West and global capital on the one hand and of the developing, largely poor world on the other, as well as the particular exploitation of women in the developing world. 'And women themselves are devalued. Because many women in the rural and indigenous communities work co-operatively with nature's processes, their work is often contradictory to the dominant market driven "development" and trade policies' (ibid.: 3).

The global inequalities involved in the inequitable experience of environmental degradation and danger have been highlighted by the anti-globalisation movement. This movement has drawn attention to the unequal balance of power and inequitable distribution of resources across the globe. This imbalance not only leads to the overuse of resources by the developed, largely Western world, but also the environmental degradation arising from that exploitation and overuse of resources.

The inequality between the powerful and the powerless has been well illustrated in the World Summits on Sustainable Development. There is often a stark contrast between those with power, land and resources and those without. Globalisation, especially economic globalisation, may be seen as partly contributing to and exacerbating such inequality. This inequality is the focus of many of the movements against globalisation.

One of the ways in which the problems have been experienced across the globe as a result of climate changes and the impact of contemporary patterns of production and consumption has been described as environmental **risk**. What do we mean by risk? Risk involves hazard and even danger. Environmental risk suggests that the planet itself is in some danger and that people may be at risk in relation to the environment in which they live. We are familiar with some of these

Plate 7.5 A protester stands in front of a wall of German police during an anti-globalisation demonstration outside the site of the G8 Summit, 2007

Source: © PA Photos

risks. They include risks in relation to the food we eat. Think of the health scares around BSE (Bovine Spongiform Encephalopathy) or 'mad cow' disease, foot and mouth disease in sheep, listeria in cheese and salmonella in eggs. All of these food scares raised questions about how food is produced, what necessary safety precautions should be taken and the responsibility of human beings who participate in the processes of production. Risks related to the production process which are identified and manifested as 'scares' demand political intervention, and it is difficult to disentangle the economic from the political. Other scares involve apparently 'natural' disasters. These include poor-quality air and increases in respiratory diseases such as asthma arising from fossil fuel burning pollution, increased incidence of skin cancer and links with depletion of the ozone layer along with floods and other 'natural' disasters affecting human health and well-being.

All such environmental hazards involve some human intervention or agency and are not simply 'natural'. They may be the result of human activity, for example, feeding herbivorous animals such as cows with meat, including offal from diseased sheep. These human actions may be motivated by the need to increase **productivity**, to reduce production costs, to make ends meet or to increase profits. On the other hand, human intervention may take the form of defining what constitutes the 'risk'. Sociologists such as Ulrich Beck and Anthony Giddens argued that we live in a 'risk society' where the perception of risk is great and people feel they should take responsibility for dealing with these perceived risks

(Beck, 1992; Giddens, 1999). It is suggested that technology in contemporary society is increasingly seen to be producing physical harm and the effect of such damage is not restricted by national boundaries. Such harm requires global management of risk (Giddens, 1999). For example, disasters such as Chernobyl have had global consequences, with impacts as far afield as the UK where it is claimed sheep cannot be eaten in the northwest of England because of contamination by caesium 137 (Stacey, 2000: 133). Beck (1992) suggests that science is no longer seen as protecting people from risks but as creating them. Environmental problems are linked to health problems; for example the depletion of the ozone layer with the increased danger of skin cancer. The idea that we could take some action to protect ourselves as individuals from these hazards creates a climate of fear and anxiety. This is exacerbated by the knowledge that the scares and even disasters may be the result of human action and not simply 'acts of God' or naturally induced. However, individuals have limited powers in protecting themselves from policies which have permitted practices that have created these problems in the first place.

The notion of 'risk' may be seen to imply an element of choice that danger does not suggest. Risk may even include some element of excitement and of gambling on one's chances, which the more material 'danger' does not imply. Beck's choice of the term 'risk' has some significance because of its focus on both the perception of human agents and its element of chance. Risk may carry less weight than danger which suggests no way of people addressing the problems they face and of effecting any changes in outcome.

Other social and material aspects of the environmental risks and dangers that accompany globalisation involve the unequal experience of these dangers. For example, natural disasters such as floods or even earthquakes have very different outcomes if they are experienced in more affluent countries such as the US, for example an earthquake along the San Andreas fault in California in the US compared with one in a less well-resourced country such as Turkey. This is most likely to be the result of a disaster which cannot be said to be induced by the actions of human beings in any way. However, this is not to say that the disaster is purely natural and that it has no social implications. Another relevant factor might be the choice of human beings to live in a particular, disaster-prone area, although this is most likely to be a very limited choice for the poor. Those who are well-off and whose communities are well resourced are better able to protect themselves with adequately built and supported housing and work accommodation.

Other disasters impacting upon the environment are more directly the result of human activity, such as at the Chernobyl nuclear power station disaster and the United Carbide plant in Bhopal, India, which killed thousands and left many more permanently disabled. These are examples of accidents resulting from the failure of those responsible for developments in technology. However, as the anti-globalisation movement and Green activists have pointed out, 'normal' economic developments and activities in a globalised world also have disastrous outcomes. The unprecedented growth of industrialised market economies over the past

200 years have led not only to higher consumption but also to the degradation of the natural environment.

Summary

- Globalisation may be seen as highlighting inequalities between different areas of the world.
- Environmental degradation can accompany globalisation and contribute to the perception of risk.
- Environmental degradation involves social and political factors as well as natural matters, and the natural and the social interrelate.
- Environmental degradation and even natural disasters impact more upon the poor than on the rich.
- Not only does massive economic expansion lead to the side-effects of environmental problems, but the poor are less able to protect themselves than the well-off.

Different views: weighing up the arguments

This discussion of some of the different aspects of the phenomenon of globalisation illustrates some of the main tensions between social science approaches. One key aspect of the tension between different approaches relates to the definition of globalisation, especially between those who see the phenomenon as a particularly important feature of the twentieth and twenty-first centuries, unprecedented in earlier times and being distinguished by the developments of new technologies of communication and political and economic networks and flows. These different views on the phenomenon of globalisation may be summarised by dividing the opposing approaches of those who argue that globalisation is a significant new phenonemon and those who claim that globalisation is not so new nor so important in explaining the experience of the twentieth and twenty-first centuries.

Those who argue that globalization has been a most significant phenomenon which has fundamentally changed social, cultural, political and economic life can be further subdivided into those who regard the changes effected through globalization as largely positive and who welcome the processes and those who take a more negative, pessimistic view.

The purpose of summarising the positions (Tables 7.1 and 7.2) is to highlight the areas of difference in order to facilitate understanding of different views and also to provide a means of questioning a theoretical position. As was suggested in Chapter 3 there are different ways of evaluating and assessing the positions taken by social scientists in order to establish the strengths and weaknesses of their arguments. In Chapter 3 it was suggested that one useful strategy was to pose the questions:

- *What is the evidence for this claim?*
- *Does the claim cover everything? What are the gaps?*
- *Does this claim make sense?*
- *Does the conclusion follow from the initial claims?*

Table 7.1 Globalists and non-globalists

	Globalists	Non-globalists
Definition of globalisation	A real change in social processes A unified global culture and economy Very limited state sovereignty and autonomy	Globalisation is not new Much economic and cultural activity is local/regional, but traditional inequalities persist
Significance of contemporary globalisation	Very important and wide-reaching changes	Fewer really fundamental changes; globalists too concerned with new technologies rather than with material divisions
Impact of globalisation	New global structures in politics, economics and cultural life; dominant financial and political institutions worldwide over and above national structures and institutions; large-scale migration of people	Nation states retain sovereignty and can determine own systems; cultural and social diversity remains and persists Migration not in any way a new phenomenon

Looking at alternative theoretical positions provides a useful entry into asking these questions. What is left out may be the focus of the alternative approach. For example, the more positive claims that are made about the opportunities of globalisation may be seen to omit the experience of the developing world and the inequalities created by the phenomenon, especially the exploitation of women, children and of some ethnic groups, which are highlighted in feminist critiques of globalisation. Asking the question 'who is left out' may well be presented to challenge claims that there can be the same experience for a group of people or even a society, which is necessarily diverse in terms of gender, ethnicity, age and disability. The more positive globalists may omit the experiences of those who are on the margins of the benefits of globalisation or who have specific experiences owing to their gender or ethnicity. As has been argued above, women's and men's experiences of globalisation are different.

Of course, there are not only two perspectives on globalisation. Table 7.2 represents only one reading of possible oppositions in thinking about globalisation. As was suggested earlier, there are approaches to the phenomenon that argue for its importance as part of the experience of living in the twenty-first century, but

Table. 7.2 Opportunities and inequalities

Globalisation: opportunities	Globalisation: inequalities
Opportunities of Internet and greater democracy through online participation	Internet dominated by wealthy areas of world; ignores differences of gender and race and material inequalities
Fast transmission of information	Speed of more importance to affluent nations
Easy access for individuals and community activists	Terrorist organisations benefit more than local communities
New opportunities for development of ideas and markets	Developing world not permitted to benefit fully; environmental risk and degradation harsher in developing world
Access to cultural products for all across the globe	Media dominated by US and Western corporations
More choice	Choice only between Western products
Easier movement of people across globe	
Spread of democratic neoliberal governance	Migration blocked for many refugees and migrants; different experiences of exploitation by women; increase in ethnic tension and exploitation of some ethnic groups; increased exploitation of women, children, older people and some ethnic groups
No state control of virtual space; opens up possibilities for democracy	No regulation of virtual space could increase exploitation and spread of violent material, sexually exploitative material and pornography

that the same phenomenon both offers opportunities and reinstates inequalities. As suggested in the work of both Giddens and Held, globalisation is seen to be transforming contemporary societies in all respects (political, economic, social), but has different impacts at different times and in different places. However, this approach challenges the dominance of a particular economy and culture and suggests that globalisation does not make everyone the same; there is scope for resistance and for more local agency. This approach rejects the polarity of a globalist versus non-globalist division and supports more complex readings of the phenomenon, which permit some space for the independence of nation states on the world scene (Giddens, 1999; Held *et al.*, 1999).

Conclusion

This chapter has introduced the idea of globalisation and has explored some of the ways in which it is defined and discussed within the social sciences, as well as the impact of some of the processes involved upon our daily lives. Globalisation is an important concept in contemporary social science and, although the phenomenon has a long history, its most recent ramifications through the twentieth and into the twenty-first century may be seen as transforming human societies across the globe. This has been illustrated by examples of marketing and the production and consumption of a whole range of goods and services worldwide, as well as by the cultural diversity that is manifest in many areas of contemporary life. The more negative dimensions of globalisation have been demonstrated by the impact of environmental degradation and political conflict which, in transgressing boundaries among states, makes everyone vulnerable and makes the vulnerable even more so. Acts of terrorism and terrorist networks have an impact on all peoples, including those in the most affluent and powerful nations, although the acts of retaliation by those more powerful nations often have the greatest and most damaging effects on those who cannot defend themselves, notably children. In the twenty-first century there have been increasing acts of terrorism, as well as fears due to the perceived threat, which may be seen as arising from the inequalities that have arisen from globalisation.

Globalisation is marked by inequality as well as by increased opportunities. This is what most concerns the social science explanations of the phenomenon. New technologies provide the possibility of optimistic readings based on greater democracy and opportunities for greater participation in political, social and economic life for all as well as speed and efficiency. However, there is still the danger of exclusion and the domination by the most powerful corporations and institutions at the expense of local communities. Optimistic readings of globalisation often underplay the differences of ethnicity and gender which are crucial to the experience of globalisation.

Chapter 8

Conclusion

How far have we come?

We have charted some of the big issues that are the subject of contemporary debate and identified some of the ways in which these issues have been addressed within the social sciences. Most of these 'big issues' are associated with change and transformation: materialities and mobilities. For example, we have considered the role of *identity* in a world that has fast-changing modes of communication and representation and a rapidly changing political landscape. Identity is a key concept for the exploration and understanding of how attachments are made and the links between the personal and the social and what connects the individual to the wider society. This has particular resonance in a world that both appears to have become more uncertain as a result of economic, social, technological and political changes and new connections and new conflicts, and has seen an increasing interest in the self in Western societies. A focus on identity provides a means of assessing the impact of change and the ways in which people make attachments in the midst of uneven and often unequal transformations. The discussion of multiple identities draws in many of the other dimensions of social relations and organisation, all of which are implicated in the relationship between the individual and society.

The question of *citizenship* raises debates about changing social networks and identities, and the ways in which some groups of people have challenged their exclusion from the mainstream of social, economic and political life as represented by full participation in citizenship. Citizenship offers another means of interrogating the extent of change and the forms it takes. As a re-formed category the notion of citizenship permits a fuller discussion of what is involved in the exclusion and marginalisation of some people and, to counter this, the key elements in the promotion of greater social inclusion.

Another key area of change is the transformation of the role of *consumption* and of the relationship between production and consumption. The notion that we live in a 'consumer society' lends the term some status and centrality in contemporary debates. The extent of this change of emphasis has been both endorsed and challenged, and the apparent shift towards patterns of consumption as assuming particular importance in contemporary societies has been the subject of some controversy. This focus on consumption raises questions about the need to explore other aspects of the process and the tension between earlier views which attributed the greatest significance to production in shaping experience and social relations and divisions and more recent postmodernist approaches, with their focus on culture and representation. Patterns of consumption, especially the enormous growth of consumption in recent years, have material consequences and illustrate the importance of materialities in explaining social change. Increased consumption of goods across the globe has created waste products and enormous problems which are both material and social. The concept of material culture has been deployed to explain the links between objects, even the objects we no longer want or need, and people.

Issues of consumption demonstrate the importance of *materialities* and material culture which see material objects as constitutive of social life. Materialities include the natural world such as the environment and the non-human as well as the materialities of social relations and culture to which objects are inextricably linked.

An intensification of migration and the movement of peoples and a greater awareness of difference and diversity have led to a concern with the links between *place* and *race*. Current debates raise questions about the importance of place in shaping social relations. Place has been the focus of shifting explanations of social divisions, which have ranged from more local considerations of where people live, as we saw in Chapter 1, to wider-scale mobilities in the places we come from, the routes we have travelled and the places that have been important on those journeys. Place is linked to the construction of race and the experience of multiculturalism in contemporary societies. Race and ethnicity, along with gender and different aspects of embodied experience, are aspects of difference that are central to current debates and thus to the issues addressed in this book.

Concern with place and mobilities, especially movement across the globe, whether of peoples, ideas, information or materials, highlights another key area of current debate. The extent and impact of *globalisation* has been of central concern both within the social sciences and in our everyday lives. We see daily reminders of economic and cultural globalisation. The globalisation of economic, social, political and cultural life presents issues that have to be addressed and assessed. However, there is considerable disagreement about the extent of globalisation and about its impact, for example, whether the phenomena associated with globalisation have been beneficial or disadvantageous to different communities and different groups of people across the world. As I have argued, it is not an even process but one characterised not only by different perspectives, but also by significant inequalities. It is experienced differently by people in different parts of the world, especially the more affluent West on the one hand and parts of the developing world on the other. Globalisation has a different impact upon women than upon men and upon people from different ethnic groups.

These are the substantive big issues that have formed the focus of each of the chapters in this book, but there are other, equally important debates involving key concepts which have been woven through the discussion. The approach taken in this book has involved focusing on an interrogation of these issues, which has introduced some of the ways of thinking and, in particular, some of the important concepts in the social sciences.

Making sense of the issues: ideas that matter

Some key ideas have emerged through the discussion of the big issues in this book. You will have noticed that there are recurring themes and concepts. Some of these ideas are in common usage in everyday life, but they have particular meanings and applications within the social sciences. These themes and concepts have been organised around particular developments in the social sciences in recent years. First are the material environment and the connections between places and people's lived experiences that are brought about through material things and processes. Second, places and lives are connected through identifications, that is, through people's sense of who they are. These connections increasingly involve mobilities of migration from one place to another and in the identities that are available in changing times. Material questions are involved in the sustainability of societies and people's engagement with material and social worlds which are interrelated. Third, social order is made or broken at different times and in different places. Governments play a key role in the maintenance of social order and security, and have to deal with risk at international and local levels as well as individuals in their personal lives.

Difference

The question of *difference* is one that has particular resonance. At several points we have considered what is meant by difference between and among people, and whether difference necessarily involves inequality, another key theme in this book. Difference is relational but as we have seen on many occasions it is also oppositional and involves the superiority of one group over another group which is identified as different, or 'other'; this is most marked in relation to race, ethnicity, gender and disability. Difference operates within the exchanges of everyday life and in the global arena, where it has been most marked in relation to global inequalities in some recent incidences of global terrorism and conflict. Difference also takes more positive forms in relation to cultural diversity and the opportunities afforded by new technologies and global transformation. In the practices and policies of neoliberal governance, diversity sometimes replaces difference in order to acknowledge the equal weighting that should be given to all groups within multi-ethnic societies.

Inequality

Inequality has been deployed to draw attention to the ways in which the trans-formations of contemporary life often manifest traditional imbalances and inequities or create new forms, for example of exclusion. We have considered a range of examples of such imbalances that underpin many aspects of social relations, structures and institutions. Traditionally there has been an emphasis on social class as the main indicator of social divisions and inequality, but the study of social divisions has been extended to encompass many other dimensions of difference that are based on unequal power relations and an inequitable allocation of resources and civil rights. There have been a wide range of examples, such as gender, class, ethnicity and race, disability and the experience of migration. In many cases differences have been interpreted as involving an unequal relationship. For example, in the case of citizenship, the assumption of a white, male, able-bodied norm has involved the inequitable treatment of those who did not conform to this norm. Assumptions of homogeneity often conceal inequality. The impact of globalisation has been uneven. The opportunities offered by new networks of communication, new technologies and economic globalisation are not experienced equally across the globe, nor within specific communities and nations. Inequality has been another major issue in this book and has been linked to different manifestations of the unequal distribution of power.

Power

The issue of who can exercise power and who is denied access or has much more limited power raises questions about what we mean by power and most importantly how it is implicated in the structure of societies and the ways in which they are divided. As we have seen, this concept too is one which is both central to the social sciences and to addressing contemporary big issues, and strongly contested. We have looked at some of the developments in addressing the question of power in order to consider how it might be applied to current debates. Power may be seen as operating in a top-down relationship or as operating more diffusely in different situations. These discussions have taken us beyond the more common-sense assumptions that power must necessarily involve coercion, and has led to some useful considerations of the ways in which power is produced, often in very indirect ways. There has been some shift from a discussion of the origins of power to an examination of how it operates, although the two are not necessarily mutually exclusive. It is possible to be eclectic, providing one supports the argument logically and with evidence. The purpose of the discussion in this book has been to show the importance of looking at both how power operates and at its sources and how it is supported. There are examples of changes, not only in the conceptualisation of the social sciences, but also in power relations both at a global level and in routine, everyday exchanges. Debates about how power operates are implicated in the experience of uncertainty in a changing world.

Change – uncertainty and insecurity

Change creates uncertainty as well as new opportunities. The two necessarily interrelate at times of change. The benefits of scientific and technological progress create high expectations, but with greater knowledge there may also be greater anxiety. Medical science may contribute to the prolonging of life, but longer life expectancy, especially if accompanied by ill health, can create more anxiety. The speed and extent of change may create insecurities as well as radical new possibilities. For example, technological change such as that related to reproductive technologies may create both new opportunities for childless people to have their own babies, but along with these benefits go all the uncertainties about identity for those born through IVF, who may be unsure about who their genetic parents are. Globalisation may be read positively as providing greater opportunities for democratisation or, conversely, as creating inequalities and tensions which promote insecurities and even conflict that, in recent years, has taken the form of terrorist attacks. Societies may be enriched by the presence of a diverse range of peoples with different ethnic and cultural backgrounds, and increased mobility may offer the chance to start a new life in different parts of the world. The web makes illegal as well as legitimate communication fast and effective. The same social phenomena can lead to both positive and negative reactions by different groups of people. Uncertainty and inequalities characterise social change, as well as greater stability, with different weightings in different situations at particular times.

Culture and meaning

The so-called 'cultural turn' has led to more of a concern with how meanings are produced and the mediation of culture in the understanding of social phenomena and relations. Many of the developments within the social sciences have turned to the need to explore the ways in which meanings are produced and have drawn attention to the crucial importance of representation and symbolic systems in shaping our perception of the world and our own place within it. For example, we have looked at some of the ways in which race is a category that is represented and reproduced rather than reflecting any fixed truth or biological certainty. The meanings and values that are associated with the construction of race and with ethnicity are deeply embedded in cultural practices and histories. One of the ways of combating racism is to uncover some of these processes and to show how race is constructed and reproduced. Similarly, I have shown some of the ways in which economic processes such as the relationship between production and consumption are mediated by culture, both through cultures of production and the production of culture. It is impossible to extricate consumption from the ways in which it is represented and the meanings that are associated with the goods and services which we consume. Throughout this book I have attempted to show that we have to unpack meanings and to show the associations that accompany symbolic systems, rather than implying that meanings are transparent and merely reflect the material world. The words, images, ideas and practices that form part of the cultural process are impossible to disentangle from the material world of which they make sense and which they represent.

Knowledge

Knowledge is both a key concept and a theme which has particular importance at this moment in history. In a 'knowledge society', the production and dissemination of knowledge has enormous significance. For example, there has been massive intensification of the ways in which knowledge is produced and communicated at speed across the globe. We started with the example of education in Chapter 1 in order to highlight the importance of knowledge in the contemporary world. In our opening example access to education was presented as offering an escape from disadvantage and exclusion and an entry into a more privileged sphere where there are choices. Knowledge is an asset in the same way that finance and capital are assets. Knowledge is often the means of accessing higher rewards. In the 'information society' economic wealth increasingly flows to those who are more active in knowledge production and the communications revolution, especially those who are involved in the production, processing and control of knowledge. Traditional sources of authority have been challenged. In some cases there has been a democratisation of knowledge, with more people being able to access information and to make decisions about their own lives on the basis of that information. Sources of knowledge have changed, especially in terms of who has authority and who is classed as 'expert'. What is the role of the social sciences in this knowledge revolution? How are the social sciences implicated in the 'knowledge society'?

How do the social sciences address the big issues?

Most of the discussion in this book has involved identifying some of the big issues of contemporary concern and introducing some of the ways in which the social sciences address these issues. We have also considered the ways in which these 'big issues' in the world are also central to debates within the social sciences. These debates begin with *questions*, notably questions about what is happening and how we can better understand the transformations that are taking place. The social sciences have specialist language just like other academic fields, and one of the necessary processes involved in doing social science research is the development of new concepts to deal with the issues and problems that have been identified. Material and cultural transformations require specific ways of thinking and appropriate concepts to make sense of them. *Concepts* provide some of the organising frameworks employed in order to make sense of what is happening in the contemporary world, and, in particular in this book, of the changes that are taking place. Concepts have to relate to the world we inhabit in the ways in which it is organised, and one of the means of exploring the usefulness of concepts is to examine the *evidence*. We have looked at many different sorts of evidence in this book, although there has not been any extensive discussion of the methods adopted by social scientists. The sources of evidence upon which social scientists draw range from quantitative material, for example relying on observational research methods and those which produce statistical data, to more interpretive, qualitative evidence, such as interview material, first-person accounts and evidence that permits more of a voice to the people who are being studied. Some of the material which we have looked at has been largely quantitative, such as the statistical data from *Social Trends*. Other sources have included media coverage of issues, such as newspaper articles and first-person accounts and interview material, such as those recorded in *The Parekh Report*, which would be categorised as more qualitative material. There is other material that can be included, such as fictional accounts, even poetry, all of which can give meaning to social issues.

Having reviewed the evidence there are *claims* that can be made, for example, about how we might understand social phenomena. The claims that may be made on the basis of the evidence we have must be translated into an integrated explanatory *theory*, drawing on the evidence that has been cited in support of the claims made and developed in relation to other theoretical positions. The work of the social sciences is dynamic and constantly developing, both in relation to the evidence that is produced and the theoretical arguments that are renegotiated and expanded. As I have suggested, one of the most important skills within the social sciences is the evaluation of different theories and the ways in which we can point to the weaknesses and omissions of one position in order to further support another perspective. There is an ongoing relationship between theories and evidence and the development of different theoretical approaches. This is what makes the social sciences exciting!

The social sciences

This book has covered the social sciences as if they constituted a shared body of concerns. Study in this area does illustrate shared characteristics across the different disciplines that make up the grouping that can loosely be called 'the social sciences'. However, each of the constituent disciplines has its own distinctive features as well as shared concerns in terms of areas of interest and methodologies. There has been a trend towards what has been called interdisciplinarity within the social sciences. For example, each of the different disciplines that make up the social sciences has addressed some of the key concepts that have been identified in this book and has approached a 'big issue' of contemporary concern, but employing some of the methods and theoretical approaches that are specific to that discipline. For example, globalisation has been of interest to all disciplines within the social sciences and, although they have taken different approaches, this can be seen as an indicator of an interdisciplinary position, where the phenomenon under investigation takes priority, rather than the traditional concerns of the discipline. However some disciplines have a different focus and you may feel that some of these areas may be of more interest to you than others.

While you have been reading this book you may well have found that you wanted to know more about the psychological issues that were raised by the material. In Chapter 2, some of the most important aspects of social identity are discussed. How are the social influences on identity experienced at a psychological level? The discipline of psychology engages with questions about the relationship between the personal and the social, with a focus on the internal processes that are taking place. The discipline covers a wide range of issues and specific methods which are adopted to explore some of the investments that are made by individuals and by groups.

One of the themes of this book is the way in which society and nature combine. Psychology is a discipline that spans these two topics. At one end of the span, it looks at how society influences and is influenced by individuals. At the other end it looks at how biology, for example the structure of the brain, influences and is influenced by individual behaviour and experience.

Psychology covers a broad range, from language and social relationships to neurons and hormones. Social psychology takes up many of the issues addressed in this book but with an emphasis on the experiences of people living within society.

While reading this book you have encountered various questions and topics that are closely related to the study of economics and its focus upon materialities We have looked at issues of work, consumption and inequality, and the relationship between production and consumption and material culture. The phenomenon of economic globalisation has had a profound impact on people throughout the world. These are all essentially matters of concern to economists and involve both the interrogation of empirical data and theoretical dispute, for example between different approaches to globalisation. Economics requires an ability to handle its concepts, use of quantitative data and techniques and an interest in its methodological approaches, some of which focus on evidence which is presented in quantitative form, such as statistical data. Economic issues also involve the workings of economies, for example particular economies in particular areas in the context of wider historical, political and cultural questions.

Many of the big issues picked out in this book have a political dimension, either directly or more widely. The discussions about gender, inequality and social class, and nation, are all relevant to political debates about social norms and political identities. Other arguments about citizenship and the environment relate directly to government policy-making and wider social debate on these issues. You are also introduced to the key political idea of power, and the discussion has included topics involved in central government policy-making areas. Different interpretations of the meaning of globalisation illustrate a topic which governments around the world are having to manage. Many of the areas of change addressed in this book involve policy making, decision making and regulation at different levels ranging from communities to national governments and the global arena. As I have argued, politics involves issues that impact upon our daily lives and may include personal and seemingly private issues related to sexuality and family as well as the more obviously public arena of decision making and formal systems of policy making and legislation. Increasingly the study of politics considers politics and government in the context of broader cultural, social and economic trends.

Many of the big debates which are covered in this book are also those which are the subject of study in sociology. What is the relationship between individuals and the wider society and between people and things? Are there more uncertainties in the contemporary world – about identity, about our perception of risk, about politics, about expert knowledge – than in the past? What new opportunities are there for forging new identities, new, more diverse forms of family and social relations, new forms of knowledge, on the Internet, through new media, different political groupings? What sorts of structures influence people's experience – class, gender, 'race' and ethnicity?

Different aspects of social change are a key concern of sociology. It addresses the social structures that mark people out as different and are also sources of inequality, such as class, 'race' and gender. Sociology too engages with the debates about global changes, ranging from discussion of worldwide scale to those changes that take place in the private, personal areas of experience. Many of the debates that are the focus of sociological study are those which also permeate the other disciplines. Sociology draws attention to the interrelationship between the personal and the social, and looks at how individuals fit into the societies within which they live in relation to the social structures, for example of gender, class, race and ethnicity at different levels and within different contexts.

Geography has a number of concerns that distinguish it from other social sciences. First, there is an interest in the distinctive character of places, and why they have developed in the way they have. Places demonstrate material inequalities, of wealth, power, unemployment, for example, and this makes a big difference to the way things develop culturally, economically and politically. Linked to this, there is interest in the uneven way places are connected, and how globalisation processes influence places in a variety of ways. Another concern of geography is to explore relationships between social change and the physical environment and between people and the material environment. Here there is concern not only at society's environmental impact, but also at the repercussions for society. This has assumed increased significance with concerns about the impact of new genetic technologies, and global environmental crisis. At several points in this book we have concentrated on place and the interconnections between place and other social, economic and political structures and some of the big debates which require attention to the specificities of location, for example in relation to identity, to race and ethnicity and to globalisation. Another aspect of this dimension is space, for example as illustrated in our discussion of the relationship between the public and the private arenas, such as the separation at certain historical points between the public arena of decision making and of paid work and the private arena of relationships and domestic life.

Social policy provides a focus on many of the concerns of sociology but includes the specific focus on social institutions and welfare. These are informed by the concerns of other disciplines and interrelate with them but social policy retains a concentration upon the relationship between the state and social institutions and ways in which decision making impacts upon individuals and communities. Social institutions include those of family work and welfare, and encompass the ordering of everyday life as well as the institutions of state which structure experience. This is an area of change which both impacts upon our everyday lives and is the subject of considerable debate both within the social sciences and popular culture. All of these disciplines have been affected by changes in the world with which they have to engage in providing explanatory frameworks as well as policy recommendations, They all share a commitment to academic rigour and the need to support the claims they make with adequate evidence. The social sciences are constantly developing and changing in response to changing times and to the questions that emerge from the research that is carried out. There have been some shared areas of change, for example in the move towards a greater recognition of the importance of the ways in which culture mediates the processes involved in the production of knowledge. Increasingly, the disciplines which constitute the social sciences have drawn upon each other's research methods and major concerns and there has been a trend towards interdisciplinarity within many areas of the social sciences. Many of the issues raised in this book are the subject of major debates within each of the social science disciplines. Matters of identity, the impact of globalisation, our perception of risk and the changes resulting from the expansion of the knowledge society are all subjects of interdisciplinary and discipline-specific interrogation.

Knowledge and the social sciences

Of course this is only the start, but we have begun to pick out not only the debates, but also some of the key questions about the role of the social sciences. Knowledge is a diverse and multi-faceted phenomenon. However, it can be subdivided according to a number of factors, including what is being studied or discussed, the subject of knowledge, the way it is produced and the form it takes, that is, how it is represented. In this book, I have concentrated on introducing some of the ways in which the social sciences produce knowledge about some of the big issues in our everyday lives. The subject is the social world. This has involved some exploration of knowledge produced at a number of different sites, ranging from those of popular culture, for example as represented in the media, fictional accounts and, of course, the sort of knowledge that is specific to the social sciences, such as that arising from empirical research, and which might be seen as having the status of expert knowledge. Social science knowledge demands systematic and rigorous investigation and draws upon evidence to support its claims; it involves the development of theoretical explanations which organise and frame the claims that are made.

It is sometimes difficult to disentangle some social science knowledge from what we might call everyday knowledge. There are many ways in which ideas and theories produced within the social sciences have infiltrated popular culture and everyday thinking. For example, the insights of psychoanalysis, drawing on Freud's theory of the unconscious, inform media discussions of self-help, problem pages, daytime television and our exchanges with our friends as well as more formal counselling and therapy. Some of the structures and concepts which have been used by social scientists to classify and organise their understanding of social phenomena have also been absorbed into everyday discourse, such as the notion of 'institutionalised racism' which, prior to the Macpherson Report, had been mainly a term used only by sociologists. Media coverage of stock market crashes and alarm over mortgage repayments and pension funds, along with corporate scandals, bring the language of economics into the everyday.

However, at a time of enormous social, political and economic transformation there are other ways in which the social sciences contribute to changing forms of knowledge and to the changes that are taking place across the globe. The social sciences have never held the privileged elite position of other sources of expert knowledge, such as scientific, medical or religious knowledge, which have in the past achieved considerable authority and status, some of which remains, although these sources of expertise have also been challenged. The social sciences, in spite of the endeavours of some earlier social scientists, have not largely laid claim to accessing some incontrovertible, objective truth. It has increasingly become the case that social scientists have pointed to the limitations of the claims of any discipline or area of study, including the natural and physical sciences, to have access to truth. It is argued that no method of enquiry and no research approach is value free or objective, however rigorous the use of experimentation and observation. All research involves some use of prejudged categories and concepts, some selection both of what is to be investigated and how knowledge will be produced. Thus 'objectivity' is an impossibility. What can be achieved is research that conforms to the standards of the discipline, employs appropriate and rational criteria and recognised, well-supported methods. Research findings are then subject to the evaluation and assessment of peers within that area of study. The claims of the social sciences are invariably challenged by different theoretical explanations. However, this is not to say that their role and, especially, their transformative potential is invalidated. Social science research, as we have seen in this book, provides an important source of information and analysis for governments, both in the collection of data about populations and social trends as well as people's attitudes to change. Social science knowledges offer diverse and multi-faceted understandings of social phenomena and of change which are necessary in a complex world where there have been significant shifts in sources of authority. The social sciences are able to engage with this diversity and complexity, to be flexible in responding to change and to provide frameworks and structures for making sense of the things that matter. Social science has been important in providing explanations, and in identifying and defining the big issues in contemporary life. I hope this introduction to some of these ideas and ways of thinking makes you want to find out more!

Glossary

Agency Action and energy which leads to activity on the part of human beings in directing the course of their own lives. Agency is often addressed in relation to structure, to indicate the tension between the choice and autonomy of individuals and groups on the one hand and the constraints of social and natural structures, mostly outside their control, on the other. While groups and individuals may be constrained by structures, those structures are also the product of human agency in many cases.

Capitalism An economic system which is organised around the investment of private capital in large-scale production in the pursuit of profit. Capitalism may also be seen as a historically specific stage of economic development, in the Marxist critique, which focused particularly on its manifestations in nineteenth-century England, as the exploitative economic system, whereby labour, as a commodity, produced profit for the bourgeoisie, the owners of the means of production, which followed feudalism.

Class A large grouping of people who share common economic interests, experiences and lifestyles. This aspect of social divisions is linked to the economic and social organisation of any society. Some social scientists give greater emphasis to the economic organisation of production, especially in relation to ownership of the means of production or relegation to selling one's labour for a wage (Karl Marx). Others stress the importance of market position; that is, occupation and the status that might be associated with different aspects of market position (Max Weber). Whatever the definition employed, class remains an important feature of social inequality. It is an issue that shapes social divisions in conjunction with other structures, such as gender, race and ethnicity with which class is deeply implicated.

Consumption The process which involves the purchase of goods and services. Increasingly, it is argued that production and consumption are inextricably linked. The production of goods and services is influenced by patterns of consumption and consumer choice, as well as consumption being shaped by what is produced. There is a focus on the links between production and consumption which incorporates the importance of culture in the interaction of the whole process.

Cultural capital This term was used by Pierre Bourdieu to describe social and cultural advantages which people are able to accrue as a result of their class position; for example, the middle classes are able to access a more sophisticated use of language, knowledge of 'high' culture such as opera, literature and drama and the more high-status sports such as golf. Working-class people tend to have less access to cultural capital or to be limited to physical, body-based means, for example boxing as a sport, and popular culture rather than more highly acclaimed cultural forms.

Diaspora The dispersal of people across the globe, originally associated with the movement of Jewish people, but now used for a diverse range of people. It is also used as a category of identity, seen as particularly useful at a time of large-scale migration and to provide a means of explaining globalised identities and identities that cannot be traced to a single origin or home and incorporate often multiple sites of belonging. Diaspora is a concept used to understand globalised identities and citizenship, which cross the boundaries of the nation state, across the globe.

Difference A relational concept, whereby something, or one group of people, is defined in terms of how it connects to something else or to another group. Difference can be oppositional, as in a binary opposition, good/bad, night/day, or it can relate to position in relation to other phenomena. For example, Tuesday comes after Monday and before Wednesday. Binaries often involve a hierarchical opposition where one of the two is rated above the other.

Discourse When deployed within the social sciences this term is often drawn from the work of Michel Foucault to go beyond the more common everyday meaning which focuses on language. For Foucault, it includes sets of ideas, practices, ways of producing knowledge and shaping what we do and think according to that specific knowledge. Truth is measured by the discourse itself, not by some external criteria. Thus a discourse is true if it is thought to be so.

Ethnicity Identities may draw upon markers of visible difference and of physical characteristics but are based upon social features such as language, narratives, rituals and religion. Human societies are characterised by membership of ethnic groups, where ethnicity is not the same as nation and transcends geographical boundaries and those of nation states. Thus an ethnic community would be a group of people whose shared identity is related to culture, history and/or language but whose relationship to territory and statehood might not be encompassed by a nation.

Gender Many social scientists use this term to describe differences based on anatomical and physical characteristics associated with sexual difference. The term gender is preferred because it includes the social and cultural dimensions of difference. Gender is used to highlight the social construction of meanings about femininity and masculinity and the importance of social divisions between women and men. This focus on gender as implicated with sexual difference allows for an understanding of the social and political aspects of sex, rather than seeing sex and gender as separate and distinct.

Globalisation This is a set of social, cultural, political and economic phenomena which are subject to many different interpretations, ranging from those who see its impact as nothing new, to globalists who argue that it is a recent and very significant phenomenon which has transformed life across the world. Some read this as a positive experience while others see it as having disastrous effects on local communities and those outside the Western, especially US, mainstream. Increasingly globalisation is seen as contributing to global conflict. Most commentators agree that it has had some transforming impact.

Identification A psychological process of association between oneself and something else, usually someone else. In the psychoanalytic work of Sigmund Freud the child identifies with the parent of the same sex and thus comes to take on the appropriate gender identity. Identification is thus a complex psychological process and not simply a matter of copying behaviour. The term has come to be used more widely, sometimes as an alternative to 'identity' because it suggests a process rather than a fixed position and thus is preferred because identification is more dynamic and complex than identity.

Institutionalised racism The systematic, structural and patterned forms of discrimination which operate at a range of different sites, based on race and ethnicity. This racism is generated by the organisation, culture and attitudes of an institution or group.

Markets In a market economy, resources are mainly allocated through exchange in markets. A market comprises all the exchanges involving a certain type of commodity. Political tensions often, especially at times of economic recession, focus on the extent to which markets can be self-regulating or how far they require regulation and intervention by the state in a neoliberal eonomy.

Materialities The material world, which includes the environment, the economy and the objects with which people interact, shapes human experience. Social life is experienced through the interaction of people, animals and things, and human life is bound up with the material world. Not only is the material world which includes different materialities connected to people; they are inextricable.

Mobilities This term is used to describe one of the characteristics of twenty-first-century social, cultural, economic and political life, which features different sorts of movement; of peoples across the globe and within nations, of the identifications that can be made in changing cultural climate, including political affiliations and alliances, and in situations where technological changes are transforming social life.

Multi-cultural A multi-cultural society is one in which civic nationalism and multi-ethnic citizenship are accompanied by public recognition and participating citizens from a diversity of ethnic groups enjoying equal status and esteem. In recent years it has been argued that multi-culturalism has failed because there has not been a positive celebration of multi-ethnic culture and deep tensions and suspicions remain, for example, in the first decade of the twenty-first century.

Nation A named and known people who recognise a solidarity and identity, which is the result of a common history, culture and sense of belonging to a common homeland. This can lead to feelings of nationalism, which involve emotive, affective identification with a political project to secure an independent nation state for the nation.

Nation state A state which has external, fixed, recognised, demarcated borders and has some internal uniformity of rule and government.

Neoliberalism This is the form of government associated with free markets and democratic states that are based on the idea their citizens are self-regulating rational individuals. Following the breakup of the former USSR and the demise of communist regimes in much of the world this form of governance was seen to have become universal. The extent to which neoliberalism is non-interventionist and permits freedom equally to all its citizens has been called into question as a result of twenty-first-century anxieties about terrorism and increased risks. Economic recession has also led to a lack of confidence in the operation of the free market and especially unregulated banking and investment services.

Power This is a much contested concept in the social sciences. It lies at the heart of social scientific enquiry in many fields as well as being fundamental to the exploration of social divisions and inequality as well as stratification, drawing on the work of Max Weber. Power may be seen as operating hierarchically from the top down or as more diffuse and present in all human exchanges. Michel Foucault argues that power is not only diffuse, but productive as well as illustrating constraint and even coercion. Power can be the power to do something as well as involving someone having the power to stop you doing something. Foucault's idea about power as everywhere and as productive as well as restrictive has had a great deal of influence, although he has also been criticised for failing to locate the source of power.

Postmodernism This school of thought has been associated with Jean Baudrillard, who is mentioned in this book, and other, often French, thinkers, including Michel Foucault. In the social sciences, it refers to a set of theories that challenge modernism and the existence of universals, even the idea that there is a unified self, as well as other overarching structures, like social class. It counters the all-embracing approaches of the 'grand theories' such as Marxism, by suggesting that there is no single organising framework of society, which is diverse and segmented. Such theories are often characterised by a focus on representation and culture, and the myriad different ways in which meanings are produced and the fragmentation of contemporary societies.

Production The transformation of resources, such as raw materials, labour and time into goods and services. Considerable stress is placed on the efficiency of production, as productivity, in order to maximise profit and more recently upon the relationship between production and consumption in influencing productivity and decisions about what is produced. The outcome of a country's production is measured as its Gross National Product (GNP).

Race This term permits social scientists to stress the political significance of race and ethnicity and the use of 'race' in inverted commas shows that race is not a fixed biological category, but a dynamic, changing social concept. Race is not now used in the social sciences to describe biological make-up but the term is retained in order to hold on to the historical and political dimensions of this aspect of difference. Race, more than the term ethnicity, allows for a recognition of racism and racist practices which discriminate against people of different ethnicities.

Risk Being exposed to dangerous situations and adverse conditions. Taking risks involves knowing that an action may prove costly and even dangerous. The magnitude of the risks that people take may be quite well known, for example through the availability of public information about them, or they may be unpredictable.

Risk society One version of the state of contemporary societies which stresses changes in the ways in which awareness of risk, uncertainty and trust in expert sources of knowledge and advice changed in the latter part of the twentieth century. The risk society account emphasises the importance of knowledge and perception of risk, especially in cultures where, although life expectancy has increased and standards of health and care have been vastly improved, there is still much more consciousness of risk and awareness of knowledge about possible risks and dangers.

Roles The society into which we are born presents us with a series of roles, which are rather like parts in a play. The scripts are mostly already written, although, depending on our social and economic position and individual attributes, we can interpret these roles in different ways. A role comes with a pattern of behaviour, routines and responses. Although not the same as identities, roles offer a useful description of the social component of an identity. Development of theories about the significance of roles is associated with the work of Erving Goffman.

Social exclusion Some groups are marginalised and cut off from full participation in social, political, economic and cultural life. These groups are not able to take full advantage of all that is available in these areas to the more affluent members of the society. Social exclusion has been the target of neoliberal governments which have sought to promote greater social inclusion and cohesion, through policies which have increasingly been called diversity policies.

State The grouping of institutions which claim ultimate law-making authority over a particular territory. The state will also claim the monopoly on legitimate use of violence and coercion.

Status The honour, prestige or social standing which is associated with different groups in society. High status may or may not be accorded to those in social groups which have considerable wealth and does not derive necessarily from economic class position or occupation.

Structure This is used, often in conjunction with agency, to describe some of the organised or systematic, coherent constraints on human activity. Structures may take the form of social institutions, for example those of the state, or discourses which organise ideas and practices, like those of gender and ethnicity, or be based in physical or biological, embodied dimensions of experience. Structures are created and shaped by human agency in different ways at different times and in different contexts.

Symbolising Making one word, object or image stand for another. For example, green at the traffic lights means you can go and red means you have to stop. The notion of symbolising is used extensively in the social sciences as part of systems of representation through which we make sense of the world.

Taste A concept associated with the work of Pierre Bourdieu (1984) on the distinction between the different dispositions of people in particular social classes, such as taste in food and drink, clothes and leisure activities. Taste has specific social conditions, especially as derived from educational experience, which are linked to class.

Unconscious The unconscious mind is that part of the mind into which all the desires and feelings we have had to suppress are deposited. For example, when a small child's needs are not met the child represses these feelings into the unconscious. These feelings can emerge, often unexpectedly, later in life, for example in dreams, in jokes or in slips of the tongue. Thus dreams can be significant in revealing the feelings we have of which we are not otherwise conscious.

Further reading

The Open University 60 points level 1 course, *DD101 Introducing the Social Sciences*, which you can study as two separate 30-point courses, DD131 and DD132, is a good place to start finding out more information. The course provides an approachable and contemporary introduction to the disciplines and subjects that form the social sciences, as well as the questions and issues that social scientists investigate and explore. The course uses three themes – *Material Lives*, *Connected Lives* and *Ordered Lives* – to address its big questions:

- How is society made and repaired?
- How are differences and inequalities produced?
- How do we know?

Find out more at http://www3.open.ac.uk/study/.

There are some major textbooks, like Anthony Giddens' *Sociology*, now in its fifth edition (Cambridge: Polity Press), which provide extensive coverage of a range of the kinds of debates that are introduced in this book, but with a more specific focus on the discipline of sociology and on a teaching and learning text, and useful reference sections in which to look up points of information and explanation. Some books which pick up on the debates introduced in different chapters of *Introduction to the Social Sciences: The Big Issues* include:

Murji, K. and Solomos, J. (eds) (2005) *Racialization: Studies in Theory and Practice*, Oxford: Oxford University Press.
Payne, G. (ed.) (2006) *Social Divisions*, Basingstoke: Macmillan.
Richardson, D. and Robinson, V. (2007) *Introducing Gender & Women's Studies* (3rd edn), London: Macmillan.
Sassatelli, R. (2007) *Consumer Culture. History, Theory and Politics*, London: Sage.
Sassen, S. (2007) *A Sociology of Globalization*, New York: W. W. Norton.
Woodward, I. (2007) *Understanding Material Culture*, London: Sage.

Bibliography

Abu-Habib, L. (2002) 'Welfare, Rights and the Disability Movement' in Grewal, I. and Kaplan, C. *An Introduction to Women's Studies*, New York: McGraw Hill.

ACORN (2009) http://www.caci.co.uk/acorn/pclookup.asp (last accessed 10 January 2009).

Adam, B. (2002) 'The Gendered Time Politics of Globalization: Of Shadowlands and Elusive Justice', *Feminist Review*, 70: 3–29.

Anderson, B. ([1983] 2000) *Imagined Communities: Reflections on the Origins and Spread of Nationalism*, London: Verso.

APACs (2007) http://www.apacs.org.uk/resources_publications/card_facts_and_figures. html (last accessed 10 January 2009).

Armstrong, G. and Guilianotti, R. (1999) *Football Cultures and Identities*, Basingstoke: Macmillan.

Arnot, C. (2002) 'Pride and Prejudice', *Manchester Guardian*, 24 July, pp. 2–3.

Asthana, A. and Smith, D. (2009) http://www.guardian.co.uk/uk/2009/jan/18/race-identity-britain-study (last accessed 22 January 2009).

Balsamo, A. (2000) 'The Virtual Body in Cyberspace' in Bell, D. and Kennedy, N. (eds) *The Cybercultures Reader*, London: Routledge.

Barthes, R. (1972) *Mythologies*, London: Cape.

Baudrillard, J. (1988) 'Consumer Society' in Poster, M. (ed.) *Selected Writings*, Cambridge: Polity Press.

Bauman, Z. (1987) *Legislators and Interpreters. On Modernity, Postmodernity and Intellectuals*, Cambridge: Polity Press.

Bauman, Z. and May, T. ([1990] 2001) *Thinking Sociologically*, Oxford: Blackwell.

Bayoumi, M. And Rubin, A. (eds) (2000) *The Edward Said Reader*, London: Granta.

BBC (2008) http://news.bbc.co.uk/1/hi/world/americas/7728513.stm.

BBC (2009) http://news.bbc.co.uk/1/hi/uk/7718436.stm.

Beck, U. (1992) *Risk Society: Towards a New Modernity*, London: Sage.

Begum, N. (1994) 'Snow White' in Keith, L. (ed.) *I Mustn't Grumble: Writing by Disabled Women*, London: Women's Press.

Benson, S. (1997) 'The Body, Health and Eating Disorders' in Woodward, K. (ed.) *Identity and Difference*, London: Sage.

Berger, J. (1984) *And Our Faces, My Heart, Brief as Photos*, London: Writers and Readers.

Beveridge, W. (1942) *Social Insurance and Allied Services* [The Beveridge Report], Cm. 6404, London: HMSO.

Bhavnani, K. K. (1993) 'Towards a Multicultural Europe?: "Race", Nation and Identity in 1992 and Beyond', *Feminist Review*, 45: 30–45.

Bhavnani, K. K. and Coulson, M. (1986) 'Transforming Socialist Feminism: The Challenge of Racism', *Feminist Review*, 23: 81–92.

Biemann, U. (2002) 'Remotely Sensed: A Topography of the Global Sex Trade', *Feminist Review* 70: 75–88.

Bocock, R. (1982) *Freud*, London: Tavistock.

Bonnett, A. (1998) 'Constructions of Whiteness in European and American Anti Racism' in Werbner, P. and Modood, T. *Debating Cultural Hybridity*, London: Zed Books.

Bordo, S. (1993) *Unbearable Weight: Feminism, Western Culture and the Body*, Berkeley: University of California Press.

Bourdieu, P. (1978) 'Sport and Social Class', *Social Sciences Information* 17 (6): 819–840.

—— (1984) *Distinction: A Social Critique of the Judgement of Taste*, London: Routledge.

Bradley, H. (1996) *Fractured. Identities*, Cambridge: Polity Press.

Brah, A. (1993) 'Re-framing Europe: engendered racisms ethnicities and nationalisms in contemporary Western Europe', *Feminist Review*, 45: 9–29.

Branwyn, G. (2000) 'Compu. Sex Erotica for Cybernauts' in Bell, D. and Kennedy, B. (eds) *The Cybercultures Reader*, London: Routledge.

British Social Attitudes (2002) National Centre for Social Research, also available online at http://www.esds.ac.uk/findingData/snDescription.asp?sn=4838 (last accessed 2 April 2009).

Callinicos, A. (2000) *Equality*, Cambridge: Polity Press.

Carvel, J. (2002) 'The Census', *Guardian*, 1 October, p. 4.

Castells, M. (1996) *The Rise of the Network Society*, Oxford: Blackwell.

—— (1997) *The Power of Identity*, Oxford: Blackwell.

Census (2008) http://www.ons.gov.uk/census/index.html.

Chua, A. (2003) *World on Fire: How Exploring Free Market Democracy Breeds Ethnic Hatred and Global Instability*, New York: Doubleday.

Collins, P. H. (1990) *Black Feminist Thought: Knowledge, Consciousness and the Politics of Empowerment*, New York: Routledge.

Connell, R. W. (1985) *Masculinities*, Berkeley: University of California Press.

Conway, E. (2009)'House Prices', *Daily Telegraph*, 1 January, p. 4.

Corker, M. and Shakespeare, T. (2002) 'Disability/Postmodernism', in *Embodying Disability Theory*, London: Continuum.

Cwerner, S. (2002) 'The Cosmopolitan Ideal: Time Belonging and Globalization', *Time and Society* 9 (2 and 3): 331–345.

Davis-Floyd, R. and Dumit, J. (eds) (1998) *Cyborg Babies: From Techno-Sex to Techno-Tots*, London: Routledge.

De Garis, L. (2000) 'Be a Buddy to Your Buddy' in McKay, J., Messner, M. and Sabo, D. (eds) *Masculinities, Gender Relations and Sport*, London: Sage.

Dinesen, I. (1975) *Lost Tales*, New York: Vantage.

Donnelly, L. (2007) 'Ministers Fail on Teen Pregnancy', *Sunday Telegraph*, 30 December, p. 1.

Donzelot, J. (1980) *The Policing of Families*, London: Hutchinson.

Douglas, M. (1966) *Purity and Danger: An Analysis of Pollution and Taboo*, London: Routledge.

Du Gay, P., Hall, S., Janes, L., Mackay, H. and Nebus, K. (eds) (1997) *Doing Cultural Studies*, Buckingham: Open University Press.

Durkheim, E. (1915) *The Elementary Forms of the Religious Life: A Study in Religious Sociology*, trans. J. Swain, London: Allen & Unwin.

—— (1964) *The Division of Labour in Society*, New York: Free Press.

Dyer, R. (1997) *White*, London: Routledge.

Economist Technology Quarterly (2007) 9 June.

Eisenstein, Z. (1981) *The Radical Future of Liberal Feminism*, New York: Longman.

Engels, F. (1972) *The Origins of the Family, Private Property and the State*, New York: International Publishers.

Erikson, E. (1968) *Identity, Youth and Crisis*, New York, W. W. Norton & Co.

ESRC (2008) (http://www.esrcsocietytoday.ac.uk/ESRCInfoCentre/facts/index41.aspx? ComponentId=12619&SourcePageId=20004.

Falk, P. (1994) *The Consuming Body*, London: Sage.

Family Spending (2007) http://www.statistics.gov.uk/StatBase/Product.asp?vlnk=361 (last accessed 15 September 2008).

Featherstone, M. (1991) *Consumer Culture and Postmodernmism*, London: Sage.

—— (2000) 'Post-bodies, Ageing and Virtual Reality' in Bell, D. and Kennedy, B. (eds) *The Cybercultures Reader*, London: Routledge.

Feuer, L. (ed.) (1959) *Marx and Engels. Basic Writings on Politics and Philosophy*, New York: Anchor Doubleday.

Foreign Policy Association (2002) http://www.fpa.org/calendar_url2420/calendar_url_ show.htm?doc_id=106979 (last accessed 2 April 2009).

Foucault, M. (1973) *Madness and Civilization: A History of Insanity in the Age of Reason*, New York: Vintage.

—— (1975) *The Birth of the Clinic*, New York: Vintage.

—— (1978) *The History of Sexuality:* Volume 1, New York: Vintage.

—— (1980) *Power/Knowledge: Selected Interviews and Other Writings*.

—— (1988) *Technologies of the Self*, Amherst: University of Massachusetts Press.

—— (1997) *Discipline and Punish, The Birth of the Prison*, New York: Vintage.

Frankenburg, R. (1993) *White Women and Race Matters. The Social Construction of Whiteness*, Minneapolis: University of Minnesota Press.

—— (1999) 'Identity without Selfhood', *Self Agency & Society* 2 (1): 53–80, Derby: University of Derby.

Freegans (2009) http://freegan.info/ (last accessed 4 January 2009).

Freud, S. ([1905] 2005) *The Interpretation of Dreams*, trans. J. Strachey, 1965, New York: Avon Books.

Fussels, S. (1991) *Muscle: Confessions of an Unlikely Body Builder*, New York: Poseidon Press.

Galbraith, J. K. ([1999] 2002) 'The Crisis of Globalization', www.igc.apc.org/dissent/ current/summer99/galbrait.html.

Garfinkel, H. (1967) *Studies in Ethnomethodology*, Englewood Cliffs, NJ: Prentice-Hall.

Gellner, E. (1983) *Nations and Nationalism*, Oxford: Blackwell.

Gerth, H. and Mills, C. (1948) *From Marx to Weber*, London: Routledge.

Giddens, A. (1991) *Modernity and Self-identity: Self And Society in the Late Modern Age*, Oxford: Polity Press.

—— (1992) *The Transformation of Intimacy: Sexuality, Love and Eroticism in Modern Societies*, Stanford, CA: Stanford University Press.

—— ([1999] 2002) *Runaway World, The Reith Lectures, 1999*, 2nd edn, London: Profile Books.

Gilroy, P. (1992) 'The End of Anti-racism' in Donald, J. and Rattansi, A. (eds) *'Race', Culture and Difference*, London: Sage.

—— (2005) *Post Colonial Melancholia*, New York: Columbia University Press.

Goffman, E. (1959) *The Presentation of Self in Everyday Life*, New York: Doubleday.

—— (1961) *Asylums*, Garden City, NY: Doubleday.

—— (1963) *Stigma: Notes on the Management of Spoiled Identity*, Englewood Cliffs, NJ: Prentice-Hall.

Goldberg, D. T. and Quayson, A. (eds) (2002) *Relocating Postcolonialism*, Oxford: Blackwell.

Goldblatt, D. (2006) *The Ball is Round, A Global History of Football*, Harmonsdworth: Penguin.

Goodley, D. and Rapley, M. (2002) 'People with Learning Disabilities' in Corker, M. and Shakespeare, T. (eds) *Embodying Disability Theory*, London: Continuum.

Grewal, I. and Kaplan, C. (2002) *An Introduction to Women's Studies*, New York: McGraw Hill.

Hall, S. (1982) 'Culture and the State' in *The State and Poplar Culture*, Milton Keynes: Open University Press.

—— (1991) 'The Local and the Global' in King A. D. (ed.) *Culture, Globalisation and the World System*, London: Macmillan.

—— (1992a) 'The West and the Rest' in Hall. S. and Gieben, B. (eds) *Formation of Modernity*, Cambridge: Polity Press, Open University Press.

—— (1992b) 'The Question of Cultural Identity' in Hall, S., Held, D. D. and McGrew, T. (eds) *Modernity and its Futures*, Cambridge: Polity Press with Blackwell Publishers and the Open University.

—— (1995) 'New Culture for Old' in Massey, D. and Jess, P. (eds) *A Place in the World: Places, Culture and Globalization*, Oxford: Oxford University Press.

—— (ed.) (1997) *Representation: Cultural Representations and Signifying Practices*, London: Sage.

Halliday, E. (2002) *Two Hours that Shook the World: September 11th 2000: Causes and Consequences*, London: Saqi Books.

Hammonds, E. M. (2002) 'New Technologies of Race' in Grewel, I. and Kaplan, K. (eds) *An Introduction to Women's Studies*, New York: McGraw Hill.

Haraway, D. (1991) *Simions Cyborgs and Women: The Reinvention of Nature*, London: Free Association Books.

—— (1992) *Private Visions*, London: Verso.

—— (1997) 'The Virtual Speculum in the New World Order', *Feminist Review* 55 (Spring), London: Routledge.

—— (1998) 'The Persistence of Vision' in Mirzoeff, N. (ed.) *Visual Culture Reader*, London: Routledge.

—— (2000) 'A Manifesto for Cyborgs' in Kirkup, G., Janes, L., Hovendon, F. and Woodward, K. (eds) *The Gendered Cyborg*, London: Routledge.

Harris, J. (2008) 'Safe as Houses', *Guardian*, 30 September, 2008, pp. 6–11.

Hawkes, T. (1988) *Structuralism and Semiotics*, London: Routledge.

Held, D., McGrew, A., Goldbatt, D. and Perraton, J. (1999) *Global Transformations*, Cambridge: Polity Press.

Henley Centre, HCFV (2009) http://www.hchlv.com/ (last accessed 10 January 2009).

Henley, J. (2008) 'I'm Waiting for Riots in the Streets', http://www.guardian.co.uk/environment/2008/jun/23/waste.pollution (last accessed 28 January 2009).

Hochschild, A. (1994) 'The Commercial Spirit of Intimate Life and the Abduction of Feminism: Signs from Women's Advice Books', *Theory Culture and Society* 11: 1–24.

HMSO (2003) Census, National Statistics online, http://www.statistics.gov.uk/CCI/nugget. asp?ID=348&Pos=2&ColRank=1&Rank=310 (last accessed 10 January 2009).

Ignatieff, M. (1993) 'The Highway of Brotherhood and Unity', *Granta* 45: 225–243.

—— (1994) *Nationism and the Narcissism of Minor Differences*, Milton Keynes: Open University Press, Centre Paper.

International Passenger Survey (2009) http://www.statistics.gov.uk/ssd/surveys/international_ passenger_survey.asp (last accessed 10 January 2009).

Jackson, S. and Scott, S. (eds) (2002) *Gender: A Sociological Reader*, London: Routledge.

Jamieson, L. (1998) *Intimacy: Personal Relationships in Modern Societies*, Cambridge: Polity Press.

Jarvis, M. (ed.) (2002) *Poems for Refugees*, London: Vintage.

Jenkins, R. (1996) *Social Identity*, London: Routledge.

Jordan, T. and Pile, S. (eds) (2002) *Social Change*, Oxford: Blackwell.

Kaplan, E. A. (1992) *Motherhood and Representation: The Mother in Popular Culture and Melodrama*, London: Routledge.

Keith, L. (ed.) (1994) *I Mustn't Grumble: Writing by Disabled Women*, London: Women's Press.

Kirkup, G., Janes, L., Woodward, K. and Hovenden, F. (eds) (2000) *The Useful Cyborg*, London: Routledge.

Klein, N. (2001) *No Logo*, London: Flamingo.

Kopytoff, I. (1986) 'The Cultural Biography of Things: Commoditization as Process' in Appadurai, A. (ed.) *The Social Life of Things: Commodities in Cultural Perspective*, Cambridge: Cambridge University Press.

Lasn, K. (2000) 'Culture Jamming' in Schor, J. and Holt, D. (eds) *The Consumer Society Reader*, New York: The New Press.

Lee, D. (2002) 'IVF Twins Mix-up Poses Complex Questions for Family Courts', *The Times, Law*, 16 July.

Lee, S. (1993) 'Racial Classifications in the US Census 1890–1990', *Ethnic and Racial Studies* 16 (1): 75–94.

Lewis, G. and Young, L. (1998) 'Windrush Echoes', *Soundings* 10 (Autumn): 78–85, London: Lawrence and Wishart.

Lutz, H. (2002) 'At Your Service Madam? The Globalization of Domestic Service', *Feminist Review* 70: 89–104.

Mac An Ghaill, M. (1999) *Contemporary Racisms and Ethnicities*, Buckingham: Open University Press.

Macpherson, W. (1999) The Stephen Lawrence Inquiry. Report of an Inquiry by Sir William Macpherson of Cluny, Cm 4262–I, London: The Stationery Office.

Marshall, T. H. ([1964] 1994) 'Citizenship and Class' in Turner, B. S. and Hamilton, P. (eds) *Citizenship: Critical Concepts*, Vol. 2, London: Routledge, pp. 5–44.

Mead, G. H. (1934) *Mind, Self and Society*, Chicago, IL: University of Chicago Press.

Meek, J. (2009) 'To Live in Remarkable Times', *Guardian*, G 2, 5 January, pp. 4–8.

Mercer, K. (1990) 'Welcome to the Jungle' in Rutherford, J. (ed.) *Identity, Community Culture, Difference*, London: Lawrence & Wishhart.

Miller, D. (1997) 'Consumption and its Consequences' in *Consumption and Everyday Life*, ed. H. Mackay, London: Sage.

Mirzoeff, N. (ed.) (1998) *Visual Culture Reader*, London: Routledge.

Mitchell, J. (1975) *Psychoanalysis and Feminism*, Harmondsworth: Penguin.

Moore, H. (1994) *A Passion for Difference: Essays in Anthropology and Gender*, Cambridge: Polity Press.

Naidoo, R. (1998) 'All in the Same Boat?, *Soundings* 10: 172–179.

National Center for Health Statistics (NCHS) (2007) http://www.cdc.gov/nchs/pressroom/07newsreleases/teenbirth.htm (last accessed 1 April 2009).

Nelson, B. (1995) Introduction to *The Ladies' Paradise* in Zola ([1883] 1995), pp. vii–xxiv.

Nicholson, L. (1992) 'Feminist Theory: The Private and the Public' in McDowell, L. and Pringle, R. (eds) *Defining Women*, Cambridge: Polity Press.

Oakley, A. (1972) *Sex Gender and Society*, London: Temple Smith.

Obama, B. (2009) In 'Obama Peace Drive', by Tom Baldwin, *The Times*, 22 January, p. 1.

ONS (2008) *Annual Abstract of Statistics*, Basingstoke: Palgrave Macmillan.

Oprah News (2009) http://www.news.com.au/story/0,23599,23482682-401,00.html.

Ortner, S. (1974) 'Is Female to Male as Nature is to Culture?' in Rosaldo, M. Z. and Lamphere, L. (eds) *Women, Culture and Society*, Stanford, CA: Stanford University Press.

Pagnozzi, A. (1991) 'Race in America: Mixing it up', Hatchette, *Mirabella*, September: 130–134.

Panorama (2006) http://news.bbc.co.uk/1/hi/programmes/panorama/5219906.stm (last accessed 10 January 2009).

Parekh, B. (2000a) *The Future of Multi Ethnic Britain, The Parekh Report*, London: Profile Books.

—— (2000b) *Rethinking Multi Culturalism: Cultural Diversity and Political Theory*, Basingstoke: Macmillan.

Parker, T. (1994) *May the Lord in His Mercy be Kind to Belfast*, London: Harper Collins.

Pateman, C. (1988) *The Sexual Contract*, Cambridge: Polity Press.

Petchesky, R. ([1985] 2000) 'Foetal Imaging' in Kirkup et al. (eds) *The Gendered Cyborg*, London: Routledge.

Phillips, A. (1999) *Which Equalities Matter?* Cambridge, Polity.

—— (2000) *Promises Promises: Essays on Literature and Psychoanalysis*, London: Faber and Faber.

—— (2001) 'The End of Identity', *The Times*, 20 November, pp. 2–3.

Phizacklea, A. (1998) 'Migration and Globalization, A Feminist Perspective' in Koser, K. and Lutz, H. (eds) *The New Migration in Europe, Social Construction and Social Realities*, London and Basingstoke: Macmillan.

Potts, L. (1990) *The World Labour Market: A History of Migration*, trans. Terry Bond, London: Zed Books.

Reich, W. (1951) *The Sexual Revolution*, London: Vision Press.

—— (1970) *The Mass Psychology of Fascism*, New York: Simon & Shuster.

Richardson, D. (2000) *Rethinking Sexuality*, London: Sage.

Rose, G. (1990) 'Place and Identity: A Sense of Place' in Massey, D. and Jess, P. (eds) *A Place in the World?*, Oxford: Oxford University Press.

Rose, N. (1991) *Governing the Soul: The Shaping of the Private Self*, London: Routledge.

—— (1996) 'Identity, Genealogy, Wishing' in *Questions of Identity*, London: Sage.

Rothman, P. (1992) 'Feminism, Subjectivity and Sexual Difference' in Gunew, S. (ed.) *Feminist Knowledge: Critique and Construct*, London: Routledge.

Roux, C. (2002) 'The Reign of Spain', *The Guardian*, 28 October, pp. 6–7.

Rowson, M. (2001) 'Suddenly I Had 10 Brothers and Sisters', *Manchester Guardian*, pp. 8–9.

Rutherford, J. (ed.) (1990) *Identity, Community, Culture, Difference*, London: Lawrence & Wishart.

Saatchi (2009) http://www.saatchigallery.co.uk/artists/artpages/tracey_emin_my_bed.htm (last accessed 5 January 2009).

Said, E. (1978) *Orientalism*, Harmondsworth: Penguin.

Sarup, M. (1996) *Identity, Culture and the PostModern World*, Edinburgh: Edinburgh University Press.

Sassatelli, R. (2007) *Consumer Culture. History, Theory and Politics*, London: Sage.

Sassen, S. (1998) *Globalization and the Discounts: Essays on the New Mobilities of People and Money*, New York: The New Press.

—— (2001) 'A Message From the Global South', *Manchester Guardian*, 12 September.

—— (2006) *Cities in a World Economy*, Thousand Oaks, CA: Pine Forge Press.

Savage, M. and Burrows, R. (2007) 'The Coming Crisis of Empirical Sociology', *Sociology* 41 (5): 885–899.

Scheper-Hughes, N. (1992) *Death without Weeping: The Violence of Everyday Life in Brazil*, Berkeley/Los Angeles: University of California Press.

Segal, L. (1999) *Why Feminism?*, Oxford: Polity Press.

Shakespeare, T. (1994) 'Cultural Representation of Disabled People: Dustbins for Disavowel?', *Disability and Society* 9 (3): 183–199.

Shilling, C. (1997) 'The Body and Difference' in Woodward, K. (ed.) *Identity and Difference*, London: Sage.

Shirky, C. (2008) *Here Comes Everybody*, Harmondsworth: Penguin.

Shiva, V. (2002) 'Poverty and Globalization', (The Reith Lectures) London: BBC, http://news.bbc.co.uk/hi/english/static/events/reith-2000/lecture5.stm. http://news.bbc.co.uk/1/hi/world/americas/7488894.stm (last accessed 5 January 2009).

Sibley, D. (1998) 'The Racialisation of Space in British Cities', *Soundings* 10 (Autumn): 119–127, London: Lawrence & Wishart.

Skeggs, B. (1997) *Formations of Class and Identity*, London: Sage.

Social Trends (2007) London: HMSO.

—— (2008) London: HMSO.

Spittle, S. (2002) 'Producing TV: Consuming TV' in Miles, S., Anderson, A. and Meethan, K. (eds) *The Changing Consumer: Markets and Meanings*, London: Routledge.

Spivak, G. C. (1990) *The Post-colonial Critic: Interviews, Strategies, Dialogues*, ed. Sara Haraym, London: Routledge.

Squires, J. (2002) 'Public and Private' in Grewal, I. and Kaplan, C. (eds) *An Introduction to Women's Studies*, New York: McGraw Hill.

Stacey, J. (2000) 'The Global Within' in Franklin, S., Lury, C. and Stacey, J. (eds) *Global Nature, Global Culture*, London: Sage, pp. 97–145.

Stallybrass, P. and White, A. (1986) *The Politics and Poetics of Transgression*, London: Methuen.

Stanley, L. (1984) 'Should "Sex" Really Be "Gender" or "Gender" Really Be "Sex"?' in Anderson, R. and Sharrock, W. (eds) *Applied Sociology*, London: Allen & Unwin.

Steans, J. (2000) 'The Gender Dimension' in Held and McGrew (eds) *The Global Transformations Reader*, Cambridge: Polity Press.

Stoller, R. (1968) *Sex and Gender*, New York: Aronson.

Teodorczuk, T. (2009) 'The Shape of Things to Come', *Media Guardian*, 5 January, p. 1.

The Times (2008) http://www.timesonline.co.uk/tol/news/world/us_and_americas/article 3628860.ece

Times Online (2008) http://www.timesonline.co.uk/tol/sport/formula_1/article3305228.ece.

Travis, A. (2008) 'Boom in Births Brings UK Population to Almost 61m', *Guardian*, 22 August, p. 9.

Thompson, G. (2000) 'Economic Globalization?' in Held, D. (ed.) *A Globalizing World? Culture, Economics, Politics*, London: Routledge.

Thomson, R. G. (2002) 'Theorizing Disability' in Golberg, D.T. and Quayson, A. *Relocating Postcolonialism*, Oxford: Blackwell.

Trinh Minh-Ha (1992) *Framer Framed*, New York: Routledge.

Tsang, D. (2000) 'Notes on Queer 'N' Asian Virtual Sex' in Bell, D. and Kennedy, N. (eds) *The Cybercultures Reader*, London: Routledge.

Twine, F. (1994) *Citizenship and Social Rights: The Interdependence of Self and Society*, London: Sage.

Urry, J. (2000) *Sociology Beyond Societies: Mobilities for the Twenty-first Century*, London: Routledge.

—— (2002) 'The Media and the War on Terrorism', *Pain's Lecture*, Milton Keynes: Open University Press.

Visvanathan, N., Duggan, L., Nisonoff and Weigersman, N. (eds) (1997) *The Women, Gender and Development Reader*, London: Zed Books.

Wacquant, L. (1995) 'The Pugilistic Point of View: How Boxers Think and Feel about Their Trade', *Theory and Society* 24 (4): 489–535.

Wakeford, N. (2000) 'Cyberqueer' in Bell, D. and Kennedy, N. (eds) *The Cybercultures Reader*, London: Routledge.

Warner, M. (1985) *Alone Of All Her Sex: The Myth and Cult of the Virgin Mary*, London: Picador.

—— (1994) 'Managing Monsters: Six Myths of Our Time', *The Reith Lectures*, London: Vintage.

Warren, J. W. and Twine, F. W. (1997) 'White Americans: The New Minority?', *Journal of Black Studies* 28 (2): 200–218.

Waste Online (2009) http://www.wasteonline.org.uk/ (last accessed 4 January 2009).

Web Ring (2009) www.webring.org (last accessed 12 December 2008).

Werber, P. and Modood, T. (1998) *Debating Cultural Hybridity*, London: Zed Books.

White, G. (2009) 'Primark to Set Up Workers' Inquiry', *Telegraph Business*, 12 January, p. B4.

Wiley, J. (1999) Nobody is Doing It: Cybersexuality' in Price, J. and Shildrick, M. (eds) *Feminist Theory and the Body*, Edinburgh: Edinburgh University Press.

Williams, R. (1981) *Culture*, Glasgow: Fontana.

Williamson, J. (1986) *Consuming Passions*, London: Marion Boyars.

Wilson, A. and Beresford, P. (2002) 'Madness, Distress and Postmodernity: Putting the Record Straight' in Corker, M. and Shakespeare, T. (eds) *Embodying Disability Theory*, London: Continuum.

Wilson, E. (1977) *Women and the Welfare State*, London, Tavistock.

—— (2001) *The Contradictions of Culture, Cities, Culture, Women*, London: Sage.

Wilson, R. M. S., Gilligan, C. and Pearson, D. (1992) *Strategic Marketing Management*, London: The Stationery Office.

Woodward, K. (1997a) *Identity and Difference*, London: Sage.

—— (1997b) 'Concepts of Identity and Difference' in Woodward, K. (ed). *Identity and Difference*, London: Sage.

—— (1997c) 'Motherhood: Meanings and Myths', in Woodward, K. (ed.) *Identity and Difference*, London: Sage.

—— (2000a) *Questioning Identity*, London: Routledge.

—— (2000b) 'Representing Reproduction: Reproducing Representation' in Kirkup, G. et al. (eds) *The Gendered Cyborg*, London: Routledge.

—— (2000c) 'Defining Moments', BBC, Open University TV programme.

—— (2002a) 'Up Close and Personal: The Changing Face of Intimacy' in Jordon, T. and Pile, S. (eds) *Social Change*, Oxford: Blackwell.

—— (2002b) *On the Ropes: Masculinity, Men and Boxing*, Pavis Centre Paper, Milton Keynes: Open University Press.

—— (2004) 'Rumbles in the Jungle. Boxing; Racialization and the Performance of Masculinity', *Leisure Studies* 23(1): 1–13.

—— (2007a) *Boxing, Masculinity and Identity: The 'I' of the Tiger*, London, Routledge.

—— (2007b) 'On and Off the Pitch: Diversity Policies and Transforming Identities', *Cultural Studies* 21 (4/5): 758–778.

—— (2009) *Embodied Sporting Practices: Regulating Bodies, Regulatory Bodies*, Basingstoke: Palgrave Macmillan.

Woolf, J. (1985) 'The Invisible Flaneuse: Women and the Literature of Modernity', *Theory, Cutlure and Society* 2 (3): 44–68.

Wroe, M. (2002) 'In Cyberspace We All Put on an Act' *Sunday Times*, Section 9, 25 August.

Wrong, D. J. (1961) 'The Oversocialized Conception of Man in Modern Sociology', *American Sociological Review* (2): 183–193.

Zola, E. ([1883] 1995) *The Ladies' Paradise*, trans. Brian Nelson, Oxford: Oxford University Press.

Index

eBooks